ACPL ITEM
DISCARDED

Our Great Spring Victory

D1616093

NOV 1 1 2010

NOV 1 1 2010

Our
Great Spring
Victory

An Account of the Liberation of South Vietnam by General Van Tien Dung, Chief of Staff, Vietnam People's Army

Translated by John Spragens, Jr.
Afterword by Cora Weiss and Don Luce

Monthly Review Press
New York and London

We would like to thank the Vietnam News Agency, Hanoi,
and Internews, Berkeley, California, for the photos.

Copyright © 1977 by Cora Weiss
All rights reserved

Library of Congress Cataloging in Publication Data
Văn Tiên Dũng.
   Our great spring victory.
   Translation of Đai thắng mùa xuân.
   1. Vietnamese Conflict, 1961-1975—Campaigns.
2. Vietnamese Conflict, 1961-1975—Personal narratives,
North Vietnamese. 3. Văn Tiên Dũng. I. Title.
DS557.7.V3513   959.704'34   76-58106
ISBN 0-85345-409-4

First printing

Monthly Review Press
62 West 14th Street, New York, N.Y. 10011
21 Theobalds Road, London WC1X 8SL

Manufactured in the United States of America

Contents

Publisher's Note

Our Great Spring Victory is based upon a series of articles that originally appeared in *Nhan Dan*, the newspaper of the Vietnam Workers' Party (now renamed the Vietnam Communist Party).

On the first anniversary of the end of the war, April 1976, the government of the reunited Socialist Republic of Vietnam wanted the people to know the story of the final military and political campaign for liberation. General Van Tien Dung, chief of staff of the Vietnam People's Army and commander of "Campaign 275," the general offensive and uprising which won the war, related the details of the fifty-five-day battle to a *Nhan Dan* reporter. When it became apparent that details of the struggle were in demand around the world, a committee was set up to work with General Dung to eliminate repetition and refine the presentation. The result is this authorized edition, translated from the Vietnamese by John Spragens, Jr., who taught English in Vietnam with the International Voluntary Service in Vinh Binh and worked with war-wounded children for the Committee of Responsibility.

Peter and Cora Weiss, invited as the first Americans to visit the reunified Vietnam in the summer of 1976, obtained permission to publish General Dung's account in an English translation. It was agreed that all profits from the sale of the book will go to the reconstruction of Vietnam through Friendshipment, a coalition of forty religious and peace groups whose major project is the building of a hospital at the site of the My Lai massacre.

vii

This remarkably frank account, given so soon after the war's end, is a dramatic and significant contribution to history, and a source of inspiration to people throughout the world who are struggling for their independence and freedom.

Translator's Note

Military ranks in the forces of the Democratic Republic of Vietnam and the Provisional Revolutionary Government (the revolutionary forces), Saigon, and the United States are not exactly parallel, the discrepancies being greatest in the case of general officers. The chart below may help clarify matters.

GENERAL RANKS IN THE REVOLUTIONARY FORCES

Vietnamese	Translation used	U.S. equivalent
Dai tuong	General	General of the Army
Thuong tuong	Lieutenant-General	General
Trung tuong	Major-General	Lieutenant-General
Thieu tuong	Brigadier-General	Major-General

(The rank of Senior Colonel corresponds to the U.S. rank of Brigadier-General.)

GENERAL RANKS IN THE SAIGON FORCES

Vietnamese	Translation used	U.S. equivalent
Thuong tuong	General	General of the Army
Dai tuong	Lieutenant-General	General
Trung tuong	Major-General	Lieutenant-General
Thieu tuong	Brigadier-General	Major-General
Chuan tuong	Candidate-General	Brigadier-General

Although Vietnamese is written in Roman characters, numerous regional spelling variations, especially of place names, present problems in translation. An example is Ton Son Nhut, the name of the air base at Saigon which will be familiar to many readers. When not equipped with the appropriate diacritical marks, this is pronounced as spelled—Ton Son Nhat. I have chosen to keep this spelling, as it is that used by General Dung and reflects the pronunciation commonly used by northerners.

The transcription of names in minority languages, such as those in the Tay Nguyen, is another problem. In this case I have used spelling which will be more familiar to Western readers, such as Ban Me Thuot, Kontum, and Pleiku rather than Buon Me Thuot, Cong Tum, and Play Cu.

All footnotes, as well as bracketed material in the text, are mine.

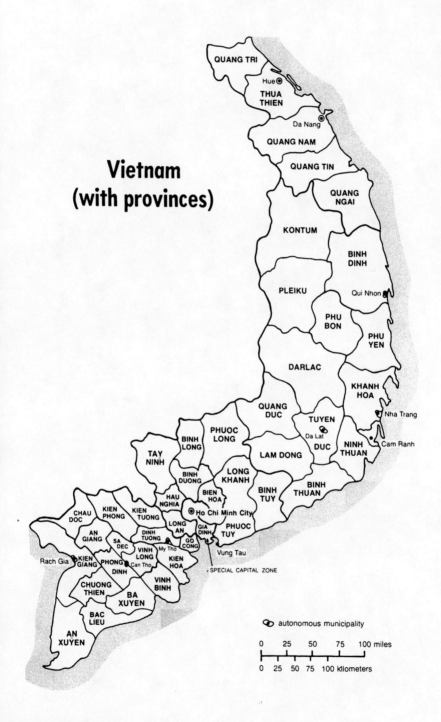

Vietnam
(with provinces)

QUANG TRI

Hue

THUA THIEN

Da Nang

QUANG NAM

QUANG TIN

QUANG NGAI

KONTUM

BINH DINH

PLEIKU

Qui Nhon

PHU BON

PHU YEN

DARLAC

KHANH HOA

QUANG DUC

TUYEN DUC

Da Lat

Nha Trang

PHUOC LONG

Cam Ranh

NINH THUAN

TAY NINH

BINH LONG

LAM DONG

BINH DUONG

LONG KHANH

BINH TUY

BINH THUAN

HAU NGHIA

BIEN HOA

CHAU DOC

KIEN PHONG

KIEN TUONG

Ho Chi Minh City

GIA DINH

LONG AN

PHUOC TUY

AN GIANG

SA DEC

DINH TUONG

GO CONG

VINH LONG

My Tho

Vung Tau

Rach Gia

KIEN GIANG

PHONG DINH

Can Tho

KIEN HOA

SPECIAL CAPITAL ZONE

CHUONG THIEN

VINH BINH

BA XUYEN

BAC LIEU

AN XUYEN

🐟 autonomous municipality

0   25   50   75   100 miles

0   25   50   75   100 kilometers

Introduction

A year has passed since the complete victory of the General Offensive and Uprising of Spring 1975 that completely defeated the aggressive war and the neocolonialist rule of U.S. imperialism and completely liberated the South. Far from blurring the details of this victory of our army and people, time has made them even clearer. Our great spring victory is engraved in history in letters of brilliant gold.

With our determination to fulfill the testament of President Ho Chi Minh, with a pace such that "one day seemed like twenty years," and with the strength of the military pressure which had built up for so many years, our army and people gained complete victory in only fifty-five days and nights, through three major campaigns: the campaign to liberate all of the Tay Nguyen* which opened with the attack on Ban Me Thuot, the campaign to liberate Hue and Da Nang and sweep the enemy from the coastal areas of Central Vietnam, and finally the Ho Chi Minh campaign to liberate Saigon-Gia Dinh and the remaining provinces of Nam Bo. The one-million-plus army and the whole administrative structure of the quisling regime

---

* Usually referred to in Western accounts of the war as the Central Highlands, the Tay Nguyen was an extremely important strategic area.

were shattered. The neocolonial apparatus which the
United States had devoted all its strength to building over
the past twenty years collapsed completely.

I had the good fortune to be one of the many comrades
directed by the party's Central Political Bureau to take
part in the 1975 general offensive and uprising, as representative of the Central Military Committee and of the
General Command to supervise the Tay Nguyen campaign directly, and as commander-in-chief of the Ho Chi
Minh campaign.

On the first anniversary of the complete liberation of the
South, *Nhan Dan* asked me to recount some of the events
of the campaign to Hong Ha. After *Nhan Dan* ran that
series of articles, many readers and publishing houses
suggested that the account be published as a book. Although it was difficult to find the time, because of the
urgency of readers' requests, I have rewritten the account
and supplemented it with additional materials for this
book, *Our Great Spring Victory*.

No single book, no single unit or individual can possibly
give a complete picture of such a significant historical
event as the great spring victory. The work of collecting
and researching the documents and of synthesizing the
experiences of this event will demand many years,
perhaps decades. So this book, *Our Great Spring Victory*,
is only a sketch of some of the events of the General Offensive and Uprising of Spring 1975, so that everyone can
witness the way in which the whole of the Political
Bureau and the Central Military Committee directed it
with strategic talent, with a spirit of determination, following the principle of revolutionary offensive, and with a
spirit of independence and autonomy, and so that
everyone can understand the extraordinary efforts and the
great sacrifices of our army and people throughout the
country.

The primary aim of this book, then, is to present an
introduction to the clearsighted leadership of the party's
Central Political Bureau and Central Military Committee,
and to the brilliance of our party, our army, and our people

in this test of strength and of wits on the strategic and campaign level, which led to the complete victory. It does not go deeply into the activities, records, and particular battles of the various military regions, corps, services, branches, units, or the various classes of the people.

This book cannot possibly recount all the thoughts and analyses of the entire Political Bureau and Central Military Committee, or of the full General Staff, when they reached their strategic decision at this key time to resolve the war according to the desires of the whole party, all the people, and the whole army. It is impossible to remember or retell all the strategic calculations of the party which led to the creative, urgent, and daring implementation on all battlefronts of the resolutions of the Political Bureau to achieve complete victory. There is no way to remember or recount all the heroic actions of the hundreds of thousands of fighters and cadres in the army, of the tens of millions of people from South to North, the wholehearted contribution of party and state agencies and of people's organizations which made this absolute victory possible. This is a task for many of our comrades and compatriots from many units and localities, of many books, articles, and works of art for months and years to come, as they contribute more materials to tell the full story of the great spring victory.

However, this book also aims to present an early refutation of certain erroneous, mistaken, and reactionary interpretations of the victory, which some who wish to distort history—those who usurped and sold out our country—would spread in defense of their shameful defeat and to denigrate the victory of our people.

Because of the tremendous scale of the victory, no one person's vision can encompass everything. Because time has been so short, this book cannot avoid a number of shortcomings. I hope that you, dear readers, will add to it and offer your comments.

—Van Tien Dung
May 1976

General Offensive and Uprising of Spring 1975
March 4–May 1, 1975

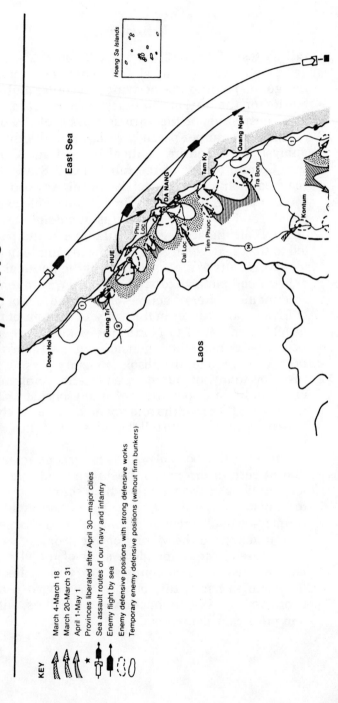

KEY

March 4-March 18

March 20-March 31

April 1-May 1

★ Provinces liberated after April 30—major cities

Sea assault routes of our navy and infantry

Enemy flight by sea

Enemy defensive positions with strong defensive works

Temporary enemy defensive positions (without firm bunkers)

Hoang Sa Islands

East Sea

Laos

Dong Hoi

Quang Tri

HUE

Phu Loc

DA NANG

Dai Loc

Tien Phuoc

Tam Ky

Quang Ngai

Tra Bong

Kontum

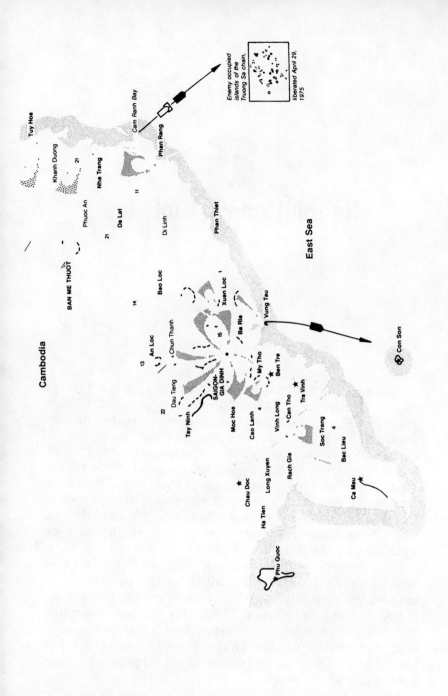

Cambodia

Tuy Hoa

Khanh Duong

Phuoc An

BAN ME THUOT

21

Nha Trang

21

Da Lat

Di Linh

Cam Ranh Bay

Phan Rang

11

Phan Thiet

East Sea

Bao Loc

14

Xuan Loc

An Loc

13

Chun Thanh

15

Ba Ria

Dau Tieng

SAIGON-GIA DINH

22

Tay Ninh

Moc Hoa

Cao Lanh

My Tho

Ben Tre

Vinh Long

Can Tho

Tra Vinh

Vung Tau

Con Son

Soc Trang

Bac Lieu

Chau Doc

Long Xuyen

Rach Gia

4

Ha Tien

Ca Mau

Phu Quoc

Enemy occupied
islands of the
Truong Sa chain,

liberated April 29,
1975

1

Revolutionary Violence

In the spring of 1974, after the New Year of the Tiger, a high-level conference of military cadres met at 33 Pham Ngu Lao Street in Hanoi. Included were representatives from all the battlefronts, all services and branches, all corps and divisions, as well as representatives of all agencies of the office of the General Command. They met to study and discuss the Resolution of the Twenty-first Conference of the Party Central Committee, which met in October 1973, and to disseminate the March 1974 Resolution of the Central Military Committee, which had been approved by the Political Bureau.

First Secretary of the Vietnam Workers Party Le Duan and Comrade Le Duc Tho called on the conference to present the Resolution of the Twenty-first Conference. At the same time, the National Assembly decided to promote a number of high-level military cadres to the rank of general. President Ton Duc Thang visited to raise people's spirits and to give assignments to the high-level cadres and to the whole army.

All the cadres and fighters were enthusiastic to have the Central Committee show them the road ahead and the bright prospects for the revolution. The instructions from

6

First Secretary Le Duan and President Ton Duc Thang represented orders from the party and the state to the whole army to advance.

By then it was more than a year since the Paris Agreement had been signed. The agreement stipulated that the U.S. imperialists had to end their aggressive war in Vietnam, pull all American and satellite troops out of the South, and pledge to respect the basic national rights of the people of Vietnam: independence, sovereignty, unity, and territorial integrity. They pledged to respect the right of the people of South Vietnam to self-determination, to end their military involvement and their intervention in the internal affairs of South Vietnam, and to acknowledge the reality that in South Vietnam there were two governments, two armies, two zones of control, and three political forces.

The agreement represented a big victory for our people and a big defeat for the U.S. imperialists and their lackeys, the result of eighteen years of determined and persistent struggle by our army and people under the correct leadership of our party. The Paris Agreement marked an important step forward in our people's revolutionary struggle, and opened up a new period in the South Vietnamese revolution: the period for completing the people's democratic revolution, and for reuniting the country. That would be the final phase of the people's democratic revolution in general, and of revolutionary war in the South in particular.

The U.S. imperialists and their lackeys tried hard to destroy the Paris Agreement on Vietnam. This was their plan, and they did it systematically. Although they had been compelled to sign the agreement, the U.S. imperialists still had not abandoned their basic policies in Vietnam: the implementation of the "Nixon Doctrine," the imposition of American-style neocolonialism in the South, and the prolonged division of our country. To implement these designs they intended from the very beginning to sign the agreement, yet at the same time help their

Saigon protégés* continue the insane war to destroy the agreement. In the southern part of our country the U.S. imperialists used many cunning measures to carry out their neocolonial war.

These included continued military and economic aid to the puppets. Before they withdrew their troops, the Americans sent nearly 700 airplanes of all kinds, 500 artillery pieces, 400 tanks and armored cars, and a great number of warships into the South. They made plans to send in a large number of technological weapons also, and increased the Saigon troops' stocks of war materiel to the relatively high level of almost 2 million tons.

The ink on the agreement was hardly dry when Nguyen Van Thieu started ranting about "flooding into all our territory." He pulled his forces together to carry out his 1973-1975 Three-Year Pacification Plan, March-August 1973 Six-Month Pacification Plan, Ly Thuong Kiet Military Plan, and 1974–1979 Armed Forces Development Plan, all with the aim of wiping out our armed forces and revolutionary organizations in the South.

The enemy urgently set about strengthening and increasing the development of their troops, especially the various branches of the regular armed forces. Their intention was to ensure that their troops would be strong enough to deal with our main-force troops under all circumstances. In 1973 the enemy drafted some 240,000 soldiers, and rounded up more than 130,000 deserters and wounded, raising their troop total to 710,000, roughly the same as in the December 1972 period total of 717,000, and more than the January 27, 1973, period total of 650,000. They also increased the size of main-force and regional-force battalions. The enemy put considerable effort into developing the air force, especially tactical and helicopter

---

* The Vietnamese almost always use the adjective *nguy*, meaning "puppet," when referring to the Saigon administration or army. Where appropriate, we have translated it with some of the more usual expressions in English; elsewhere we have merely referred to Saigon.

forces, increased the number of tanks and armored cars, and began using the M-48 tank in place of the M-41. The enemy had basically completed the organization of battalions and groups of security forces, and the elevation of those security forces to the status of mobile reserves for sector and subsector levels. At the same time they increased the number of civil guards from 1,100,000 (230,000 of them armed) to 1,500,000 (400,000 of them armed). Thus by the end of 1973 Saigon's troops had taken a stride ahead in organizational strength and had gained important technological weaponry.

With this foundation the enemy threw their strength into carrying out their pacification and encroachment plans, with the intention of wiping out our lower level forces, destroying the scattered bases which we held in their zone of control, imposing an economic blockade on the border zones, and encroaching on the zones that had been liberated before the Paris Agreement was signed. Their scheme was to eliminate the existing situation, in which there were two zones of control, two armies, and two governments, and turn the South into a single zone entirely under their control. During the eleven months from the signing of the Paris Agreement until the end of 1973, the enemy used 60 percent of their main forces and all of their regional forces to begin more than 360,000 blockade and encroachment operations and security sweeps, and brought together large forces for major operations against our liberated zones in Sa Huynh, northern Kontum, Chu Nghe, Kien Duc, Quang Duc, north and south of Route 4 in My Tho, in Chuong Thien, Nui Dai, Tri Ton, and elsewhere. They pushed into almost all the zones we had liberated in our January 1973 campaign, and seized a number of the liberated areas scattered in their zone of control. Besides that, the United States kept a force in Southeast Asia—called a deterrent force— including air force units, forces of the Seventh Fleet, and their bases in Thailand. At the same time they increased their diplomatic activities aimed at placing limits on our big offensive potential.

Our people could not sit quietly by and watch the United States and their puppets cynically violate the Paris Agreement, beating the drum while they robbed the house. In this critical situation, the Twenty-first Conference of the Party Central Committee met in October 1973 and put forth the watchword: "Coordinate the political and military struggle with diplomacy." They also pointed out clearly: "The revolutionary road for the South is the road of revolutionary violence. Whatever the situation, we must firmly seize the opportune moment,* maintain a course of strategic offensive, and give active guidance to advance the revolution in the South. The problems of gaining people, gaining administrative control, and developing the real strength of the revolution are the urgent and basic demands in the new phase. . . ."

In March 1974, the Central Military Committee met to reach a clear understanding of the Resolution of the Twenty-first Conference of the Party Central Committee and to discuss concrete plans for its implementation on the military front. They affirmed: "The Vietnamese revolution may have to pass through many transitional stages, and can only gain victory through revolutionary violence—carrying out popular uprisings, relying on our political and military forces, or in the event that large-scale war returns, carrying out revolutionary warfare to gain complete victory. The revolution in the South must hold firmly to the concept of an offensive strategy. . . . We must resolutely counterattack and attack, keep the initiative and develop it in all respects. . . ."

The spirit of the resolution was: *If the enemy do not implement the agreement, and continue the policy of Vietnamization, which is essentially a neocolonial war* aiming to take over the whole of the South, then there is

---

* In Vietnamese, this is *Thoi Co*, a fundamental concept in military strategy.

3 1833 05569 3458

no other course for us but to *conduct revolutionary warfare, destroy the enemy, and liberate the South.*

The Twenty-first Conference of the Central Military Committee not only emphasized the slogan "counterattack and attack," but also spelled out the basic directions for putting the slogan into effect in each region, and the types of actions to be taken on each battlefield. The conference also set the task for all of the armed forces: to carry out active political work with the aim of constantly increasing the overall political quality of the armed forces, to create a strong new transformation in thought, organization, ability, and conduct in every unit, in every cadre, and in every fighter. In particular the goal was to raise the will to struggle, step up organizational discipline, and guarantee that all three kinds of troops [main-force troops, regional-force troops, and local guerilla militia] would victoriously complete every mission in the new period. The Political Bureau approved the resolution.

As soon as the resolution reached them, the General Staff, along with the General Political Office and the General Logistics Office, began research and planning both for general strategy and for the campaigns on each battlefield, together with the urgent organization and training of all main-force units and technical branches. They spelled out preparation and maintenance plans, and at the same time directed all battlefields to step up activities, carry out offensives and uprisings, preserve and develop the strategic initiative, and change the situation on all fronts, thereby creating conditions for widespread, large-scale offensives in 1975.

All regions and all units, from Tri Thien* to western Nam Bo (South Vietnam) and the region surrounding Saigon-Gia Dinh, carried out strong actions from April through October 1974, attacking and counterattacking

---

* Tri Thien included the former province of Thua Thien, where Hue is located, and that part of the former province of Quang Tri south of the 1954 demarcation line.

the enemy with no let up, winning greater victories each day, at a greater pace. In every place where the Resolution of the Twenty-first Conference of the Central Committee and the Resolution of the Central Military Committee were understood clearly, where the standpoint of revolutionary violence and the concept of taking the offensive were grasped firmly, not only was the area able to destroy the enemy's "pacification" plans and preserve our liberated zones and our bases scattered through the enemy-controlled zones, but they were even able to expand many liberated zones and back the enemy into a position of confused passive resistance.

We paid particular attention to the battle which knocked out the district town of Thuong Duc in Zone 5. This was a test of strength with what were said to be the enemy's best-trained troops. When we knocked out Thuong Duc district town, the enemy sent a whole division of paratroops for days of continuous counterattacks to take it back. But we inflicted heavy casualties on them, held Thuong Duc, and forced the enemy to give up.

From this battle for Thuong Duc and the battles where we wiped out enemy main-force units at Chu Nghe, at Dac Pet in the Tay Nguyen (Central Highlands), and other locations, the General Staff concluded that the fighting ability of our mobile main-force units was superior to that of the enemy's mobile main-force units, a conclusion it reported to the Central Military Committee. The war had moved into its final stage. The balance of forces had changed. We had grown stronger, while the enemy had weakened. Thus we could and should move on from attacks intended mainly to wipe out the enemy's effective forces to attacks which, besides wiping out the enemy, would be intended to liberate people and hold territory; instead of operating primarily to destroy enemy main-force units on mountain and jungle battlefields we could now wipe out the enemy and liberate people and land even in the border zones, the lowlands, and the towns. If we wanted to defeat the enemy on a large scale and hold the newly liberated zones, it would no longer be appropriate to use only independent and coordinated divisions. We would need mobile commands and specialized branches combined on a larger scale, to deliver a powerful punch, which could be used at the most important opportune moments, could go into action along the principal thrusts, and could take on primary responsibility for destroying large enemy main-force units.

The Political Bureau and the Central Military Committee agreed unanimously with this conclusion, and directed us to proceed immediately with the organization of mobile commands directly subordinate to the General Command. From October 1973 onward, these corps were established one by one, brought together for combat training as combined units, and deployed in the best positions for strategic mobility. The development of high-level mobile commands allowed us to carry out campaigns with large-scale combined units, including many corps and divisions, which were strong enough to mount large assaults, had both high mobility and the strength for sustained combat, and could operate successfully in strategic campaigns. Along with the reorganization of our forces, an urgent task was to replace the equipment of our army with better and more modern materiel. Massive amounts of tanks, armored cars, rockets, long-range artillery, and antiaircraft guns, which the Americans tried unsuccessfully to destroy in their twelve-day B-52 bombing blitz against the North in December 1972, were now sent to the front one after another. And for the first time self-propelled long-range artillery and some of our good tanks got all the way to the rubber forests of the Nam Bo plains. This was a big step toward maturity for our army, and at the same time was a most positive preparation of our forces for the coming offensive.

Now that we had our large forces and our still inadequate modern equipment, we needed to organize the field of battle so that we could fully exploit the strength of those large forces and that modern equipment. The rule of revolutionary warfare is to progress from small units to large commands of coordinated combat branches to destroy the enemy's forces on a large scale, and finally to attack the cities, attack the nerve centers, and smash the enemy's administration. Only then would the enemy be brought to their knees and the Fatherland liberated. And so we needed enough communications routes and motorized transport to bring sufficient food, ammunition, and weapons to the front. A key problem was to develop a system of roads for good mobility. The project to build a strategic road east of the Truong Son mountain range began in 1973 and was completed by the first part of 1975. Carried out at the most urgent pace, it was a labor project of more than 30,000 troops and members of the Vanguard Youth. The finished road ran from Route 9 (in Quang Tri) down to eastern Nam Bo, and increased the total length of the strategic and tactical roads, old and new, constructed during the war to more than 20,000 kilometers. The state and our people poured a great amount of strength and material into this project. Thousands of motorized vehicles of all kinds, tens of thousands of soldiers, workers, engineers, Vanguard Youth, and volunteer workers overcame innumerable hardships and suffering caused by the climate and weather, and by enemy bombs and shells, flattening mountains and passes, turning them to gravel to build the road, constructing culverts and bridges—a proud exploit in the western part of our land. It was indeed "our eight-meter-wide road," permitting large trucks and heavy combat vehicles of all kinds to drive quickly in both directions in all four seasons. Day and night they enthusiastically carried hundreds of thousands of tons of supplies of every description down to the stockpiles for the various battlefields, to ensure the success of our large-scale attacks.

Alongside the strategic road to the east of the Truong Son range was a 5,000-kilometer-long oil pipeline which ran from Quang Tri through the Tay Nguyen and on to Loc Ninh, crossing rivers, deep springs, and tall mountains with peaks more than 1,000 meters high, capable of supplying fuel to tens of thousands of vehicles of all kinds going back and forth along the road.

It was a picture to be proud of. In that region of towering mountains in the western sector of our Fatherland were more than 20,000 kilometers of strategic roads running north to south, with campaign roads running west to east—strong ropes inching gradually, day by day, around the neck, arms, and legs of a demon, awaiting the order to jerk tight and bring the creature's life to an end.

Telecommunications lines also reached down to Loc Ninh, making it possible to speak from Hanoi directly with many battlefields. Just when the people of the South were pushing the enemy back almost everywhere, trying to gain the right to rule their own lives, in the North from every village and neighborhood, every government agency, every school and factory, tens of thousands of spirited youth answered the call of the party and the Fatherland to join the army, and set out on the road to the front. The Resolution of the Twenty-first Conference of the Party Central Committee and the Resolution of the Central Military Committee, along with the correct and timely directions given by the Political Bureau, had transformed the battlefield situation to our advantage and mobilized the might of the entire country to support the front lines.

2

The Opportune Moment

During the months of July, August, September, and October of 1974, all the agencies of the General Staff were bustling and tense. Comrades on the Central Military Committee and the Political Bureau kept track of the situation each day and directed the research and proposed strategic combat plans. Then a cool, pleasant breeze wafted through our entire party and people: the revolution in the South had soared since the Resolution of the Twenty-first Conference of the Party Central Committee and the March 1974 Resolution of the Central Military Committee. The situation on the battlefield was developing to our advantage. Our army and people had taken firm, positive steps to advance the position and strength of the revolution, had mounted sustained counterattacks and offensives against the enemy, and had gained increasingly large victories at a rapid pace.

Zone 9 had grasped the concept of strategic offensive and defeated each of the enemy's encroaching operations, swept away more than 2,000 enemy outposts, and liberated more than 400 hamlets with a population of more than 800,000. Zone 8 had wiped out more than 800 enemy outposts and liberated an additional 200 hamlets with more than 130,000 people. Zone 7 had maintained its offensive position, defeated enemy blockage operations, and held the strategic base area to the north of Saigon. The area surrounding Saigon had stepped up its struggle on all fronts to hold onto its scattered liberated areas, and had inflicted heavy casualties on counterattacking enemy troops. Zone 5 had gone more and more strongly on the offensive, expanded its bases in the border zone (Nong Son, Thuong Duc, Tuy Phuoc, Minh Long, Gia Vut, etc.), stepped up attacks against the enemy in the lowlands, wiped out nearly 800 outposts, and liberated 250 hamlets with 200,000 people. In the Tay Nguyen we had attacked and wiped out or forced withdrawal from Dac Pet, Chu Nghe, Mang But, Mang Den, and Ia-xup, and expanded the liberated zone and the strategic corridor. In Tri Thien we had continued to tie the feet of the marine division, Saigon's strategic mobile division, had moved in close to the border area, and had stepped up resistance to "pacification" in the lowlands with results that were improving daily.

The enemy became passive, and started to decline everywhere. Their "pacification" and encroachment plans had been significantly thwarted in many of the lowland areas, especially in the Mekong Delta. The morale and fighting strength of the Saigon troops had clearly fallen: 170,000 had deserted and left their ranks since the first of the year. Their total troop strength had fallen by 20,000 compared with 1973; the number of combat troops had decreased greatly. The enemy's strategic mobile forces had bogged down (the marine division in Tri Thien, and the paratroop division at Thuong Duc). The decrease in American aid had made it impossible for Saigon troops to carry out their combat and force-development plans. In the 1972–1973 fiscal year the Americans had given their protégés $1,614 million in military aid. In fiscal year 1973-1974 it was only $1,026 million, and in fiscal year 1974–1975 it fell to $700 million. Nguyen Van Thieu had to call on his troops to switch to a "poor man's war": according to their own documents, fire support fell nearly 60 percent because of the shortage of bombs and shells;

mobility also decreased 50 percent because of a shortage
of aircraft, vehicles, and even fuel. This situation forced
them to change over from large-scale operations and
deep-penetration helicopter and tank assaults to defense
of their outposts, digging in and carrying out small search
operations.

In sum, the principal characteristic of the situation in
the South after nearly two years of struggle for the implementation of the Paris Agreement was that although
U.S. and satellite troops had been forced to withdraw from
South Vietnam, a revolutionary war was still taking place
in which we coordinated military attacks and political
struggles to oppose the enemy's neocolonial war. The most
significant point about this daily expanding struggle was
that as *we increasingly took the initiative and grew
stronger, the enemy grew weaker and more passive
every day. This was a new step forward in the balance of
forces which was advantageous to the revolution.*

As we were developing our position and strength on the
battlefield in the South, we were making great efforts to
develop and strengthen every aspect of the socialist North
and, step by step, to recover from the serious effects of two
wars of destruction. Production had reached roughly the
1965 level. The people's living conditions had been
stabilized. In the two years 1973 and 1974, hundreds of
thousands of fighters had been mobilized for the front.
Preparations for battle were proceeding actively, especially from the former Zone 4 south, and in the air
defense-air force branch.

In October 1974, as the late autumn weather began to
turn cold, we military cadres were reminded of the campaign season ahead. The Political Bureau and the Central
Military Committee met to hear the General Staff present
its strategic combat plan. The Combat Planning Office of
the General Staff had made quite complete preparations
on every aspect of the enemy's situation and our own, and
the developments on all battlefronts since the signing of
the Paris Agreement, with maps, charts, and statistical

comparisons covering the four walls of the meeting room. Through the reports and discussion the conference reached a unanimous evaluation of the situation in the South, summed up in five points:

First, the Saigon troops were growing weaker militarily, politically, and economically every day. Our forces were stronger than the enemy in the South.

Second, the United States was meeting difficulties at home and abroad, and its ability to give political or military aid to its proteges was declining every day. Not only had the United States had to decrease its aid to Saigon, it also faced increasing opposition to any effort to "jump back" into the South. And even if troops did intervene, they would not be able to rescue the collapsing Saigon quisling administration.

Third, we had set up strategic positions linking North and South, had increased our forces and our stockpiles of materiel, and had completed the system of strategic and tactical roads.

Fourth, movements calling for peace, improvement of popular welfare, democracy, and national independence, and demanding that Thieu be toppled, gained momentum in the towns.

Fifth, our people's just struggle had the sympathy and the strong support of the world's people.

One question was posed and discussed heatedly at this conference: Did the Americans have the ability to send troops back into the South when our large attacks led to the danger of the Saigon army's collapse? Everyone saw clearly and paid special attention to the fact that since they had signed the Paris Agreement on Vietnam and had been forced to withdraw their troops from South Vietnam, the Americans had grown more confused and were in greater difficulty than before. The internal contradictions within the United States administration and between the American political parties, too, were growing sharper. The Watergate affair had agitated the whole country and brought about the resignation of an ultrareactionary president: Richard Nixon. The United States was in an economic recession, inflation was increasing, unemployment had become serious, and the fuel crisis was continuing. At the same time America's allies were quarreling with it, and those countries subordinate to the United States were seeking some means of escaping American control. American aid to the Saigon quisling administration was on the decline. Le Duan put the important conclusion into a resolution: "Now that the United States has pulled out of the South, it will be hard for them to jump back in. And no matter how they may intervene, they cannot rescue the Saigon administration from its disastrous collapse."

When we discussed the strategic combat plan for 1975, another important question was raised: What should be the principal battlefield? On every southern battlefield the enemy had deployed their forces in positions of "strength on two ends." Specifically, in I Corps next to the socialist North the enemy had five divisions of main-force troops; in III Corps, including the defensive perimeter around Saigon, the enemy had three main-force divisions, but they might also be prepared to call in one or two of the three main-force divisions in IV Corps. Then in II Corps, which included the Tay Nguyen, the enemy had only two main-force divisions, and these had to be spread out both to hold all of the provinces of the Tay Nguyen and to protect the coastal provinces of southern Trung Bo from Binh Dinh to Binh Thuan.* But the Tay Nguyen was a very mobile field of battle with many positional advantages that could be developed to the south along Route 14 or down to the east along Routes 19, 7, and 21. The area comprises a high

---

* Under the Saigon governmental structure the four "corps"—more properly called corps tactical zones—were used for both military and civilian purposes. On the civilian side, they were administrative districts below the national level but above the province level. The same thing was true on the military side, and they corresponded to similarly numbered army corps. Thus Saigon's First Army Corps was responsible for I Corps, and so on.

plateau with negligible variations in altitude, convenient for road-building, where technological weapons could operate easily and develop their full might. In short, this was a most important strategic area.

The conferees unanimously approved the General Staff's judgment and chose the Tay Nguyen as the main field of battle for large-scale widespread offensives in 1975. But the Political Bureau saw that to reach a final decision on determining strategy, it was necessary to research the situation more carefully and supplement the strategic combat plan to make it still more complete. At the same time it was decided that it was urgent to step up work on many fronts in order to carry out this resolution. The Political Bureau called all the leading party members and battlefield commanders from the South to come together in Hanoi to report on the situation, discuss it carefully, and come to an agreement on the strategic decisions.

In early December 1974, Pham Hung, member of the Political Bureau and secretary of the southern party branch, General Tran Van Tra, Phan Van Dang, Central Committee member from Nam Bo, Vo Chi Cong, Central Committee member and party secretary for Zone 5, and General Chu Huy Man from Zone 5 came to Hanoi one after the other. The Political Bureau worked individually with those responsible for each battlefield, and heard reports about every aspect of the situation. From December 3 to 5, the Standing Committee of the Central Military Committee heard reports from our comrades from Nam Bo and Zone 5 on their intentions and combat plans. These were preparatory meetings for an extremely important conference of the Political Bureau which lasted from December 18, 1974, until January 8, 1975. Taking part in the conference, besides the members of the Political Bureau, were the leading party members and commanders from all battlefields, members of the Central Military Committee, and the vice chiefs of staff in charge of combat operations. All the members of the Political Bureau took turns expressing their own opinions and discussing them carefully. It must be said that during the twenty-day conference the Political Bureau sharpened their perceptions of the situation and their own opinions each week, gaining a clearer idea of the grand strategy each day, and each day strengthening their firm resolve.

During the time the Political Bureau was meeting, there was fine news from the South: the main-force infantry of eastern Nam Bo, joining together with the regional forces, had opened a campaign for Route 14 and Phuoc Long and had scored a big victory. In some twenty days we had killed and captured over 3,000 of the enemy, captured 3,000 guns of all kinds, and liberated Phuoc Long town and the whole province of Phuoc Long. This was the first province in the South to be completely liberated.

The victorious Route 14-Phuoc Long campaign was most significant, marking a new step toward collapse for the Saigon forces. Their main-force units no longer had the strength to mount large-scale encircling operations to recapture regions, bases, or important towns which we had captured on battlefields in the mountains and jungles and in the border zones. This victory also gave a clearer indication of United States designs and their ability to intervene in South Vietnam. Most important of all, the big victory in the Route 14-Phuoc Long campaign showed the vast new abilities of our army and people. That victory strengthened the strategic determination that had been confirmed in the conference of the Political Bureau and provided an additional impetus to gain a great victory when the opportune moment came.

At first the United States belligerently sent the nuclear aircraft carrier *Enterprise* with a special task force from the Seventh Fleet steaming from the Philippines toward the coast of Vietnam, and put the third marine division on Okinawa on alert. Pentagon hawks threatened to resume bombing the North. But in the end U.S. Secretary of Defense Schlesinger had to pass over the "Phuoc Long business" and announce, "This is not yet an all-out offensive by North Vietnam." He turned a cold shoulder to Thieu's heartrending cries. United States "Ambassador" Martin in Saigon told Thieu, "We have no authorization to give you American support at this time." By now the U.S. position had weakened; they could no longer do whatever they pleased.

The analysis of the Political Bureau conference was that the enemy's weakness was a signal that a new opportunity was on the way. But if we wanted to create a big opportunity we would have to have big, destructive, shattering battles to wipe out and disperse the enemy. The situation now had infinite possibilities for us. In the South there might be a crisis on the enemy's side that could give us a great opportunity. If we struck hard, systematically, and quickly, then it would surely lead to the collapse of the Saigon administration sooner than we had foreseen.

On January 8, 1975, two days after the victory at Phuoc Long, Le Duan concluded the conference, saying: "Our conference has been exhilarating, with a high degree of agreement. This time we have had our comrades from Nam Bo and Zone 5 come up to take part. The situation has become quite clear. We are resolved to complete our two-year plan. Two years is short, and yet long. The struggle in the South has, with the addition of the power of the North, the strength of the whole country. Now the Americans have withdrawn, we have our troops in the South, and the spirit of the masses is rising. This is what marks an opportune moment. We must seize it firmly and step up the struggle on all three fronts: military, political, and diplomatic. That is a special characteristic of Vietnam. . . .

"In the South we have new strength: we have the initiative on the field of battle, and have linked our positions together from Tri Thien all the way to the Mekong Delta. We have formed a powerful fist. In Zone 8 and Zone 9 this fist is also appearing and developing. We have formed battlefields around the towns; in the towns there are mass movements; the world supports us. . . ."

After analyzing the weakening position of the enemy, Le

Duan continued, "We must strike the strategic blow in 1975. In Nam Bo we must link our positions together throughout the region, increase the pressure on Saigon, wipe out more enemy main-force troops, and give all localities the strength to burst out when the opportune moment arrives. And in the Mekong Delta we must put more pressure on My Tho. We agree that the year will open with attacks on the Tay Nguyen."

Pointing to the map hanging behind him, he said: "We must open with attacks on Ban Me Thuot and Tuy Hoa. In Zone 5 we must liberate from Binh Dinh on up. In Tri Thien we must gain control from Hue to Da Nang. Such great victories will greatly change the balance of forces. We must sustain the fighting until the rainy season and pile up repeated victories. If we strike powerfully, the enemy will face the danger of disintegration sooner. To fight around the cities we must smash the enemy's main-force troops. When we enter the cities, we must crush the enemy's nerve centers. The North must guarantee adequate material and technical support to the infantry. These are the basic principles for victory. When the opportune moment comes, we will win. We must see if there is any way we can strike faster. The General Staff must consider this problem further."

The December 18, 1974–January 8, 1975 conference of the Political Bureau was one of historical significance. It correctly evaluated the essence of the situation, took firm hold of the rules of revolutionary warfare, and discovered new principles in time to determine the correct strategy. It was clear by the end of the conference that the Political Bureau was placing greater emphasis on the need to strike quickly. This desire was based on a scientific analysis once we had discovered our opportunity and grasped it. It would have been a crime against the nation to have let this opportunity slip.

Le Duan's conclusion was accepted by the conference with complete unanimity, and drawn up as a resolution: "Never have we had military and political conditions so perfect or a strategic advantage so great as we have now;

complete the national democratic revolution in the South and move on to the peaceful reunification of our Fatherland—now when the movement of the three Indochinese countries is strongly on the offensive, winning greater victories each day. . . ."

The Political Bureau expressed the determination to "mobilize the greatest efforts of the entire party, army, and people in both parts of the country, and in the 1975–1976 period to step up the military and political struggle, in coordination with diplomatic struggle, to change the balance of forces on the southern field of battle quickly and completely to our advantage, to step up preparations with the greatest urgency and complete every aspect of these preparations, so that conditions will be ripe to carry out a general offensive and uprising, to wipe out the puppet troops and make them fall apart, topple the quisling administration from central to local level, put power in the hands of the people, and liberate the South. . . .

"We must still guard against the possibility that the United States may intervene with its air and naval forces in the event that the puppet army is in danger of a big collapse and conditions are such that they can prolong their resistance. But no matter how the Americans may intervene, we have the determination and the conditions to beat them, and they cannot possibly save the Saigon administration from the danger of collapse."

The strategic resolution of the Political Bureau was put into effect through the 1975–1976 two-year strategic plan: in 1975 we would strike unexpectedly with large, widespread offensives, and create conditions to carry out a general offensive and uprising in 1976. In 1976 we would launch the general offensive and uprising to liberate the South completely.

Besides the basic two-year strategic plan, the Political Bureau had foreseen another tendency and included in the 1975 plan another essential course of action: *if the opportune moment presents itself at the beginning or the end of 1975, we will immediately liberate the South in 1975.*

3

An Important Battlefield

The day after the Political Bureau conference had concluded, on January 9, 1975, the Standing Committee of the Central Military Committee met. Vo Chi Cong, Chu Huy Man, Hoang Minh Thao, and Le Trong Tan were also invited, as the meeting was to thoroughly discuss and implement the Political Bureau's resolution. We heard a report from the General Staff on the goals and requirements of the Tay Nguyen campaign. While in session, we received information that the enemy were keeping their paratroop division in position to defend the Da Nang area. This meant that the enemy had not yet discovered our forces and preparations in the Tay Nguyen.

It was only in the course of this meeting that the idea of striking Ban Me Thuot really began to take shape. Everyone saw the significance of an attack on this town, but it would take practical investigations on the spot before we could decide how to attack for a quick victory.

The meeting had just begun when Le Duc Tho opened the door, came in, and sat down to meet with us. We later realized that the Political Bureau was still ill at ease because they saw that the idea of attacking Ban Me Thuot was not yet clearly spelled out in the plan of operations. So they had selected Le Duc Tho to meet with us and to offer the opinion that we absolutely must strike Ban Me Thuot. Le Duc Tho was animated: "We must pose the problem of attacking Ban Me Thuot unambiguously. If we have nearly five divisions in the Tay Nguyen but can't take Ban Me Thuot, where are we?"

General Vo Nguyen Giap, secretary of the Central Military Committee, concluded by affirming the region and the objective of the offensive, the mission of the campaign, the direction it would move, and the use of forces. He called for opinions on fighting methods, and emphasized the motto of boldness, secrecy, and surprise. He said we must make a great number of deceptive manœuvres so the enemy would concentrate their attention on guarding the northern sector of the Tay Nguyen. The Tay Nguyen campaign was given the code name "Campaign 275."

Meanwhile, on the Tay Nguyen front, Brigadier-General Vu Lang, the front commander, along with a number of cadres, set out for Ban Me Thuot to investigate the situation. As Le Duan and Le Duc Tho had proposed, the Political Bureau appointed me to go to the Tay Nguyen battlefield on behalf of the Political Bureau, the Central Military Committee, and the General Command to command operations directly on the spot. The historic meeting ended. All the members of the Political Bureau embraced me in turn, shook my hand, and wished me a safe trip and great victories. For a revolutionary soldier it is a great pleasure to be able to go to the front. To be able to go to carry out an important party resolution which I understood clearly was a joy and a great comfort to me, as it had been when I went to the Route 9 campaign in spring 1971, and the spring-summer campaign in Quang Tri in 1972. After the meeting of the Political Bureau with the representatives of all the battlefields, I told Tran Van Tra, "I'll go down now to fight in the Tay Nguyen until just before the rainy season, and when we've finished I'll come on down to Nam Bo to investigate the battlefield with all of you and prepare for big attacks in the 1975-1976 dry season."

284683

The whole army was excitedly preparing to go to the front. On January 26, 1975, I went with Brigadier-General Phung The Tai, a vice chief of staff, to visit the First Army Corps stationed at Ninh Binh to give them their specific assignment for 1975. This corps was the first established, and included units with many illustrious traditions and glorious exploits in the two resistance wars against the French and the Americans. Now it had become a force with a great combat strength, great mobility, and powerful assault strength. I spoke to encourage the troops:

"This corps' actions must follow closely, must mesh with the activities of the field of battle. The rhythm of the corps must blend with the rhythm of the South. The blows which this corps strikes must be mighty, must mesh and be in time with other mighty blows, and must hit the mark to make the enemy 'measure his coffin.' I hope that the corps' battle drums will throb and the corps' trumpets of victory will resound in time with the symphony of the whole army and people. So let me ask you: Can all you musicians here do that? If you musicians are all in agreement then your conductors, the Central Military Committee and the General Command, are prepared to raise our baton at the proper time, when the opportune moment arrives."

From the ranks of the troops a shout resounded: "We can do it, we can do it! We're determined to win, determined to win!"

In the Tay Nguyen at this time we had the 320th, 10th, and 968th divisions, all of which had gained a great deal of combat experience in the mountains and jungles and in the Tay Nguyen. At the end of December 1974, the General Command decided to dispatch the 316th division to this front as well. This division had glorious traditions; it had fought for twenty years, traveled far, and been victorious during the anti-French resistance. During the resistance against the United States and its hirelings, this division had gone for an extended period to fulfill its in-

ternational duty.* Before they set out, I went with
Brigadier-General Dam Quang Trung, commander of
Zone 4, to visit and talk with the division, then stationed
in western Nghe An.

After I explained the situation and the resolution of the
Political Bureau and the Central Military Committee to
the cadres and fighters of the unit, I told them, "There are
two lines from a poem which burn in my heart. I cannot
remember the author, but they express the resentment,
suffering, and bitterness which every Vietnamese must
reckon with: 'For thirty years our land has taken up the
gun, yet still the disk of our moon is split in two.' Given the
battlefield, the opportunity, and the mission, this is the
day we set out—with the whole people—to make that full
moon whole again. The enemy we meet is different in
many ways from the enemy you have met in the past:
obstinate and cunning, with more experience, more
weapons and equipment, and shrewder combat tech-
nique. But they are still an enemy without justice on
their side, with a tradition of defeat on the field of battle,
who are encountering difficulties on every side, who are
being spiritually and materially impoverished, whose position and strength are weakening. There is no reason
the 316th division cannot defeat Saigon's troops in their
weakened position when the revolution in the South is
rising."

The cadres and fighters of the division raised their
hands high and their chests swelled to bursting; they
shouted, "We are determined to win, determined to win!"
and promised, "We will travel far, go all the way, and fight
until we win."

In addition to myself, the Political Bureau and the Central Military Committee chose as battlefield representatives from the Central Military Committee and the Gen-

* This phrase refers to the logistics and combat support the Vietnamese
gave to the resistance movements in Laos and Cambodia. Western Nghe
An, where this division was stationed, is adjacent to Laos.

eral Command Major-General Dinh Duc Thien, chief of
the General Logistics Department, Brigadier-General Le
Ngoc Hien, vice chief of staff, and a number of experienced cadres from the agencies of the General Staff and
the various specialized branches.

Dinh Duc Thien had had a great deal of experience
during the anti-French resistance in organizing transportation to ensure supplies for the front, especially in the
Dien Bien Phu campaign. In the resistance against the
United States, he had directed the Logistics Department
in overcoming the difficulties as well as the dangers of
fierce attacks, guaranteeing transportation to supply the
soldiers who defeated the enemy's war of destruction in
the North, and supporting the battlefields in the South—
especially to ensure victory in the Route 9 campaign in
spring 1971 and the campaign to liberate Quang Tri in
1972. He was an active revolutionary cadre who never
spoke of retreat. He was cheerful and adventuresome,
with daring and great ability, but because he had passed
his sixth decade he was easily upset, so when he wasn't
satisfied with something he often became agitated. We
had known each other and come to understand each other
since the days we were in French colonial prison together,
before the August Revolution.* I clapped Dinh Duc
Thien on the shoulder and said, "The time has come, and
the Political Bureau has given us our assignments. If we
win this battle, then this old body can rest in peace when
it closes its eyes."

Le Ngoc Hien had fought with us since the first general
uprising in Zone 2 in 1945 and in the 320th brigade
(known as the Delta Brigade) until the end of 1953. He
had been on many fronts during the fighting against the
United States, and then had returned to the General Staff.

---

* In August 1945, the Vietminh took over the government of Vietnam
from the defeated Japanese and in September Ho Chi Minh proclaimed
the independent Democratic Republic of Vietnam. During 1946 the
French gradually reconquered Vietnam, and the resistance war began,
first in the South and later in the North.

After receiving a briefing and his assignment, he set out for the Tay Nguyen ahead of me to investigate the battlefield and prepare operational plans.

The cadres from the agencies of the General Staff and the various specialized branches in our army had also gone with me during the 1971 and 1972 campaigns. They were enthusiastic and resourceful, experienced in planning the coordination of various branches. All were in high spirits at being able to go on this campaign.

In combat, all our commanders followed certain common principles. But each person had his own style of fighting. The party had sent me to a fifteen-day military training course before the August Revolution, and it was only after the complete liberation of the North that I was able to go study at a foreign military academy. But the party had trained me, and I had matured in struggle during the time I was a party member in an independent underground cell, and had taken the initiative in revolutionary activity during the period when communications with the party were broken off.* So this process had given me an independent, daring spirit.

In early 1952, when I was commander of the 320th brigade, my comrades in that command and I organized and carried out an assault on Phat Diem. We sent our troops in, avoiding enemy positions in the outer perimeter along a twenty-kilometer stretch of road, and unexpectedly struck right in town, wiping out the nerve center of the enemy command, taking the town in one day, and only then sending the troops out to destroy the perimeter outposts. We called these tactics the "paratroop" tactics, or the "blooming lotus."**

* After his September 1941 escape from French guards while being transferred from Son La prison to a new location, Dung was under a cloud of suspicion and unable to work in direct contact with the party. He carried out anticolonial activities independently, first working as a carpenter, then posing as a Buddhist monk. He was welcomed back into the party in spring 1943.
** The image of the "blooming lotus" describes the way this style of

We thought a great deal about the coming battle. Home of immortal ballads and of popular resistance heroes like Ma Trang Lon, Nup, and Bok Vuu, the Tay Nguyen was a celebrated and indomitable region of the Fatherland. Its people had loyally followed the party, Uncle Ho, and the revolution from the first days of the resistance against the French and the Americans, and had given their all for the victory of the revolution. We must liberate the Tay Nguyen, and most immediately Ban Me Thuot, the largest town in the region. But how could we attack Ban Me Thuot most quickly, in the best order, and with the greatest surprise? The victory at Phuoc Long had shown that in 1975 we had considerable ability to liberate towns and cities. Yet certainly the towns in the Tay Nguyen would be harder to attack than Phuoc Long.

At that time the Tay Nguyen included five provinces— Kontum, Gia Lai, Phu Bon, Dar Lac, and Quang Duc—and was a battlefield of mountains and forests, blending into border zones filled with obstacles. At the time we were preparing for the attack on the Tay Nguyen the enemy had there one main-force division, seven ranger groups (the equivalent of ten regiments), and four armored groups of tanks and armored cars, deployed in well-organized defensive positions. But because they had miscalculated our intentions, thinking that if we attacked the Tay Nguyen we would strike in the north, they had concentrated their forces to hold Pleiku and Kontum, leaving reduced forces in the southern Tay Nguyen, particularly in Dar Lac. Ban Me Thuot, province town for Dar Lac, with a population of 150,000, was a political and economic center for the enemy and location of the headquarters of their 23rd division. This reflected another mistake in the enemy's evaluation of us. They thought that in 1975 we would not yet have the strength to attack large towns and cities, and that even if we attacked we would not be able to hold on when they

---

attack began in the center of town, then gradually opened out into the outlying areas like a flower bud slowly opening its petals.

counterattacked. Thus, although Ban Me Thuot was a vital position, before we attacked the enemy had not deployed their forces in strength and had neglected many things. The more deeply one went into the town, the thinner the troops were spread. If we successfully liberated Ban Me Thuot, we would successfully smash the enemy's defense system in the Tay Nguyen, thereby setting up a dangerous, mobile field position which could cause sudden changes in the battlefield situation.

When the decision to attack Ban Me Thuot was definitely confirmed, I rushed a telegram to the Tay Nguyen to instruct Le Ngoc Hien not to come to Hanoi to report as planned, but to stay there and investigate the situation in Ban Me Thuot further, and then come up to the headquarters of the 559th, the Truong Son force, to meet me on my way to the Tay Nguyen.

I went to see Truong Chinh before I set out. He inquired carefully about the situation of the army and the preparations, and bid me go out and bring back a victory. As we parted he reminded me to give careful consideration to the thoughts he had expressed in the Political Bureau meetings about the task of directing the campaign. I recalled his clear foresight about the essential direction of a revolutionary war: "We must strike strategic blows as devastating as Dien Bien Phu. We need only a few such blows and the enemy will collapse at once. We must firmly take the initiative and strike at places which will force the enemy to take cover. When they take cover, they will fall into our trap. . . ." Then Le Duc Tho took my hand, saying, "If we win this big battle, we will certainly create a new position, one extremely favorable to us. Remember to take care of your health."

One day toward the end of January 1975 I went to bid farewell to Le Duan. He reminded me that the importance of the attack on Ban Me Thuot and the Central Highlands was to create this new opportunity, and then asked if I had adequate forces. I answered, "We have enough troops. If we know how to use them, we can gain the advantage."

But he asked again, "Do we need to send any more forces in?" When I set out on campaigns before it was always like this. Le Duan always made a point of asking if anything was lacking in the preparation of forces, and if we needed any help from the central level. This time he added a warning: "You must think a great deal about the correct method of attack. The Tay Nguyen battlefield can be a great success. A victory could lead to the possibility that we have foreseen, that the South could be liberated this year."

I bid farewell in turn to Vo Nguyen Giap, Song Hao, Hoang Van Thai, and Le Quang Dao of the Central Military Committee. We were in agreement. Our hearts were united. We didn't say much to each other as we parted, but those who went to the battlefield and those who stayed at home were agreed on one thing: this time we absolutely must effect a change quite different from those of any previous campaign.

4

The Road to the Front

We went to the Tay Nguyen front with the code name "Detachment A-75." Because of the need for secrecy it had been decided that in our communications, exchanges of information, and discussions during this campaign, Vo Nguyen Giap would have the code name "Chien" and I would have the code name "Tuan."

Each year in the days leading up to Tet—the lunar New Year—I prepared some small gifts and letters of New Year's greetings to send to the families in the revolutionary base area who had helped me in my years of secret activity. This time I prepared gifts and Tet greetings in advance, so that after I had begun my journey, my family could send them on as usual. I also signed in advance the telegrams of congratulation for the armed forces anniversaries of the Soviet Union and the German Democratic Republic in February and of Mongolia in March 1975, so that they could be sent on the appropriate days.

On the morning of February 5, 1975, the twenty-fifth day of the twelfth lunar month, we went out to Gia Lam airport to board the airplane for Dong Hoi. Only Brigadier-General Phung The Tai, vice chief of staff, and Brigadier-General Le Van Try, commander of the air defense-air force troops came out to see us off.

At exactly 10:30 A.M. the AN-24 airplane took off. Hanoi

35

was filled with flowers, preparing to greet the spring. Hanoi, the heart of the whole country, from which the Political Bureau's strategic decision had come, heroic Hanoi was today immeasurably beautiful. In the airplane we remembered the admonitions of our comrades on the Political Bureau and the Central Military Committee, and thought of the tremendous responsibility they had given us and of methods for the coming attacks in the Tay Nguyen. As Le Duan had cautioned us, we "must think a great deal and have the correct method of attack."

As we went into this campaign it was the same everywhere, from the leading cadres to each individual soldier, everyone was optimistic and eager, anxious to do a good job. We were impatient, wanting to get to the battlefield that very day to carry out the plan of attack we were nurturing, and we attentively followed the enemy's every action.

According to our intelligence information, on December 9 and 10, 1974, Thieu had met in "Independence Palace" with the commanders of all his armed forces and military regions to estimate what actions we would take in 1975. They judged that this year we might attack on a larger scale than we had in 1974, but not on the scale of our attacks in 1968 or 1972; we did not yet have the capability to attack large towns or cities, and even if we did attack them, we could not hold them. We could only attack small, isolated towns like Phuoc Long and Gia Nghia. Our primary objective in 1975 would be to gain two million people in the Mekong Delta and expand the liberated zone in the mountain regions. Our goal would be to score victories to force them to implement the Paris Agreement on Vietnam. They thought that the main thrust of our offensive in the first part of 1975 would be to attack III Corps, primarily Tay Ninh, with the aim of taking Tay Ninh as a capital for the Provisional Revolutionary Government of South Vietnam. As to the timing of the offensive, the enemy estimated that we would strike just before or after Tet and continue until June 1975, then stop when the rainy season

started. Because of this assessment, Thieu ordered his
generals to attack us furiously before that time to smash
the plans we had prepared. Saigon's prime minister, Tran
Thien Khiem, met with sector and subsector commanders
to open an "immediate accelerated pacification" campaign, to run for three months beginning January 1, 1975,
to "halt the Vietcong winter-spring campaign." Because
of their assessment, they did not change their two-pronged
strategic troop deployment (I Corps and III Corps), nor did
they increase their forces much in II Corps, which included the Tay Nguyen.

At the beginning of 1975 they had 1,351,000 troops,
including 495,000 main-force troops, 475,000 regional-
force troops, and 381,000 armed "civil guards." This included thirteen main-force divisions and eighteen ranger
groups. Their troops were deployed as follows:

In I Corps they had five divisions (including two divisions of general reserves) and four ranger groups,
twenty-one battalions, and a number of companies and
platoons of artillery with 418 pieces; five armored regiments and six tank and armored-car platoons with 449
vehicles; and one air force division with 96 fighter planes.
Most of the enemy's main-force troops were holding Hue
and Da Nang.

In II Corps they had two main-force divisions and seven
ranger groups, fourteen regiments and a number of companies and platoons of artillery with 382 pieces; five armored regiments and thirteen tank platoons with 477 vehicles; and two air force divisions with 138 fighter planes.
Most of the enemy main-force troops were spread out holding the Tay Nguyen, the plains, and the coastal region.

In III Corps they had three main-force divisions and
seven ranger groups, fourteen battalions, and a number of
companies and platoons of artillery with 376 pieces; seven
armored regiments and fifteen tank and armored-car platoons with 655 vehicles; and two air force divisions with
over 250 fighter planes. All of the enemy's main-force
troops were set out in an arc to the northwest, north, and

northeast to guard Saigon from a distance of fifty kilometers, more or less.

In IV Corps they had three main-force divisions, eighteen groups of security forces, fifteen battalions and fifty-five companies of artillery with 380 pieces; five armored regiments and seventeen tank platoons with 493 vehicles; one air force division with 72 fighter planes, and 580 ships and boats of all kinds. The main-force units held the Can Tho-Chuong Thien region, Route 4, and the Cambodian border front.

The enemy's position had weakened, and they had made big mistakes in strategy and in evaluating us, which had led to incorrect troop deployment plans and mistaken operating premises, and signaled the great defeat which was coming for them.

When the airplane landed at Dong Hoi, Major-General Dong Si Nguyen and a group of cars from the 559th division command which had come up from Quang Tri were waiting to meet us at the airport. We got in the cars to go to Quang Tri. The road through Le Thuy and Ho Xa was badly pockmarked from the years of fierce enemy attacks, so the car lurched along heavily. This now represented one of the most firm, heroic sections of road in our land, because of its supply role in the South's years of struggle.

At the Ben Hai River we got into a motorboat to go up the river. The day was bright but strangely cool. In the waning afternoon we landed at a dock on the south side of the river and went into the headquarters of the 559th force, west of Gio Linh. The 559th force, as their name indicates, came into being in May 1959, and was subordinate to the General Logistics Department. Its history, like that of our army's logistics branch, was one of a process of building, fighting, and developing. This unit embodied the revolutionary ideal of attack; it understood the concept of revolutionary violence and had the farsighted vision needed to serve the struggle effectively. All of its accomplishments were battle exploits.

Tran Dang Ninh, a member of the Central Committee

and a firm revolutionary fighter who twice escaped from the prisons of the French colonialists, played an important part in building our army's logistics branch. If he were alive today he would be most gratified to see the powerful logistics force our army has now—one he had hoped for in earlier days.

Now more than 10,000 transport vehicles traveled these roads, including many sent from the military zones and local areas as well as many sent from the Ministry of Transport as reinforcements. Like a resourceful house-keeper, the logistics branch served the annual plans of the army, was careful and thrifty, husbanding its forces daily and weekly on the southern battlefront to await the big opportunity; it carried out its responsibilities to the troops at home, and fulfilled its international duty towards our brother countries. One thing that was especially exciting was to see our fighters using motorized transport to go into the campaign, and knowing they had enough to eat on the front lines. Even our dry rations, such as type A-72, were quite good. Also, this campaign marked the first time our fighters on the front had received a number of large guns and shells made in our own country by our national defense workers. This was a first step in the technological revolution in our national defense industries.

The farther we went toward the front, the more we saw the vast might of the rear, the socialist North. The rear area is one of the factors that is usually decisive for victory in battle. The heroic people of the North had borne every sacrifice and hardship to carry out every task. They had sent everything needed to serve the front, even their most precious husbands and sons.

Arriving at the headquarters of the 559th force we saw Le Ngoc Hien, who had come by car from the Tay Nguyen as he had promised.

In the thatched house night had long since fallen, but we had not been able to sleep because of our thoughts of the coming campaign. How could we carry out the Political Bureau's resolution on liberating the South? How would we win in the Tay Nguyen? And especially, how should we attack Ban Me Thuot so the enemy would collapse quickly? I remembered our nation's traditional style of fighting, the fighting style of our army for the past thirty years and more. Then again my own familiar style of fighting returned to my mind: unsuspected by the enemy, strike like a bolt of lightning straight at their command center and smash it right at the first. But would the actual situation allow for that?

The next morning we got up early and set to work. Le Ngoc Hien reported on the situation on the Tay Nguyen front and on his proposed operational plans. Dinh Duc Thien and Dong Si Nguyen reported on the status of logistics preparations and informed us that they had carried plenty of everything needed to serve the fighting to the front. They proposed that when we strike, we strike big, and however much rice, ammunition, gasoline, however many troop transport vehicles we needed, there would be plenty. That set our minds at ease. In terms of logistics, if we mounted large attacks, won big and won fast, that would decrease the level of supplies needed, and we would be able to seize material and technical resources from the enemy to supplement our own.

The very next day Dinh Duc Thien returned to Quang Binh to supervise the transfer of ammunition stores from there to add to those in the Tay Nguyen, to give directions on which type of ammunition to move first and which to move later, while we continued on our way south. The license plate on our car was repainted, adding the letters *TS* and the number 50, which meant that our car had top priority in the Truong Son zone. Colonel Phan Khac Hy, deputy commander of the 559th, was assigned to go with our group to guard against any problems along the way and ensure that we arrived quickly at the Tay Nguyen front headquarters.

Along the strategic roadway all our fighters were busily building and repairing the road. The Vanguard Youth girls, who were singing, laughing, and chattering as they worked, circled around our car. "Oh, Commander, it's nearly Tet and we haven't gotten any letters from home yet." We gave them a few hundred hair clasps to share among themselves as presents. And convoys of big trucks roared along the road on their way back to the North, having carried ammunition to the front. The men drove with one arm hanging out of their cabs. "Say, Commander, it's the eve of Tet already, but we don't have any cigarettes left." So we gave the truck drivers some cigarettes as Tet presents.

Along the road we met the 316th division on an operation. It was the first time a whole division had gone on a mechanized operation, going out to the front in 500 large trucks. The division had orders that from the time they set out until they opened fire they were absolutely not to turn on their radios, in order to preserve secrecy. We could intercept enemy communications as they called to each other saying they had lost track of the 316th division and didn't know where it was going. Our fighters sitting in the trucks—strong, healthy, and happy—waved their hats, waved their hands, and sang amidst the rumbling of the tanks, armored cars, trucks pulling long-range artillery and antiaircraft guns, and all kinds of transport vehicles bumper to bumper in a long, endless line like a great waterfall rushing out to the front.

5

Taking Up Positions

On the eve of Tet we stopped over at the headquarters of
the 470th construction division stationed at Ia Drang. A
few days before, an enemy A-37 had bombed nearby and
set two of our vehicles on fire. But the cadres and fighters
of the headquarters group still had a proper Tet celebration. Everywhere in the unit there were electric lights
shielded so they couldn't be seen from the air. On the
morning of the first day of Tet we enjoyed the celebration
and wished each other a new year full of new exploits in
battle. When we reached the Tay Nguyen, we set up our
headquarters west of Ban Me Thuot, near the headquarters of the Front Command. We were in a green jungle
next to a forest of *khooc* trees, whose dry fallen leaves
covered the ground like a golden carpet. Whenever someone stepped on them, the leaves under their feet sounded
like crisp rice crackers shattering, causing a commotion
all through that part of the forest. Here the smallest spark
could start a forest fire. This meant that those working
hardest were the communications fighters: whenever
there was a fire and communications lines were broken,
they went out to fix them and came back black as coal
miners. Another problem was the elephants, which
traveled in herds of forty or fifty, and would pull down and

break the networks of communications lines even when they were quite high in the trees.

In a meeting with the comrades responsible for the front, as had been decided, I announced on behalf of the Central Military Committee and the General Command that a Central Highlands front command was being set up, including Major-General Hoang Minh Thao, commander; Senior Colonel Nguyen Hiep (Dang Vu Hiep), political officer; Brigadier-General Vu Lang and Senior Colonels Phan Ham, Nguyen Lang, and Nguyen Nang, deputy commanders; and Senior Colonel Phi Trieu Ham, deputy political officer.

We reviewed the situation at the front. So far the enemy still had only one main-force division in the Tay Nguyen, along with seven ranger groups (the equivalent of ten regiments), four armored regiments, eight artillery battalions, and one air force division, concentrated mostly for the defense of the northern Tay Nguyen. In the northern Tay Nguyen they had eight infantry regiments and four armored regiments, while in the southern Tay Nguyen they had only two infantry regiments.

They were deployed like this because Saigon's Brigadier-General Pham Van Phu, commander of II Corps and of their Second Army Corps, felt that Pleiku would surely be hit as it was the most important position in the Tay Nguyen. The army corps command was there; it would be a convenient springboard from which to strike down at Binh Dinh; and more than that it was close to our supply corridors and near the rear bases of the Liberation Army. Phu was obsessed by the saying, "He who controls the Tay Nguyen will control all of the South." And he thought that the decisive blow from the Liberation Army in the Tay Nguyen must be against Pleiku and Kontum. If Pleiku and Kontum were lost then Ban Me Thuot would also be lost.

Although the enemy were stretched out all through the Tay Nguyen to hold many positions, and although their mobile forces in the region were limited, they still might be able to mobilize a certain force to deal with us by bringing in more from I Corps and III Corps, providing we were not able to carry out attacks on those battlefields in close coordination with those in the Tay Nguyen, and providing their ability to send in reinforcements to hold the Tay Nguyen still existed. They were very confident of their air-mobile capabilities.

Our forces taking part in the campaign included the main-force units of the Tay Nguyen, the General Command, and Zone 5, relatively well prepared, with high determination and a spirit of enthusiasm, and reinforced so their ranks were relatively full. Many of the units were familiar with the battlefield and were very experienced in combat. The road network for campaign mobility had been completed, the soldiers were relatively well supplied, and command centers had been set up and stabilized at all levels. Compared with the enemy throughout the campaign area we were not greatly superior in infantry. But because we had concentrated most of our forces in the main zone of the campaign, we had the advantage over the enemy in that area. In infantry we had 5.5 soldiers to the enemy's 1; in tanks and armored cars we had 1.2 to the enemy's 1; in large artillery we had 2.1 to the enemy's 1. But our infantry still suffered from a number of shortcomings: for example, their level of ability in concentrated combat operations was still uneven, we had little experience in attacking cities, and large-scale coordinated combat operations were still new to some of the branches.

In our discussions at the Front Command, we quickly reached agreement on the tasks and the principal objectives of the campaign. But it took us longer to discuss fighting methods. In the end we all agreed, and developed some new ideas. In the Tet Mau Than general offensive in 1968, we had used troops who were for the most part well trained, to attack towns and cities under conditions where we were still inferior to the enemy in the balance of forces, and for that reason we were unable to hold any town or city completely. In 1972 we attacked for a month, wiped

out the enemy's 3rd division, and liberated all of Quang
Tri province exactly on May 1. Later, during the rainy
season, our battlefield activities throughout the South decreased. The enemy concentrated their paratroop and
marine divisions and a number of other units and counterattacked, with U.S. air and naval support, to recapture
Quang Tri. After successively defeating enemy counterattacks throughout an eighty-six-day-and-night battle to
protect the citadel and the town, in the end we were only
able to hold the area north of the Thach Han River. The
enemy recaptured Hai Lang district, part of Trieu Phong
district, and the ruins of the citadel and town.

This time we had learned from the experiences of previous campaigns, but the important thing was to proceed
from the task at hand, the strategic requirements, the
special characteristics of the situation, and the concrete
conditions on the battlefield. So for our attack in the Tay
Nguyen campaign, we would on the one hand have to use
relatively large forces, of regiment and division size, to cut
Routes 19, 14, and 21, thereby establishing positions
which divided the enemy's forces; strategically, this
would cut the Tay Nguyen off from the coastal plains, and
tactically, it would isolate Ban Me Thuot from Pleiku and
Pleiku from Kontum. At the same time, we needed diversionary maneuvers to tie the enemy's feet and draw their
attention and their forces toward the northern Tay
Nguyen, enabling us to maintain secrecy and surprise in
the south until we began the attack to take Ban Me Thuot.

On the other hand, the main aspect was to set things in
motion on the key front for the campaign to capture Ban
Me Thuot. We would use a relatively strong, coordinated
assault force of regimental size, not set in place in the
positions from which the attack would be launched, but
assembled at a distance and moved in, bypassing the
enemy's outer defense perimeter positions, and unexpectedly striking deep within the town. This assault force
would coordinate its attack with sapper and infantry units
that had been stationed there secretly ahead of time, im-

mediately wipe out the command nerve centers and other crucial positions, and only when the springboard positions inside were firmly under control, strike out from the town to wipe out the isolated posts. These posts would have lost their commanders by then and would be in a panic. At the same time we needed an extremely strong coordinated reserve force which could be quickly summoned if needed to beat back any enemy counterattack aimed at recapturing Ban Me Thuot.

It was impossible to carry out the plan to strike directly into Ban Me Thuot right at the first of the campaign, because when we reached the front our comrades there had already deployed a strong force around Duc Lap and on as far as Dac Soong in order to wipe out the enemy and liberate a stretch of Route 14, opening a strategic corridor down to Nam Bo. To have shifted those troops would have cost us time and created many difficulties, especially in maintaining secrecy. So we had to decide to go ahead and hit Duc Lap, then go on to strike Ban Me Thuot the very next day after isolating Ban Me Thuot and spreading our forces around the town in a tight encirclement.

We continued our careful investigation of the situation in the town of Ban Me Thuot. One cadre who led a reconnaissance group to infiltrate Ban Me Thuot came back and reported, "This town is big! It's almost as big as Hai Phong city." We knew that Ban Me Thuot wasn't as big as Hai Phong, but it was a big town with a wide outer fringe, with many tall buildings, and lit at night with neon lights, so it seemed even larger to the men in the reconnaissance patrol. Some people in the revolutionary structure in town had been asked to come out to report on the situation. Bui San (Dang Tran Thi), a member of the standing committee of the party committee in Zone 5, and Huynh Van Man (Can), secretary of the Dar Lac provincial party committee, also came to our headquarters to tell us about the political situation and the local political movements, and the status of our network within the town. When we met Vo Chi Cong at the conference of the Central Military

Committee back in Hanoi, we had suggested that Zone 5 should send people ahead to get a good grasp of the situation so that when we reached the Tay Nguyen we could meet with them and speed up the work. We had also captured a spy from the enemy's 45th regiment, and from interrogating him had gained additional information about the situation. Throughout the time we were making preparations, we followed the enemy's troop positions and troop movements closely from hour to hour. By following enemy radio transmissions we knew that their commanders had ordered their reconnaissance units to find out where our 10th division was located. The Campaign Command ordered our forces to conceal themselves more carefully than ever, and new orders were given to cadres and reconnaissance agents to go out and continue diversionary actions so the enemy would think the 10th division was still stationed in the northern Tay Nguyen.

For days on end the enemy fired artillery in the vicinity of Ban Me Thuot to support groups of spies and rangers operating far out in our direction. Enemy planes bombed our defensive positions north of Kontum. Every day enemy reconnaissance planes flew over Duc Co and northeast of Kontum. And they assigned extra troops to Pleiku.

On the night of February 25, 1975, in a jungled section of Dar Lac, amid the noise of enemy artillery sounding the watch, we met with the Tay Nguyen front command to discuss the direction of the attack on Ban Me Thuot, both the direction if the enemy should increase their forces and the direction if the enemy stayed as they were now. On behalf of the General Command, I approved and signed the map determining the assignments, forces to take part, and our routes of attack on Ban Me Thuot. Hoang Minh Thao, the commander, and Nguyen Hiep, the political officer, signed their names next to mine. We shook hands and wished each other victory. After the signing I expressed some of my thoughts.

"If we strike the enemy in ways and at a time which they cannot possibly anticipate—completely unexpectedly—it will be extremely dangerous for them. We must pool our ideas completely and make every effort to preserve secrecy and surprise so we can attack as we have planned before they can increase their forces. If the enemy should increase their forces and be on guard, then we will use the second method. This may be more difficult, but we will surely win.

"So far it has not occurred to the enemy that we might organize a large-scale attack, nor do they yet know when we will attack. They have no clear idea of what forces we have in the Ban Me Thuot area, unless we are discovered while we are on the move. In the days ahead we must keep the enemy certain that the main thrust of our attack will be against Kontum and Pleiku. Our opportunity lies here. We must step up our coming actions at Kontum and Pleiku to make the enemy still more firmly convinced in this error.

"At this time there are several problems to raise. First, what are the forms of attack to use against large towns and cities? In the final phase of revolutionary war, in conditions where we are stronger than the enemy, we definitely must carry out large annihilation attacks and liberate the towns and cities. There is no other way. For the attack on Ban Me Thuot we are in a stronger position than the enemy. We have nearly three divisions, while the enemy have only one main-force regiment of the 23rd division and three groups of security forces, so they are relatively weak and isolated. But they are in a town that is spread out, with a complex layout, and with organized defenses in place. Attacking a large town and using large coordinated forces are still new to us. These are things we must pay attention to.

"In attacking Ban Me Thuot we will take a force many times stronger than the enemy, organize powerful combined assault units, coordinated with the sapper and infantry battalions already in position, to strike immediately into the center of town, capture the two airfields, and quickly disable the command nerve center of the enemy.

Only then will we move back out to wipe out the enemy outside the town. There are two difficult problems in this type of attack: first, we must organize the coordinated fighting and command each wave of the attack so they are all on schedule and operating according to plan, crossing the rivers and passing all the enemy defense posts, both those farther out and those in close to town. Second, we must preserve secrecy and keep the enemy unsuspecting until the minute we open fire. If we can do these two things well, then the enemy will be toppled quickly, not in seven to ten days as you predicted at the outset. The balance of forces here allows us not only to smash the enemy and capture them, but to have a powerful reserve force to wipe out counterattacking enemy units, preserve our victory, and carry the offensive forward, because the whole Tay Nguyen will be isolated from the southern battlefield, not merely from Ban Me Thuot. And that is without mentioning that our activities on all other battlefields will be coordinated with those in the Tay Nguyen, even further limiting the enemy's ability to mobilize sizable reinforcements for the Tay Nguyen front.

"I must add that in all these battles it will be best if we can destroy the command headquarters and capture the enemy's top commanders, as we will then be able to end the battles more quickly. Naturally that is a difficult task, because the enemy's command nerve centers are always deep inside the town and are well defended. We must also realize that the battle for Ban Me Thuot is the key opening battle of the campaign. Toppling the enemy quickly, wiping them out, liberating and holding the town, defeating enemy counterattacks and pushing ahead—all are closely linked aspects not only for Ban Me Thuot but for the whole Tay Nguyen campaign. If we can maintain surprise about our objective, our timing, our forces, and our method of attack, if we can isolate the town and still remain stronger than the enemy without the enemy discovering it, then we can guarantee that the battle will be less costly and victory will be more rapid. The dry season is very important to us. We cannot waste a single day, a single hour. We must race with time to sustain our attacks and gain continuous victories.

"In sum, this method of attack aims at saving time by quickly wiping out the enemy and liberating a large town like Ban Me Thuot, thereby transforming the battlefield; it is a creative manner of attack which will put into practice the spirit of an active offensive by the revolutionary army. That is the result of a process of careful investigation and research, of meticulous and scientific consideration of every problem to reach a precise solution and to carry out a high development in the art of combat. If we can put our resolution into practice we will have additional experience to carry with us as we liberate other towns in the Tay Nguyen, such as Phu Bon, Gia Nghia, Pleiku, and Kontum.

"Second, we have the correct method of attack, and now we must organize the fields of battle: we must closely organize each regiment, each battalion, down to the smallest units; we must coordinate each wave, each spearhead, each specialized branch; and we must especially organize the mechanized assault units which will strike deep inside the town, as well as the combined fighting inside the town. If we have a high spirit of determination and a bold concept, but are not tightly organized and do not make our assignments clearly, we may get strung out and worn down.

"Third, we must recognize that the town of Ban Me Thuot is a political and economic center, and a center for the ethnic groups and religions in the Tay Nguyen. Members of various ethnic groups, as well as Catholics, Protestants, and Buddhists, and bourgeoisie, plantation owners, and foreigners have all lived under neocolonialism for many years, making the situation very complex. When our soldiers enter the town they must have the correct attitude and behavior, strictly carry out the policies and regulations that have been issued, help the local committee build a basic-level revolutionary administration, win the hearts of the people, and quickly stabilize people's life after liberation.

"Fourth, we must organize a military administration after liberation. There is work to be done; there are services that must have someone to head them. Many tasks in this military administration will be new and unfamiliar, and we will discuss these problems with Bui San and the Dar Lac provincial committee. But the main thing is to be organized, to have people to take charge, and to have the army take part. Then we will be able to do it. Colonel Y Bloc, a man from one of the ethnic groups who has the confidence of the people and is loved and respected by everyone in the area is here. After discussing it with the Zone 5 command, we have proposed to the Central Military Committee and the General Command that if we completely liberate the town we will ask that Y Bloc be promoted to the rank of senior colonel and appointed chairman of the Ban Me Thuot military administrative committee.

"Fifth, Ban Me Thuot is the rear base for the 23rd division, and contains the rear bases of all the division's regiments. It has a large system of storage areas, as well as many factories and a considerable industrial base belonging to the bourgeoisie. We must protect this whole infrastructure and get it back in operation. This will be a complex task to organize. We will confiscate public property, but we must not touch the property of the people, and we must correctly follow the policies on property of the bourgeoisie. Nguyen Nang, our deputy commander in charge of logistics, must help the local authorities with this work. We must confiscate all military vehicles, resources, weapons, and equipment. Staples and other food, and anything that can be used for the army, must be kept and guarded and properly administered.

"Sixth, we know from our experience at Phuoc Long that after liberation we may be able to use newly captured prisoners of war, especially soldiers from specialized branches like artillery, and drivers of cars, tanks, armored cars, road repair vehicles, and so on. When we are in a strong, victorious position, we can do this. In sum, we must give the utmost attention to using war booty and prisoners of war immediately for the battle. Naturally we must be on guard and supervise them.

"The final matter I want to talk with you about is that there is not much time before we begin the attack on Ban Me Thuot. If we drag out our preparations, we may be found out. We must attack on time, according to our proposal, because all the other fronts are using our timing as the standard for coordination. We must realize that it will be very difficult for the enemy if they have to deal with us on the whole southern battle front. Ban Me Thuot is the most important town in the Tay Nguyen, but other places are also important for the enemy because they are closer to Saigon and Da Nang. So, when they are being hit with a barrage of attacks on many battlefields, the enemy will be forced to look at the overall situation, and consider where the main strategic thrust of our offensive is. For that reason, they will not send their general reserves out immediately, but the enemy will first respond with the forces of the Second Army Corps. But the Second Army Corps doesn't have many forces, the roads to the Tay Nguyen have been cut, and any attempt to land troops by air will be limited and will make it easier for them to be wiped out. Our work is most urgent, and we must do everything possible to preserve secrecy. Those of you from the front must go all the way there to help our units, especially the 316th division who have just arrived and are not yet familiar with the field of battle. We cannot strike too soon, but if we do not make our preparations quickly and time stretches on, that will not do either.

"The Central Military Committee and the General Command recognize that the attack on Ban Me Thuot will seriously upset the enemy's overall situation. A victory in the Tay Nguyen campaign along with victories on all the other fields of battle may cause important developments which will push the enemy into a position where there will be a large-scale metamorphosis. There is no other way.

Since the enemy is embarked on a counter-revolutionary war, we have to embark on a revolutionary war. The longer the enemy continue the war the weaker they become; the more we carry forward this kind of revolutionary war, the stronger we become.

"I think you all have much work yet to do. We have already reached agreement and drawn up our resolution on these matters which we have discussed together, so we must cooperate fully with each other to see that our assignments are carried out well. In other words, we must do what is needed to smash the enemy, liberate Ban Me Thuot, push the offensive forward to liberate the Tay Nguyen, and liberate the whole of our beloved South. In the Front Command we must assign responsibilities for some to take care of preparations for the attack on Ban Me Thuot, and for others to take care of overseeing and helping direct units as they deploy their forces and take up blocking and encircling positions for the campaign according to our plans.

"Today we have had a relatively full meeting, with representatives from all divisions, specialized branches, and agencies. On behalf of the Central Military Committee and the General Command, let me approve the resolution and the operational plans of the Tay Nguyen front command. We must do a great deal of work, using all our energy and cunning, before our artillery shells explode on the enemy's heads in Ban Me Thuot, yet we must still maintain surprise, strike quickly, and finish the battle quickly. We must see to it that party committees at all levels and our cadres and fighters understand the full significance of this battle, raise their spirit of courage, shrewdness, and creativity in combat, and understand and correctly carry out the methods of attack we have discussed. Then we will certainly achieve a lightning victory."

The enemy were still concentrating on defending the northern Tay Nguyen. We again stepped up our diversionary activities, mobilizing people in the liberated zones of

Kontum and Pleiku provinces to go out noisily to build and repair roads and carry supplies, and soldiers joined with local authorities to organize meetings welcoming the soldiers back to liberate Pleiku and Kontum.

On March 1 the 968th division wiped out two outposts on Route 19 west of Pleiku, right on the edge of Thanh An district town. The enemy became all the more certain we were preparing the field for an attack on Pleiku. They hastily shifted the 45th regiment from Thuan Man (where the road forks off from Route 14 toward Phu Bon) up to Thanh An on March 3. Seeing that the enemy were "hooked," I reminded Hoang Minh Thao to instruct the 968th division to strike harder, to send more big shells for the division to fire into Cu Hanh airfield, and to warn Thanh Son, the division commander, to "strike once and shout ten times."

On March 3 the 95th regiment and the 3rd division from Zone 5 smashed a chain of bases and cut Route 19 in two places—east and west of An Khe. The enemy shifted two regiments of the 22nd division up from Binh Dinh to break the blockade east of An Khe and the 2nd cavalry brigade down from Pleiku to break through west of An Khe. Pham Van Phu stuck his neck out further still to increase his defenses in the northern Tay Nguyen, primarily Pleiku. He sent the 4th and 6th ranger groups on sweeps northwest of Kontum and Pleiku to look for the 10th division and the 320th division, two divisions which had dealt the enemy painful blows from 1972 to 1974. Enemy artillery and airplanes concentrated their strikes on any place they suspected we might have troops encamped or might have a fire base.

At that time the 320th division was still lying quietly to the west of Route 14, only five kilometers from the road—along the stretch from the Ia Leo bridge to Chu Xe. On March 3 the division had sent its 9th battalion across Route 14 to circle around to the east of Thuan Man district town, ready to set up a blocking position on the road from Thuan Man to Cheo Reo when the order came, to keep the enemy from coming up from Phu Bon to reinforce Route 14 or from breaking and running from Thuan Man to Cheo Reo. I must say that the actions of this battalion were extremely clever and well concealed. They split off for independent actions far from their division, but even strung secret telephone wires across Route 14 to maintain communications with the division twenty kilometers away. And it was this same 9th battalion which was the first unit of the 320th division to cut the enemy formation to the east of Phu Bon when they broke and ran from Pleiku toward Phu Yen along Route 7.

Meanwhile, the 10th division was secretly positioning its troops and firepower in next to Duc Lap and Dac Soong to the southwest of Ban Me Thuot, urgently preparing everything so they could open fire at the exact time planned. And on March 5 the 25th regiment came out and cut Route 21 along the section east of Chu Cuc, destroying a unit of more than eighty vehicles. Thus by March 5 the enemy in the Tay Nguyen were isolated from the lowlands. But they could still go back and forth between the northern and southern Tay Nguyen, because we didn't yet intend to cut Route 14. Some sixty to eighty military and civilian vehicles a day traveled back and forth as usual.

Here we should clear one thing up. We didn't cut Route 14 at the same time we cut Routes 19 and 21 although our plan included, besides the strategic roadblocks, the campaign blockade of Route 14 in order to cut Ban Me Thuot off from Pleiku. The problem was when we should put it into effect. If we cut Route 14 too soon, our intention to attack Ban Me Thuot might be discovered. And if we wanted to cut Route 14 in two places—north and south of Thuan Man district town—we would have to attack and capture the town. But once we captured it, the enemy would know that we had a division positioned north of Ban Me Thuot; they would find some way of bringing in more forces to reinforce Ban Me Thuot, and break the blockade by using helicopters to land troops or by fighting through along Route 14. The fighting here could "break out" too soon, and the element of secrecy would be lost. Our intention was to hit Thuan Man and cut Route 14 when we began the attack on Ban Me Thuot. But we also had to have a large force ready so that if the enemy should discover our intention to attack Ban Me Thuot before we had cut the road, and send reinforcements of regiment size or larger down Route 14 from Pleiku, we could immediately set in motion an ambush campaign to smash that force and simultaneously block off Route 14. Foreseeing this possibility, we deployed the 320th division, which was familiar with campaign-style fighting and had a great deal of experience cutting and blocking roads, in this area. But it was not simple to carry out this intention. It required constant monitoring of the situation, and intense thinking, especially for the person in direct command there, the commander of the 320th division. Meanwhile, enemy vehicles were still going up and down the road as usual. In battle we cannot always know precisely what the enemy's intentions and actions are. More than that, this enemy were crafty and strong, and could still use their air power. So we had to calculate carefully and quickly when to give the order to the 320th division to attack the enemy and cut the road.

There was one incident. At noon on March 5, the 320th division used a battalion to wipe out a convoy of fourteen military vehicles, and captured two 105mm artillery pieces on Route 14, north of Thuan Man on the way to Ban Me Thuot. They seized all their weapons and took prisoners including an artillery major and his wife. Then they reported to the Front Command that during the past two days the enemy had sent an extra battalion of the 45th regiment to Thuan Man for regular patrols west of Route 14 to look for us. The 320th division avoided them without firing and so maintained secrecy, but as the level of enemy movements along Route 14 was increasing daily, they judged that the enemy were gradually bringing their 45th regiment in to reinforce Ban Me Thuot and decided to attack that day. They proposed that the Front Command allow them to seize its roadblock position on Route 14, attack Thuan Man and wipe out the whole battalion of the 45th regiment reinforcing the town.

Vu Lang reported the situation to me and asked for instructions. I sympathized with the concern and responsibility of the 320th division, and also sympathized with the tension felt by a large unit forced to keep silent and wait for the right moment to be of greatest service to the whole front. They had to hide and avoid the enemy's probing artillery fire and spies, as well as the small units the enemy deployed by helicopter or sent out on foot. The enemy were hunting, and were also worried.

But as we reviewed the enemy's activities over the past few days, it seemed they were still responding cautiously and did not yet have any clear plan of action. They were still concentrating their attention on the northern Tay Nguyen and were concerned with breaking the blockade of Route 19, so they had not changed their old assessment. We had been able to maintain secrecy, and should keep it up, so as to further deceive the enemy and draw them off, and urgently prepare for the opening of the key front.

After discussing things further with Le Ngoc Hien, I directed the Front Command that the 320th division should remain silent, avoid exchanging fire with spy patrols, not fight on Route 14 without orders, and hold closely to the resolution that had been confirmed. At the same time I ordered the Front Command to delegate a cadre to go immediately to question the Saigon artillery major who had just been captured. At midnight my secretary came to report that the prisoner of war had said their convoy was carrying a company from the 45th regiment and a number of other personnel back to their rear base in Ban Me Thuot to rest, and on the following day would carry recruits up to reinforce the regiment's positions in Pleiku. So the fourteen vehicles going from Pleiku to Ban Me Thuot represented ordinary traffic, and the enemy were not yet reinforcing Ban Me Thuot. But in any case the enemy had been attacked and knew that we had forces along Route

14, about thirty kilometers south of Pleiku. My secretary
also reported that the Front Command had learned that a
group of cadres from an artillery regiment went to scout
the terrain on March 5 and encountered the enemy north
of Ban Me Thuot. One of our fighters was wounded and
captured by the enemy. He was carrying a diary with him.

I thought, there are four days left before we begin the
attack on Ban Me Thuot. What will the enemy do in these
coming days? So far the enemy have been mistaken in
their perception of the primary direction of our attack. But
if there are more incidents like these that break secrecy,
we will certainly have to reconsider. Now the enemy are
trying to figure out our intentions and activities. I called
Vu Lang to remind him to keep each fighter under control,
to carry out the decisions about maintaining secrecy most
strictly.

On the morning of March 6 a military intelligence staff
cadre reported that according to intercepted enemy information, they had sent the 3rd battalion of the 53rd regiment, along with an armored platoon and a battalion of
security forces, to strengthen Quang Nhieu, eleven
kilometers northeast of Ban Me Thuot. Right after that the
chief of the Front Command's operations office reported
by telephone the specific position of each enemy spearhead, how they were searching in this area, and the
direction in which our artillery and tank units and our
engineering units which were preparing roads and staging areas had to pull back to avoid being discovered by the
enemy. But if they continued their searches until March 8,
it would affect preparations for our attack on the town
from the north.

Perhaps it was because they had captured our fighter
with his documents that the enemy had become suspicious of this direction. But even if they knew we had an
artillery unit north of Ban Me Thuot, the enemy would not
necessarily have realized that we were preparing to attack
the town. If they didn't find out anything else, they might

think that we were preparing to shell the city as we had in the past.

I discussed matters with the combat operations staff section of the General Command, then appointed Le Ngoc Hien to go down to the Front Command headquarters to lay out the following problems for them. Near Quang Nhieu we should continue to avoid the enemy and not let them discover us, but prepare forces so that if they should come in deeper, to our assembly point, then we could surround and thoroughly destroy each enemy thrust. We should follow enemy activities in this direction closely to make concrete arrangements for every contingency. If by the afternoon of March 6 the enemy had not pulled back to Ban Me Thuot (as a rule, they usually sent out one-day patrols when they suspected something, and if they did not uncover anything they pulled back), then we should order the 320th division to prepare to destroy the Chu Xe strongpoint (on Route 14 north of Buon Ho) on the morning of March 7 in order to draw the enemy in that direction and enable our units off toward Quang Nhieu to continue their preparations. If by March 7 the enemy were still continuing their search, then on March 8 the 320th division would attack and capture Thuan Man district town and subsector headquarters, cut Route 14 and suck the enemy up from Ban Me Thuot, and at the same time be prepared to fight enemy forces coming down from Pleiku.

Just as we had guessed, at noon on March 6 we intercepted information from the enemy that our fighter who had been seriously wounded had been taken to the hospital by the Saigon troops. There they had amputated his leg and treated him so that the commander of the 23rd division could come down to interrogate him personally. But our fighter was unconscious and had not yet come to. (We later learned that we liberated Ban Me Thuot before they had a chance to interrogate him. Then he was carried by his brothers from the enemy hospital back to his unit.)

On March 7 we smashed Chu Xe in thirty minutes,

allowing us to strengthen our blockade of Route 14 but still the enemy did not pull back from Quang Nhieu. On the morning of March 8, the 320th division captured Thuan Man district town and cut Route 14. By noon the enemy force at Quang Nhieu had hurriedly abandoned their operation and pulled back to Ban Me Thuot.

On March 9, exactly according to plan, we captured Duc Lap district town, Dac Soong, and Nui Lua, completely opening up the North-South strategic route east of the Truong Son range. To the north we had wiped out Thanh An district town on Route 19, and had closed in on Pleiku from the west.

So by March 9 we had completely set out our forces in their strategic and campaign positions, had cut the Tay Nguyen off from the lowlands, had cut the northern and southern Tay Nguyen apart, and had completely surrounded and isolated Ban Me Thuot. The first stage in our test of wits with the enemy was over, and the victory belonged to us.

But the enemy were still being subjective, and our actions only strengthened their mistaken assessment. Until we wiped out Duc Lap district town, they still thought that we were attacking to open Route 14 into Nam Bo, and they were still concerned with responding west of Pleiku. By this time, however, even if they had known for certain that we were going to attack Ban Me Thuot, it would already have been too late. It was hard for them to move. The field positions were set and nothing could spoil them.

On the afternoon of March 9 I sent a telegram to the Political Bureau and the Central Military Committee to report on the results of the fighting from March 1 until after the liberation of Duc Lap, and the main features of the campaign as a whole. (I did not report before this in order to maintain secrecy.) In closing the telegram I wrote:

ON MARCH 10 WE WILL ATTACK BAN ME THUOT. WILL CABLE FURTHER ON HOW THE SITUATION DEVELOPS AND IF THERE ARE ANY IMPORTANT OBSERVATIONS. WE ARE STILL

HEALTHY. BROTHER THIEN AND THE 559TH HAVE ASSISTED
THE CAMPAIGN MOST POSITIVELY. THEY HAVE TRIED TO
GUARANTEE EVERY NEED. THE TROOPS ARE WELL FED,
FORCES ARE LARGE, WEAPONS AND EQUIPMENT PLENTIFUL;
THERE IS AN ATMOSPHERE OF EXCITEMENT, AND SPIRITS
ARE HIGH. NEVER BEFORE HAVE THERE BEEN ATTACKS HERE
SO STRONG AND CONCENTRATED AS THIS YEAR. I WISH ALL
OF YOU ON THE POLITICAL BUREAU AND MILITARY COMMIT-
TEE WELL.

TUAN

After supervising the reserve stores of ammunition in the
rear area and planning for continuing transfers to await
the opportune moment, Dinh Duc Thien came along the
west of the Truong Son range to headquarters. For several
days he had been rechecking all logistics preparations one
final time. At 19:00 hours on March 9, we telephoned each
unit one after the other. Every location reported that all
preparations were complete and that they had arrived at
their appointed positions. This had been particularly com-
plicated and difficult for units that had to cross Route 14
and cross the Se-re-poc River on bamboo rafts carrying
their artillery with them. All the units that were to strike
into town from the south were also in their staging areas for
the attack. The coordinated assault units which had to wait
for the shooting to start before setting out in their motorized
transport and evading enemy outposts were also deployed
in formation. All the commanders pledged their determination to carry out their missions. I wished them lightning
victories, few losses, quick attacks, and completion of their
missions, and sent greetings to all the fighters before they
set out for the front.

On the night of March 9 we sat at headquarters and
continued to follow the situation and wait for "H" hour.
None of the staff cadres sitting around could hide their joy
and excitement as the momentous hour came nearer. For
a soldier in battle, the night spent waiting for "H" hour is
like waiting for midnight on New Year's Eve. From the

highest ranks to the lowest, we had been waiting years for this New Year's Eve. Although this night in the Truong Son mountains was peaceful, tens of thousands of people were moving toward their objectives. Every commander had someone standing over him, their hair falling together on the maps as they checked their plans one final time. And on this night, too, the quislings from Saigon to the Tay Nguyen surely had not yet been able to guess where we would act or imagined our strength; they had been led by us from one error to another, making us confident that when "H" hour began we would enjoy a great advantage. At this hour our rear base was very busy, and surely all our comrades on the Political Bureau and the Central Military Committee were wide awake following the situation on this front. The rear area had responded to every request of the front lines for a great attack and a great victory. That heroic rear area, that great rear area!

I told Major-General Hoang Minh Thao, front commander, on the telephone, "We are continuing according to plan. Nothing is changed. We must guarantee good command and communications so we will be certain of the situation. Keep in close touch with me by every possible method so that we can exchange opinions in time and consider every eventuality. When we know what the situation is and have made a decision, we must give our orders promptly so the lower levels can act quickly and decisively. We must not drag out our discussions. I wish you victory."

6

A Knockout Blow

At exactly 2:00 A.M. on March 10, sapper troops opened
fire on the Hoa Binh airfield, the rear base of the 53rd
regiment, the town airfield, and the Mai Hac De supply
depot, raising the curtain for the attack on Ban Me Thuot.
At the same time, all kinds of artillery and rockets poured
a tempest of fire into the enemy's 23rd division headquarters and kept up the barrage until 6:30 A.M., putting the
enemy nerve center in an uproar and paralyzing them.
With the practiced fighting methods of our special action
troops, our sappers had taken most of the town airfield in
just one hour, in the wink of an eye destroying seven
enemy aircraft, and had captured one corner of the Hoa
Binh airfield and all of the Mai Hac De supply depot.

Under cover of the thunder of the artillery and the sound
of gunfire, vehicles pulling artillery and antiaircraft guns,
as well as our tanks, armored cars, and troop transports
roared in toward town from all directions. When we heard
the firing of the guns, those of us at headquarters looked at
each other and breathed easier, because that meant we
had gotten past a period that is especially tense for
commanders—the period of positioning their forces for the
attack. Indeed, this is an extremely difficult and complex
problem. How can you in one night move a large force
including twelve regiments of infantry and the special

63

technical branches into their proper positions safely and on time? A number of units had to take positions in close to town secretly, and the main body of mechanized infantry and tanks for the deep thrust, waiting at their positions far out in different directions, had to follow different routes to their predetermined objectives in town.

Some tank units forty kilometers from Ban Me Thuot had to evade barricades and slip past enemy outposts along the road, then roar straight into town. On the Se-re-poc River modern ferries were set up quickly; tanks, armored cars, antiaircraft guns and mechanized artillery crowded each other across the ferry. The mountains and forests of the Tay Nguyen were shaken by the storm of fire. Because our coordination was well organized, safeguards were perfect, and command and control were tight, every spearhead of the attack moved in at the correct time. So we had scored our first victory over the enemy at Ban Me Thuot.

The sky gradually grew light. The enemy positions in town appeared in clear detail before the eyes of our artillerymen. At 7:15 A.M. our artillery groups joined together on signal, vying with each other to aim their shells into the headquarters of the 23rd division, the sector command, and the armored units' compound. Before that, under cover of the still-dark sky, two of our infantry battalions had secretly advanced into town from the south and taken a number of targets. Taking advantage of the artillery attack, they had quickly struck the six-point crossroads in the center of town, then had fought over to the area of the enemy's military chapel and taken positions to the west of the 23rd division headquarters. The enemy sent in bombers and infantry in a desperate counterattack to force us out. It was an extremely desperate battle. At 9:00 A.M. we sent in infantry coordinated with tanks in an attack on the sector command post, the command nerve center for the security forces and civil guard in the province. The enemy put up a strong resistance, and we had to send in more reserve troops to organize waves of continuous attacks. It was 13:30 before our troops could go through the gate of the sector headquarters. Enemy troops in guardhouses continued to mount a resistance, but we stayed on course, wiping out all resisting enemy groups. At 17:30 we were in complete control of the sector headquarters of Dar Lac province.

After taking care of the sector headquarters, we detached a force to move on to the adminstrative nerve center of the Saigon government, knock it out, and capture many of their government officials alive. Then we continued on, taking the military police compound and completely wiping out an enemy company northeast of the town airfield. In coordination with the northeast thrust, the northwest wing of troops had quickly captured Chu Bua Peak, a control point and fort outside town, and following that had used infantry coordinated with tanks to attack and capture the armored units' compound, the artillery compound, and the rear base of the 1st battalion of the enemy's 45th regiment.

By 15:00 hours we were in complete control of these objectives. The enemy troops had been almost completely wiped out, and the remaining few fled to the 23rd division headquarters. Toward the southwest, one of our vital deep-strike spearheads made up of infantry and tanks leapfrogged the Mai Hac De supply depot while the enemy were still reeling, thrust in and captured the communications center and closed in on the 23rd division from the west. The enemy used bombers to cut us off and organized waves of counterattacks, resulting in a tug-of-war between us and the enemy over each building, each street corner.

That day we captured most of the town, except for the area of the 23rd division headquarters and a few objectives east of the sector headquarters. The enemy had been hit unexpectedly and had responded haphazardly; their artillery and armor were completely paralyzed right from the first. Nevertheless they remained extremely stubborn and sent eighty bomber sorties to halt us and sought every

Tay Nguyen Campaign
March 4–April 3, 1975

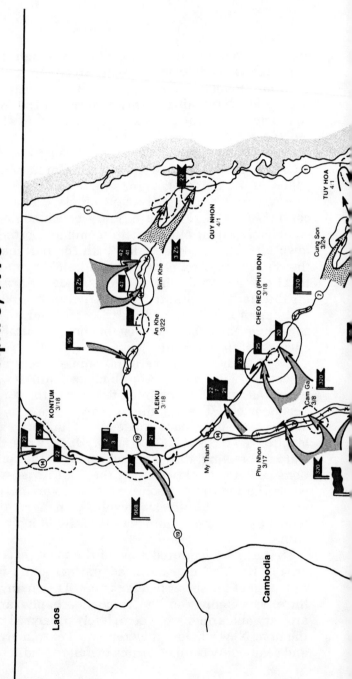

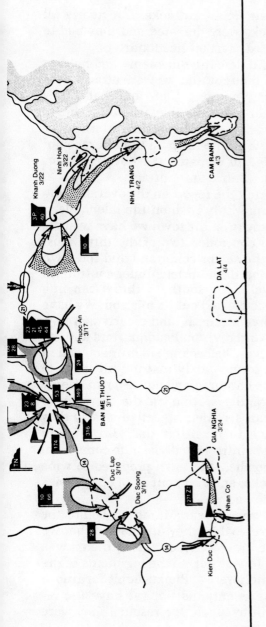

Key

March 4-March 18
March 22-April 3
Advance group of General Staff (ours)
Campaign Command (ours)
Army corps level (ours)
Army corps level (enemy)
Division level (enemy)
Enemy group/squadron/brigade
Roads blocked or cut
Military zone level (ours)
Division level (ours)
Regiment level (ours)

Brigades (ours)
Battalion level (ours)
Enemy defensive positions with strong defensive works
Temporary enemy defensive positions (without firm bunkers)
Enemy wiped out in flight
Enemy retreats to defensive positions or regroups after our attack

Z: zone
MF: main force
AF: air force
P: paratroops
TN: Tay Nguyen

opportunity for desperate counterattacks. But nearly all the enemy counterattacks were defeated and they had to fall back to hold the 23rd division headquarters.

In spite of their painful defeats, the enemy had not lost their subjectivity. They thought that we were attacking at the same level as we had in spring 1968, and that if they could hold on for three or four days they would be able to bring things back to normal. Apart from the 21st ranger group, which had been sent into town on the afternoon of March 10, they intended to dispatch the 45th regiment from Pleiku to continue their counterattack.

That night, after hearing the report on the overall situation, I reported to Hoang Minh Thao on the telephone.

"In the first day of attacks on the town we have won big victories, captured and controlled two of the three most important objectives—the sector command and the town airfield—and brought Hoa Binh airfield under control. All thrusts have fought well. The southern thrust ran into more difficulties, but has carried out its mission. We have used up little of our force strength, and clearly can now quickly finish off their 23rd division headquarters and the other remaining objectives, before the enemy can send in new forces. You must immediately instruct all units to hold the areas they have captured and chase down enemy remnants; prepare carefully so that on the morning of March 11 when they can see their objective clearly they can organize the attack to finish off the 23rd division headquarters; direct the entire 10th division to come from Duc Lap back to the northeast of town prepared to wipe out enemy counterattacks; and carry out all of our policies well when they enter town."

It must also be said that it was March 10 before the enemy stirred themselves, when they understood that we were striking to capture Ban Me Thuot. But by then it was already too late. Route 14 was cut, so the regiments of the enemy 23rd division which were at Pleiku didn't dare move down the road, but the enemy did not yet have the resources to bring them in by air for the rescue. They were absolutely panicked, vacillating because most of their families, their wives, and children lived in Ban Me Thuot. We shelled the Pleiku airfield heavily, obstructing enemy efforts to bring troops down to Ban Me Thuot by air.

On the morning of March 11 we received a report that at 7:20 A.M. our heavy artillery had fired into the 23rd division headquarters, and that our tanks and infantry were on the way to assault the 23rd division headquarters. The enemy howled disaster. Thirty minutes later our tanks and infantry flooded into the 23rd division headquarters from four directions. Enemy troops received orders to defend it to the end.

At 8:15 A.M. we learned that the deputy commander of the 23rd division and his staff section had fled the division headquarters. We continued our attack and the fighting grew intense and desperate. We had found two underground bunkers and captured Colonel Nguyen Trong Luat, province chief and sector commander of Dar Lac, and the assistant to the 23rd division's deputy commander. When we seized the rest of the bunkers, we captured thirteen more of them, including four captains and the deputy division commander, Colonel Vu The Quang, who was captured out in a coffee plantation. By this time many enemy locations had run up the white flag.

At 10:30 A.M. Saigon's 21st ranger group radioed their superiors: "At present the group command, the 23rd reconnaissance company, and the artillery are in a very strained situation; the Dar Lac sector headquarters is already lost, and the 23rd division headquarters is already lost. The rear base of the 21st group is already lost. The advance base of the 24th battalion is also lost. The 72nd and 96th battalions are now behind the sector command post, where there are many Vietcong tanks. The 21st group is powerless and cannot rescue the 23rd division headquarters. We are almost out of ammunition, with only two artillery pieces and 100 rounds left. If you cannot resupply us it will be very dangerous."

After we captured the 23rd division command center,

we flooded into the rear base of the 45th regiment. Then we took care of the military police, police, communications regional forces training compounds. Our troops from all directions met at the 23rd division headquarters. Our armed special action unit had entered Ban Me Thuot. We had basically wrapped up Ban Me Thuot by 10:30 A.M. on March 11, 1975.

We were happier than words can express. The soldiers were ecstatic. Large as the town was, we had completed our attack in just over thirty-two hours. Indeed the enemy could not possibly oppose our strength now.

One comrade at headquarters said, "It is truly incredible, taking Ban Me Thuot in just over a day and a night of fighting. I have been on this front for eleven years now. This time we really prepared meticulously, and the troops went out in fine spirits. What a joy! This is the first time we have gone to the attack in trucks. In 1968 the attack on Pleiku was quite laborious. We were only able to capture the radio transmitter, and three days afterward had to pull out. This time with such a large town it is truly amazing for us to finish things off so quickly."

We directed that the two Saigon colonels be interrogated at once to give us a better grasp of the situation in time for our coming moves. Major Mac Lam of the Military Intelligence Agency, a person with considerable experience in interrogation, was selected to go question the deputy division commander, Colonel Vu The Quang, directly. Quang told him: "Your attack on Ban Me Thuot was not foreseen by our General Staff or even by the Americans. After the Phuoc Long battle we estimated that in the coming period you might hit a number of small towns like An Loc and Gia Nghia, but you could not yet strike large towns like Ban Me Thuot, Pleiku, and Tay Ninh. When Ban Me Thuot was attacked, we still thought it was a diversion for an attack on Gia Nghia.

"If they want to defend II Corps now, Saigon must hold Nha Trang, where they have a second headquarters for the Second Army Corps, the 5th supply command, an air-

port, and a seaport. They need one regiment to hold the Mo
Drac Pass, one regiment to hold the area from the Ca Pass
on down, and one regiment to defend Nha Trang. Nha
Trang and Phan Thiet are more important than Qui Nhon.
Qui Nhon is only important while we still hold Pleiku and
Kontum. The 23rd division may be re-formed, but will only
be up to 50 percent strength after three months.

"If you strike Nha Trang now it would be to your advantage because they are in a panic. You have to watch out for
naval artillery, mainly 76mm, and just a few 122mm. The
air force can act more easily at Nha Trang, but there
aren't many of them. There are only thirty F-5 strikes a
day for the whole region, plus those made by the A-37s.
Troops can be supplied more easily by sea, but morale
among the soldiers is very low and the defensive positions
have not yet taken shape. Saigon is relying only on the
paratroops and the marines. But the paratroopers lack
confidence. If you inflict heavy casualties on the paratroopers or the marines now, the morale of Saigon's armed
forces will collapse."

Knowing that Quang had once been mayor of Cam
Ranh, we asked about the enemy defensive situation at
that port.

"Cam Ranh has no defenses at all. It just looks strong
from the outside. The Army has built all their buildings
facing toward the sea to catch the cool breeze. The way
you fight, you can take it right away. If Cam Ranh wanted
to organize defenses it would take at least three months.
But it is not even certain they could organize, because
they are short of many things. Since the Americans pulled
out they've been short of sandbags, barbed wire, cement,
and vehicles. It's a very fragile situation."

We could see the enemy more clearly. On the morning of
March 11 I sent a telegram to Vo Nguyen Giap, which
read:

TO COMRADE CHIEN,

WE ARE IN COMPLETE CONTROL OF BAN ME THUOT. WE HAVE

TAKEN AND HELD ALL LARGE OBJECTIVES SUCH AS THE 23RD
DIVISION HEADQUARTERS, DAR LAC SECTOR HEADQUARTERS,
THE ARMORED UNIT COMPOUND, AND THE AREA OF THE
TOWN AIRFIELD. WE ARE CHASING DOWN THE REMNANT
TROOPS HIDING IN TOWN. ACCORDING TO PRELIMINARY
FIGURES WE HAVE TAKEN NEARLY 1,000 PRISONERS OF WAR,
AND HAVE SEIZED A LARGE QUANTITY OF WAR BOOTY. WE
ARE IN CONTROL FROM DUC LAP TO DAC SOONG. WE HAVE
CONFISCATED TWELVE ARTILLERY PIECES AND NEARLY 100
TONS OF ARTILLERY AMMUNITION.

WE ARE PROCEEDING ON TO WIPE OUT ALL THE SURROUND-
ING TARGETS—THE 45TH REGIMENT BASE, THE 53RD REGI-
MENT'S REAR BASE, BUON HO, AND BAN DON, AND ARE
SENDING REINFORCEMENTS TO CAPTURE AND SECURE HOA
BINH AIRFIELD.

ON MARCH 11 THE DAR LAC MILITARY ADMINISTRATIVE
COMMITTEE WILL ANNOUNCE ITS WORK. WE PROPOSE COM-
RADE Y BLOC BE AWARDED THE RANK OF SENIOR COLONEL
AND BE APPOINTED TO CHAIR THE COMMITTEE.

BASED ON THE FACT THAT ENEMY MORALE IN THE TAY
NGUYEN IS COLLAPSING AND THEY ARE WEAKENED AND ISO-
LATED, AND CONSIDERING THAT OUR FORCES ARE STILL
STRONG AND IN GOOD SPIRITS, GUARANTEED WITH LOGIS-
TICS, AND THE WEATHER IS STILL TO OUR ADVANTAGE, OUR
PRELIMINARY INTENTION IS TO: (1) BOTH STRENGTHEN BAN
ME THUOT TO FIGHT ENEMY COUNTERATTACKS, AND PROCEED
TO THE OUTLYING AREAS TO TAKE COMPLETE CONTROL OF
DAR LAC PROVINCE; AND (2) CONTINUE TOWARD THE EAST
TO PHU BON (POSSIBLY WIPING OUT OR ENCIRCLING IT),
THEN FROM THERE TURN BACK UP TO SURROUND AND WIPE
OUT PLEIKU, AND ISOLATE KONTUM TO TAKE CARE OF LATER.
WE CAN POSTPONE MOVING TOWARD THE SOUTH. I HAVE
DISCUSSED THIS WITH COMRADES DINH DUC THIEN AND LE
NGOC HIEN, WHO ARE IN AGREEMENT.

WE PROPOSE YOU DISCUSS THIS IN THE MILITARY COMMIT-
TEE AND REPORT TO THE POLITICAL BUREAU, AND AFTER-
WARDS SEND US YOUR GUIDANCE.

The same day Le Duan told some cadres in agencies of the General Staff that they ought to consider whether the battle of Ban Me Thuot might be the opening battle of our big general offensive.

The Ban Me Thuot battle struck the enemy like a thunderbolt, leaving them reeling and disorganized. The quislings in Saigon wanted to conceal this serious defeat, and did everything they could to claim that Ban Me Thuot was still in their hands. Their spokesman held a press conference, saying, "I tell you that it is not correct that Ban Me Thuot is lost, absolutely not correct." French journalist Paul Leandri, who had just reported that we were in fact in control of Ban Me Thuot, was immediately called in by the police and shot dead at police headquarters.

We recommended to the Central Military Committee and the General Command that we did not need to report immediately on the Ban Me Thuot battle in our papers and on our radio. We could just let the enemy brag, and later they would be all the more dead on their feet. When we had finished liberating all of Dar Lac province it would not be too late for the papers and radio to carry the news.

On the afternoon of March 11, Hoang Minh Thao ordered our units to do certain urgent jobs immediately, such as finishing off the bunkers still surviving in town, finding and rescuing our brothers and sisters who had been held by the enemy in Ban Me Thuot prison, and wiping out positions a bit farther out from town, such as Buon Ho, Se-re-poc, Lac Thien, Ban Don, Duc Xuyen, and Khanh Duong. They especially ordered that we deploy forces ready to attack enemy reinforcements coming into Ban Me Thuot from the east. Meanwhile they would waste no time in firming up our organization and supplementing our technological weaponry to prepare to move ahead on a broader front.

The problem for a commander at that time was to take complete advantage of the opportunity that had been created to push the victory ahead immediately. Only by pushing on could we solidify the victory that we had won and create opportunities to gain new, faster, and larger victories. But how to move on, in what direction, at what level, and with what forces, were problems we had to weigh and consider closely and carefully. This was a race with the enemy and with the heavens to expand our victory. In the Tay Nguyen at that time the enemy still had a large main force of their Second Army Corps and the regional forces stationed at Kontum and Pleiku. Of the Second Army Corps' main-force units, two regiments remained—the 44th and 45th, detached from the 23rd division—which were still stationed at Pleiku. Then there was the entire 22nd division which was having to counter our forces in Binh Dinh, and the ranger groups. They were capable of sending each regiment in to counterattack to recapture Ban Me Thuot, or of reinforcing the defenses of the positions and towns they still held in the Tay Nguyen, fighting to open up communications routes, and trying to defend their positions while waiting for the rainy season. Another thing that had to be figured in was that the enemy might still be able to dispatch one or two divisions from other battlefields if our activities were weak there.

There were only about two months left before the rainy season began in the Tay Nguyen. This would be a great obstacle to the activities of our soldiers, especially large units equipped with heavy technological weapons. In that two-month period we had to figure out how to attack thoroughly and quickly so we could hold what we had won, and so after the rainy season we could continue our offensive. Or within that time period, with our soldiers in higher spirits each day, with our actual strength greater every day, with the enemy increasingly weak, there was the prospect that we might immediately gain victories surpassing the 1975 plan, and even carry out all of the 1976 Tay Nguyen plan before the rainy season. I began, along with Dinh Duc Thien, Le Ngoc Hien, and a number of our comrades at headquarters, to exchange opinions and estimates about this problem during the night of March 11 and the morning of March 12. We reported to the Political Bureau and the General Command on the situation in the Tay Nguyen and on our action suggestions. At the same time we proposed that the General Command issue an order urging the Tri Thien Front to attack boldly down Route 1 to coordinate with us and hold the enemy down there so they could not dispatch troops up to the Tay Nguyen.

It must also be said that in just this one battle—the battle of Ban Me Thuot—besides the excellent advances which had made that lightning victory possible, we had also discovered some weak points on our side that needed to be repaired quickly, such as taking too much time to get things done and an outmoded style of fighting.

But the thing we thought and speculated most about was what actions the enemy would now take on the Tay Nguyen battlefield. What would the enemy do on the whole southern battlefield? How would the Americans and the chieftains of the puppet army and administration react? That time, in the face of our strong, rapid attack and our dangerous style of fighting, the enemy in the Tay Nguyen had quickly fallen apart. In just over a day and a night they had lost two important nerve centers: the regional forces command system of Dar Lac province and the headquarters of their 23rd division. It was certain that they would counterattack to recapture Ban Me Thuot, but Ban Me Thuot was isolated. All the roads were cut, and the big airfields had been captured so that if they wanted to land troops by air they would be limited. If they used mobile troops from the main body of the Second Army Corps, and even if they used their general reserves as well, it would not be easy to recapture Ban Me Thuot once we had strong forces deployed to attack approaching enemy reinforcements.

Since March 10 all our other battlefields in the South had actively coordinated their actions, so the enemy would also have to consider the battlefield as a whole to decide whether they had a hand free to concentrate forces on Ban Me Thuot. These military difficulties were going hand in hand with the political, morale, and economic difficulties that the United States and Saigon were facing. It was not yet certain that there would be supplementary U.S. aid. And the Ford administration had other difficulties in the Middle East and at home in America.

As for us, we had won quickly and massively in the battle of Ban Me Thuot, giving all our units and all our battlefronts great confidence and enthusiasm. Our units were still strong, we had used up little of our supplies, and we had supplemented our stores with what we had taken from the enemy. Talking about the food and ammunition situation, Dinh Duc Thien spread out his hands and said happily, "We invested one, and the profit was not just four but ten!* We still have plenty, lots, not just enough to use until the rainy season, but enough for the dry season next year besides. We still have plenty of our own vehicles and our own ammunition, and we've also taken lots of enemy vehicles and munitions at the Mai Hac De supply depot in Ban Me Thuot. Let us strike more powerfully, let us strike bigger, and the faster we strike the better."

The problem was that we had to move on rapidly, without giving the enemy a chance to respond, and without letting the weather become an obstacle. So a race with the enemy as well as with the heavens began on the morning of March 12.

Our thoughts and considerations at headquarters came together on one point: we would use the bulk of the campaign forces to move back up toward the north along Route 14, smash and liberate Pleiku, and isolate Kontum. To put that plan into effect, we had to rapidly wipe out the enemy still in the outlying areas around Ban Me Thuot and liberate all of Dar Lac province on the one hand, and be prepared to strike enemy reinforcements counterattacking to recapture Ban Me Thuot and hold on to the liberated zone on the other hand.

And in Ban Me Thuot the military administrative com-

---

* According to a traditional Vietnamese belief, the maximum profit one can get on an investment is three or four times the original amount.

mittee had to make its appearance before the people soon to call on Saigon troops and administrative officials to present themselves and turn in their weapons, to organize antiaircraft defenses, evacuate the people, organize grassroots administrative bodies and self-defense forces for the town, and restore activities to guarantee the people's daily livelihood—hospitals, school, markets, electric plants, waterworks, shops, factories, and so on.

The largest and most urgent problem for Ban Me Thuot at that time was to supply staples and other food to the people in town and in the outlying areas. We immediately distributed some of the captured stores of enemy rice, salt, canned goods, and medicines.

On the afternoon of March 12 I received a telegram from Vo Nguyen Giap saying that the Political Bureau and the Central Military Committee were excited about our troops' tremendous lightning victory, and sending words of warmest praise to all cadres, fighters, party members, Vanguard Youth members, national defense workers, and people on the Tay Nguyen front. The Political Bureau and the Central Military Committee had met, and they concluded that the strategic and campaign plans issued by the Political Bureau and the Central Military Committee were correct. The victories at Ban Me Thuot, Duc Lap, along Route 19, and in all the other directions illustrated that we had the ability to gain tremendous victories at a faster pace than had been anticipated. One point that had been brought into relief was that the enemy's morale was extremely low, making it urgent that we be daring and take advantage of the new opportunity in time to gain big victories. Le Duan, Le Duc Tho, and Vo Nguyen Giap agreed that we must rapidly wipe out the remaining enemy units in Ban Me Thuot, and both move out into the surrounding area and be prepared to hit enemy reinforcements; we must quickly move on toward Phu Bon, wiping out enemy forces in each area; and we should immediately set up encircling positions around Pleiku, then move on to wipe it out. As for Kontum, we should isolate it and take it later. Moving on toward the south would be the next step.

Just a few minutes later we received a telegram from the General Command informing us that according to the latest information the enemy intended to rely on their remaining troops—one element of the 53rd regiment, the 21st ranger group—and on positions adjacent to Ban Me Thuot, especially Buon Ho and Phuoc An. They planned to dispatch an additional one or two main-force regiments plus rangers to mount a counterattack along with the enemy air force to try to recapture Ban Me Thuot.

At headquarters some more new information revealed that the 45th battle group and the main command of Saigon's 23rd division had used helicopters from Pleiku to land in Buon Ho at noon on March 11, and another battle group would land at Phuoc An on March 12. Saigon's air force was being mobilized at a high level. So the most urgent task for us was to regroup our forces and rapidly wipe out the enemy units and bases surrounding Ban Me Thuot, and wipe out their reinforcements.

Those two telegrams strongly mobilized and stimulated us. The clearsighted perceptions and principles, the sympathy and unanimity between the leadership at the central level and command elements in the field were one of the essentials that determined victory at the front. Enthusiastic about the victories we had gained and confident of victories to come, we quickly laid out our assignments. Le Ngoc Hien went immediately to meet with the Tay Nguyen front command for additional concrete discussions about the direction in which to push the victories of the campaign ahead. Dinh Duc Thien left headquarters and went down to the front logistics agency and all the relay stations and storage sites to supervise and direct their work.

We contemplated moving our headquarters forward to keep up with the developing situation. The staff cadres at headquarters were following the situation throughout the day, and at the same time investigating roads and the terrain around Pleiku, and discussing proposed methods of fighting and deployment of troops and firepower for the attack on Pleiku. They had also telephoned Hanoi to ask for weather forecasts for April and May 1975 in the Tay Nguyen.

On March 12 Thieu sent a telegram to his II Corps commander, saying "You must hold Ban Me Thuot at any cost. The commander of the 23rd division is in charge of unified command responsibility for this front." As late as March 13 the enemy had not yet acknowledged that we had liberated Ban Me Thuot. Western radio stations and news services were still vague and unclear about it. The enemy's Second Army Corps was seeking some way to respond on its own. Flights of A-37s made high-level bombing runs over Ban Me Thuot, and enemy reconnaissance aircraft hovered over the area east of town.

As we had foreseen, the 45th regiment of Saigon's 23rd division had been brought from Pleiku by helicopter and set down east of Ban Me Thuot, in the Phuoc An area, where we had already deployed our troops to wipe them out. Another key battle in the Tay Nguyen was about to begin.

7

Smashing the Counterattack

From noon on March 11, until the early morning hours of March 14, the atmosphere at Front Command headquarters was animated and tense, but full of excitement. Information poured in from all our units and from our radio interceptions. The race with the enemy had begun in earnest as soon as the guns had fallen silent in Ban Me Thuot. The sound of the guns of our attacking troops spread out rapidly along Route 14, to Buon Ho, to Ban Don, to Dat Ly, to the base of the 53rd regiment, to the rear base of the 45th regiment, and farther. Our technological weapons fanned out toward all the targets surrounding Ban Me Thuot.

The 320th division dispatched one force south along Route 14 to fight its way down and liberate Buon Ho district town and chase the enemy toward Dat Ly, and another force to fight northward to the Ia Leo bridge to take firm control of an eighty-kilometer stretch of Route 14. The 10th division was shifted forward to the east of Ban Me Thuot and spread out in good positions, prepared to strike enemy reinforcements coming to break the blockade of Ban Me Thuot. By noon on March 12 we had completed our encirclement of Phuoc An subsector and district town. Saigon's subsector commander fled along with the police.

The units of the 316th division and the 95-B regiment had swept the bunkers in town clean of the enemy, liberated our brothers and sisters who had been held by the enemy in the Ban Me Thuot prison, advanced and captured the 23rd division training school compound, chased down and captured a number of remnant troops who had reached the rubber forests west of town, and issued an appeal to the enemy's civil guard groups and regional forces platoons. The sapper troops held on at Hoa Binh airfield, beating back enemy units from the 53rd regiment base who had come to try to recapture the airfield. Our artillery units had all changed their aim to fire toward the west of town and around Hoa Binh airfield. The antiaircraft units took up positions east of town, ready to hit enemy troops being airlifted in.

Our tank and armored car units had come to the regroupment areas and were preparing new assault routes along the stretch of highway from Ban Me Thuot to Lac Thien and Phuoc An. Inside the town, when the sound of gunfire fell silent, the people began digging air defense bunkers, or were evacuated to the outskirts of town. Military police units were set up to direct people to leave to the west of town, meanwhile blocking intersections leading eastward, arresting obstinate reactionaries trying to flee. We distributed rice and salt to poor families before they were evacuated. Tongues of fire from our antiaircraft guns formed an umbrella over the town, striking back at enemy aircraft coming to bomb or carry out reconnaissance.

Within the confines of Dar Lac province the enemy resembled a snake that has lost its head. At Ban Don the greatest part of the enemy soldiers broke ranks, and some fled their positions. A Saigon major, rear-base commander for Saigon's 45th regiment, had to command his own troops plus remnants from the 53rd regiment. The commander of Saigon's 53rd regiment sent a telegram for help to his superiors, suggesting that they drop incendiary bombs on our formations so they could escape. Along the route of our advance around Ban Me Thuot, our troops ran into groups of enemy who had broken ranks, so they confiscated many enemy vehicles and 105mm artillery pieces. Groups of A-37 planes came to bomb Ban Me Thuot, and enemy reconnaissance planes stepped up their activities over the Phuoc An area and Hoa Binh airfield.

At our headquarters the working map was covered with red circles with two diagonal lines indicating places our troops had knocked out and taken over targets—red arrows showing our units' routes of advance, and green arrows showing the routes of the enemy's flight in the outlying forests.

The phones rang incessantly. The person answering, much as he tried to be calm and collected, could not stifle his joyful laughter as he received reports of victories from everywhere. Those serving at headquarters did their work quietly, walking softly and affectionately bringing cigarettes sent from the rear to the staff cadres answering the telephones.

It was early spring. The *khooc* forests of the Tay Nguyen had not yet put out new leaves, and the noon heat was all the more sultry. The sounds of all kinds of insects and the cries of the peacocks beside the building blended with cannon fire echoing in the distance, the thrumming of OV-10 reconnaissance planes hanging overhead searching for targets, and the "Hello! This is ZA-75!" from command headquarters.

Then, at noon on March 12, when the enemy counterattack was at its most intense, all telephone lines to headquarters were suddenly broken off. We had heard no bomb explosion, no sound of any airplane. We called here and there to the outside, but got no answer. All commanders stopped working, shook their heads and looked at one another in silence. The communications cadre started, then raced out of the bunker to find the cause. At the same time there came the trumpeting of a herd of elephants, gradually growing louder, about 300 meters from headquarters.

Disturbed by the bombs and shells of the battlefield, a herd of elephants started "evacuating" past our headquarters, headed for the Vietnam-Cambodia border. The headquarters guard unit was sent out immediately to block these wild elephants who had such a "low level of political consciousness." But they were ordered not to open fire and kill the elephants, to follow the regulations on protecting valuable wild animals, and to avoid making them angry, so they wouldn't trample our headquarters. Everyone was ordered to go down into the reinforced Bunker A to escape if necessary, because "there's nothing wrong with running from elephants."

Fortunately the herd of wild elephants passed by to one side of our headquarters, with our troops using a "passive blockade." It was only hard on the communications cadre who had to go repair the telephone lines. Not only were the lines broken, but whole long sections were missing: the elephants had dragged them off.

On the nights of March 12th and 13th we took turns sleeping, and the duty cadres took turns following the situation. The nighttime jungle was often completely quiet, but it was impossible to sleep long or peacefully. I tossed and turned, thinking of one problem, then another, until I had just drifted off for a moment, and then a "Hello" would echo across from the telephone in the duty bunker, or there would be the sound of a stag at the creek, or the hurried footsteps of the duty cadre coming to report.

On March 12 a flash telegram came from Hanoi. As soon as the cryptographic service had decoded one part, they would bring it for me to see. Vo Nguyen Giap was relaying to me the reactions of the Political Bureau and the Central Military Committee to my cabled report. They informed us that the other battlefields had begun good coordinated actions, and cautioned us to check and supervise the job of wiping out counterattacking enemy units, destroying a large number of the enemy forces in Ban Me Thuot and the surrounding area, and quickly encircling Phu Bon.

The Political Bureau and the Central Military Commit-

tee anticipated that if the enemy had a large portion of
their troop strength knocked out, if Ban Me Thuot and
many district towns were lost, and if Route 19 were cut,
then the enemy forces remaining in the Tay Nguyen
would regroup at Pleiku and might even be forced into a
strategic retreat, abandoning the Tay Nguyen. Thus they
directed us to set up a blockade of Pleiku immediately,
completely cutting all enemy roads and air routes, and
make preparations to wipe out the enemy in either case.
They had quite early on anticipated an enemy strategic
withdrawal from the Tay Nguyen. And the campaign positions we had taken up before we opened fire on Ban Me
Thuot, which had been chosen with a new view to preventing the enemy from sending reinforcements up to
rescue the Tay Nguyen, would not allow the enemy to flee
the Tay Nguyen easily, either.

Flights of enemy helicopters continued to land troops in
the Phuoc An region and to the west of Hoa Binh airfield.
The 44th regiment and an element of the 45th regiment,
plus the remnants of the 53rd regiment which had fled
there, had passed through their most terrifying moments.
Before they even landed, they shuddered at the antiaircraft guns shooting up at them, and saw their comrades
who had been shot down all around. When they set foot on
the ground, before they could even get into formation, they
had to scatter to escape salvoes of shells raining down
from our artillery and our infantry firing straight at them.
They were most terrified when they saw our tanks and
armored cars surging into their formations.

One after the other, the units which the enemy airlifted
in were smashed. Those who remained scattered and ran
to one another in confusion, then, clinging together,
gradually pulled back toward Route 21. As they fled, the
enemy troops pulled Saigon's local troops and administration and the rangers along with them, and left behind
many vehicles, artillery pieces, guns, and ammunition.

Our units shifted over to motorized pursuit, following
the direction of the main road, leapfrogging ahead of their

fleeing column, and setting up blocking positions along the road to capture the remnants. The intelligence and operations staff cadres were beginning to have trouble marking enemy symbols on the map, because all over the battlefield the enemy column was in chaotic flight. In the air their radios were broadcasting blind, and we couldn't distinguish who was calling for help and who was coming to their rescue. The flights of planes hovering high overhead were unable to support the enemy troops on the ground.

Early on the morning of March 14, from the summary report of the night duty officer we concluded that the main forces of Saigon's 23rd division, including the 44th and 45th regiments east of Ban Me Thuot, had been wiped out in two days of operations. The remnants of the 53rd regiment and the 21st ranger group had shared the same fate. The counterattack of their Second Army Corps in the Tay Nguyen had been smashed. And the enemy had been bogged down still more in their passive, defeated position.

We continued on according to the plans we had made, which had been ratified by the Political Bureau and the Central Military Committee. On March 14, after discussing it with staff members at headquarters, I cabled to the Political Bureau and the Central Military Committee that we had received all their telegrams, and that we were very enthusiastic about the principles for carrying the campaign forward which they had adopted. We promised that we would try to organize the campaign's implementation in such a way as to fulfill our superiors' request, namely, to cut the time allotted to achieve victory, and to complete the anticipated 1976 Tay Nguyen campaign within a few months in 1975.

So that they could have a better grasp of the situation, we reported on the first days of the campaign and told them how we had guided the enemy according to our own intentions, causing them to misjudge the main thrust of our attack, and how we had continued to strengthen that mistaken perception until the moment when we made our main attack in order to maintain the element of surprise. From March 1 to March 9, 1975, before attacking Ban Me Thuot, we had spread out into our campaign positions, drawn the enemy's attention toward Kontum and Pleiku, cut the roads, and isolated our main objective. So only when we were about to open fire on Ban Me Thuot did the enemy know. They sounded the alert and wanted to increase their forces, but they were too late and their forces were tied down everywhere else.

We reported that our attacks on the main objectives in Ban Me Thuot had comprised coordinated operations by combined special branches in four wings, coordinated with those elite units and infantry units who had secretly moved forward and deployed in advance, evading enemy outposts on the outskirts of Ban Me Thuot, and using large mechanized forces following the main roads at high speed and striking directly into town to smash the two enemy command nerve centers, the 23rd division headquarters and the sector headquarters.

From the south we had deployed two advance infantry battalions, one to attack the 23rd division headquarters and one to attack the sector headquarters, at the same time that two other wings, each including infantry, tanks, artillery, and antiaircraft weapons, struck the middle of town from the west and northeast. Moreover, we had organized a spearhead consisting of an infantry battalion and a tank company to strike simultaneously at the main objective from the southwest. One infantry company in armored cars went in along with the tank company, and the other two infantry companies had been deployed in advance about two kilometers from the main objective, the 23rd division headquarters. They waited for the tank unit to come in and coordinated with them in one spearhead; so a full infantry battalion with tanks and armored cars struck directly at the main objective just as our artillery shifted away from that target. The enemy had not been able to raise a hand in time, and had not been able to command their other forces.

The battle of Ban Me Thuot represented the implementation of a daring and unexpected style of fighting, very complex, which therefore demanded truly good organization of the coordinated units. We had tried to carry it out, but after the enemy had been smashed, some weak points were revealed in various units which we needed to overcome quickly. We were not moving ahead from our recognition of the situation to decisive action in time. In these new, more demanding conditions, we were still caught up in the old style with its many long, drawn-out meetings. No one had yet stood up to make decisions and organize action rapidly. In some situations the infantry were out of hand. They had field radios, but instead of using them went rattling around stringing telephone wires. They had vehicles taken from the enemy and POWs who knew how to drive, but didn't dare use them to drive the troops, and instead, just kept on walking. It was not as if the enemy were organized, waiting for us with defenses prepared; they were disorganized, falling apart, yet when we attacked we still demanded full discussion, and had to prepare at night, then wait until morning before attacking. The enemy air attacks were limited and at high altitude, and when they dropped their bombs their aim was not precise, yet we still did not send our troops into battle during the day—waiting, late, wasting time. We had to go over these problems time and time again, and we were overcoming them.

Big problems broke out very fast, and more opportunities to gain new victories were appearing every day. Local committees at some levels were now overwhelmed by all the work they needed to do. The old way of thinking, organizing, and acting ran counter to the demands of the newly developing situation. We had to work on a larger scale and work more rapidly. This situation might not exist only in the Tay Nguyen, but on other battlefields as well. It arose from an evaluation of the enemy, from a style of thinking and determining how to act that were not yet in tune with the new conditions. Now we needed to be quick, dynamic, lively, to save time and at the same time raise our organizational and command capabilities. Our leaders, once they had been given their assignments, needed a spirit of making judgments and accepting responsibility—"dare to act, dare to accept responsibility"—rather than assuming that the "whole village" [everyone] would bear responsibility. After this campaign the Tay Nguyen cadres and soldiers would have taken a giant step toward maturity because of the new operational situation.

We needed to set aside more time to train soldiers in a dynamic, lively style of action, and to nurture the capability for organization and for urgent, sustained combat command. We needed to train cadres and fighters to drive enemy vehicles, to use our own and the enemy's field radios. The specialized branches needed to study how to use enemy weapons, technology, and equipment. We would soon have to pay a great deal of attention to taking enemy equipment to fight the enemy.

We were in complete agreement with the propaganda steps set out in Vo Nguyen Giap's telegram. While the enemy were still using tactics of coverup and deceit, there were a number of tasks we had to carry out in time and carry out to perfection. When we had basically completed the liberation of Dar Lac province, we could report it in the papers and on the radio, and along with it we would also report the declaration of the military administrative committee of Dar Lac province, the composition of the committee, the results of the fighting, and statements of prisoners of war.

8

A Turning Point in the War

On March 15, 1975, I received a cabled reply from the Political Bureau, signed by Le Duc Tho, and one from the Central Military Committee, signed by Vo Nguyen Giap. At a meeting in Hanoi members of both bodies had carefully read the telegram I sent from the front on March 14, agreed with our assessment, and accepted our proposals. The sections talking about our experiences in diversionary activities to deceive the enemy, methods of attack, methods of training cadres and fighters to use technological weapons taken from the enemy, and weak points of command behavior had been sent by the Central Military Committee to the General Staff to be sent on quickly to all other battlefields. The Political Bureau and the Central Military Committee had reworked the proposals on coordinating battlefields into instructions and sent them to all military zones for implementation.

After we received these replies we met to discuss the implementation of plans to move north, based on the latest situation in the Tay Nguyen. The Tay Nguyen front command fully agreed with the plan and determined to concentrate all their efforts to carry it out, because after so many years of fighting the United States on that battlefield, they were more excited than anyone about the recent victories, and were confident of the victories to

89

come. In 1968 and 1972 we had mounted big attacks in the Tay Nguyen, but there had been no tremendous lightning victories like those of this year. Our forces had not been so strong then as they were now, and the logistics structure and road system were not yet adequate. Then, the enemy were still relying on the extremely strong fire and logistics support of the United States, and had a free hand in other areas so they could concentrate on dealing with us in the Tay Nguyen. Now there was a clear prospect of our liberating the Tay Nguyen. If we acted quickly and well, we might finish before the 1975 rainy season. So, all saw clearly what their responsibilities were in this vast, honorable undertaking, just as they were immeasurably elated and proud as they thought of the immediate prospects.

Hoang Minh Thao often confided to us: "Among many other important reasons, one reason the southern revolution has so far gained victories is that we have been in control of part of the Tay Nguyen, and the heroic, indomitable people of the Tay Nguyen have made great contributions of their labor power to revolutionary victories throughout the two resistance struggles against France and the United States. Day and night I hope for the complete liberation of the Tay Nguyen so that our compatriots of all ethnic groups can soon receive their freedom and escape their poverty, hunger, and suffering."

On March 15 and the morning of March 16, we received some radio interceptions and some short commentaries from Western radio stations. Although they were scattered and fragmentary, they were extremely important to our assessment of the enemy's situation in the Tay Nguyen at that time. For example, one American news agency reported that the price of an airplane ticket from Pleiku to Saigon had risen to 40,000 piasters. Why were people crowding in to buy tickets to Saigon on March 15? At noon on March 16, we intercepted information from enemy air force planes taking off from Pleiku, calling each other about landing at Nha Trang. Why were enemy airplanes taking off from this one place and landing at another place farther on, even though by the morning of March 16 we had not shelled the Pleiku airfield heavily? At 15:00 hours on March 16, Hanoi telephoned to inform us that the advance headquarters of Saigon's Second Army Corps and the American consul had moved to Nha Trang. At 16:00 hours the same day, information reported from Thuan Man said that our reconnaissance station at the Ia Leo bridge had seen a long convoy of vehicles at the My Thanh crossroads heading toward Phu Bon.

Instead of looking only at the Ban Me Thuot area when we read the maps, we began to pay special attention to the area of Pleiku, Kontum, Route 14, and Route 19. Any news about Pleiku, about the Second Army Corps, or about the strategic roads leading to the plains got particular attention.

At about 19:00 hours on March 16, after we had received all the above information, there was a heated discussion at headquarters among all the staff cadres. Although we reached no conclusions and no one was certain, still everyone felt that the enemy in the Tay Nguyen was doing something after receiving two painful defeats in a row, at Ban Me Thuot and in the counterattack by the 23rd division. One person raised the possibility that the enemy were concentrating their remaining troops from the Tay Nguyen in Nha Trang, and then along with their general strategic reserves would counterattack along Route 21 to recapture Ban Me Thuot. Another comrade pointed out that the telegram from the Central Military Committee had raised three points: one was the possibility the enemy would reinforce and counterattack; the second was that if they were attacked they might pull back to Pleiku, so we should immediately set up a blockade of Pleiku; and the third spoke of the assumption of a strategic withdrawal by the enemy. So, the information we received today suggested that the enemy might reinforce to counterattack, but might also retreat toward Nha Trang.

If they retreated, would they pull out the whole second Army Corps, or would only the corps command flee to a secure place? If they pulled out, how would they pull out, and what route would they take? It certainly wouldn't be easy to follow Route 21 and counterattack to recapture Ban Me Thuot! Encountering the defeated troops fleeing along Route 21 toward Nha Trang would be enough to destroy the morale of the counterattacking group.

Many other comrades tended to think that the enemy were fleeing, because the telegram from the Central Military Committee had raised these three possibilities, but practically speaking we had hit the counterattacking troops and were prepared to do so again, and we were discussing preparations to transfer forces up to encircle Pleiku. And perhaps after their two great defeats the enemy were hurt too badly, could not send reinforcements, and felt that they would be wiped out anyhow, so there was nothing to do but flee the Tay Nguyen. So there were two tasks we had to do well: wipe out counterattacking troops quickly, and make urgent preparations to move our forces into position to encircle Pleiku. If the enemy were retreating, our campaign positions were already prepared and the stategic roads had all been cut; if the enemy couldn't come up they couldn't get through on the way down, either.

We thought a lot about these reports and listened carefully to the debate. Indeed the Political Bureau and the Central Military Committee had foreseen all three possibilities, and we, too, when we finished destroying Ban Me Thuot, were prepared to wipe out reinforcements, not just once but many times; we were prepared not just to attack Saigon's Second Army Corps, but to fight the general reserves they sent in on the ground and landed by air, because the strategic roads, Routes 19, 14, and 21, had all been cut and firmly blockaded. This would keep the enemy from coming in and would also keep them from pulling out.

Now the circumstances might change quite rapidly, because the enemy, not being objective and so completely surprised at the beginning, might panic after these two painful battles and make even more mistaken assumptions. If they sent reinforcements to counterattack, things would be all the more difficult for them, they would get bogged down and wiped out even more. But if they fled they would still face more death, and would go further downhill.

We still had far too little information, but even so, we could discern many bases for thought and action. We re-checked the communications systems and the stations intercepting enemy information, called Hanoi to ask more about the general situation on the whole battlefield, and turned on the radio to listen to the daily news reports from around the world. We urged the Tay Nguyen command to keep on top of the situations of the 95th and 25th regiments and the 320th and 10th divisions on Routes 19, 14, and 21, and warned them to be ready to reinforce the 25th regiment on Route 21.

At 21:00 hours on March 16 the duty officer received information that the enemy were fleeing Pleiku. A convoy had passed the My Thanh crossroads heading down along Route 7, the ammunition dump at Pleiku was exploding, and there were many fires in town.

Our headquarters came alive. A map of the Tay Nguyen road network was spread out on the table, with flashlights and magnifying glasses spread out along Routes 19, 14, and 7 to find points we could "cork up," encircling routes, and attack routes, and measuring the distance between the nearest unit and Route 7 to calculate the time for each action.

I picked up the telephone and talked directly with Kim Tuan, who was then commander of the 320th division. Before we attacked Ban Me Thuot I had asked many times about Route 7, and it was reported that Route 7 had long been abandoned, bridges were out, there were no ferries, and the enemy could not use it. Two days before, I had again asked Kim Tuan about this road, and he, too, had given the same answer. Now, having heard that the enemy were retreating along Route 7, but that his unit still had no concrete hold on that road and was not yet urgently pursuing the enemy, I spoke very severely to the unit's highest responsible person. I emphasized twice to Kim Tuan, "That is a shortcoming, negligence that deserves a reprimand. At this time if you waver just a bit, are just a bit negligent, hesitate just a bit, are just a bit late, you have botched the job. If the enemy escape it will be a big crime, and you will have to bear responsibility for it."

At such times I do not want my subordinates to present excuses for trying less, I just want them to carry out their missions most strictly and completely. Having taken part in many battles and campaigns with them, having encountered the most complex and urgent circumstances, I, as commander, made strict demands on these men, and they understood me, so when they got their orders, all were determined to carry them out, and they usually succeeded.

Setting the telephone down, I conjured up in my mind images of enemy retreats in the wars against France and the United States—scenes of the flight of Charton and Le Page on Route 4 during the 1950 Border Liberation Campaign, of the rout of the American marine regiment at Khe Sanh in 1968, that of the 1st division, Saigon's paratroop brigades, and marine brigade on Route 9 and in southern Laos in 1971, and that of Saigon's 3rd division in Quang Tri in 1972. The enemy had many times fled before the strength of our attacks, and usually employed a variety of ruses as they withdrew. But now if a whole Saigon main-force army corps was fleeing at full tilt, abandoning the whole Tay Nguyen—a most important strategic area— then why? On whose orders? Had our two thunderbolts striking in the southern Tay Nguyen shaken the enemy troops so badly? It was indeed a knockout blow which had only begun to sink in several days later. The enemy were reeling and in disorder. This was another very big strategic mistake on their part.

If the order to pull the Second Army Corps out had been issued by the central government in Saigon, then the matter had surpassed the bounds of this campaign and had reached strategic proportions. For the first time in the Indochina War, within the bounds of a campaign an enemy army corps with modern equipment had had to abandon an important strategic area and flee. This situation would lead to other important developments, and might lead to our quickly and victoriously concluding the war. But this would not be an easy thing for the enemy to swallow. It would cause a military and political chain reaction that would reach even to America. Even the United States, however, could not set this chaos straight.

Our big opportunity had begun. If we wanted to grasp that opportunity firmly, the first thing we had to do was wipe out the fleeing enemy troops if possible, destroying them right here on the Tay Nguyen battlefield, and not letting them escape to the plains. We must knock them out quickly and thoroughly to stimulate the process of a quick change in the war situation.

Recalling events of the past and thinking of the events of the present, we were both happy and impatient. Throughout the night of March 16 we urged on the critical activities of the 320th division, and ordered the Tay Nguyen command to mobilize more armored cars and transport vehicles, more artillery and materiel to ensure that the 320th division could pursue the enemy and wipe them out. At the same time we ordered the advance command of Zone 5 in Binh Dinh to send regional forces from Phu Yen into action to block Route 7 to keep the enemy from escaping toward Tuy Hoa. The 968th division also got orders to advance quickly to Pleiku, leapfrogging positions along the road to stick close to the fleeing enemy column and attack them from the rear. The 559th force command sent their 470th engineer division in to carry on administration of Kontum and Pleiku, put out the fires, lead the people to safe places, and take up administration of supply depots left behind by the enemy.

From the time we issued orders until the units implemented those orders, especially the order to pursue and wipe out the fleeing enemy, we were extremely impatient, hoping for news and feeling that time was passing too slowly. In fact the 320th division, after receiving their orders, set out at high speed on the night of March 16. By the morning of March 17 one unit had quickly cut through the jungle and blocked Route 7, halting the enemy east of Phu Bon. The enemy piled up east and west of Phu Bon.

On March 18 a large force of ours caught up with the enemy, charged in and liberated Phu Bon town, wiped out the enemy soldiers piled up there, and continued fighting down to Cung Son. At that same time two regional infantry battalions from Phu Yen advanced and cut the Son Hoa bridge and, joined by the 320th division, entered and liberated Cung Son.

Enemy troops scattered in a panic. Almost all of six ranger groups and three armored regiments, not to mention all the offices of the Second Army Corps, were destroyed, and tanks, artillery, construction and transportation vehicles were lost.

Saigon Colonel Pham Duy Tat, ranger commander attached to the Second Army Corps, gave us the following statement about the withdrawal of Saigon's troops in the Tay Nguyen:

"On the afternoon of March 14, when I was going to all the units to check on the defense situation for Pleiku, the corps command called me to a meeting at the office of Pham Van Phu, the corps commander. Phu informed us that he had just been to a meeting at Cam Ranh with Nguyen Van Thieu, Tran Thien Khiem, Cao Van Vien, and Dang Van Quang. According to Phu, Thieu asked Vien, 'Do you have any reserves to reinforce the Second Army Corps?' And Vien answered, 'None left.' Then Thieu turned and asked Phu, 'Without reinforcements, how long can you hold on?' He replied that he might be able to hold on for a month, on the condition that he had maximum air support, air supply of adequate materiel, weapons, and ammunition, and that he had enough additional troops to replace recent heavy casualties. He added, 'I will remain in Pleiku to fight, and I will die there.'

"Thieu said that he could not meet those conditions, but that the Liberation Army was mounting strong attacks, so we must withdraw from Kontum and Pleiku to preserve our forces, and send those troops to hold the coastal plains where they could be supplied more easily. He asked Vien if he could withdraw along Route 19. And Vien answered, 'In the history of warfare in Indochina there has never yet been a force that has retreated along Route 19 without being wiped out.' Thieu then asked, 'So how about Route 14?' And Vien replied, 'Route 14 is even more impossible.'

"Everyone at the meeting saw that only Route 7 was left. It had not been used in a long time, and although it was in bad condition, it would create an element of surprise. Candidate-General Tran Van Cam, deputy commander of the Second Army Corps, asked, 'And what about the province chiefs, the regional forces, and the people? Should we organize them to withdraw?' Phu answered, 'According to Mr. Thieu's orders, we are to abandon these forces, and we may not inform the province chiefs, but are to let them continue their resistance. When we have completed our withdrawal then whoever knows will know. The regional forces are all montagnards, so let's give them back to the mountains.'

"After he had finished his presentation, Phu ordered Cam and Ly, chief of staff of the Second Army Corps, to make plans for the retreat. On the morning of March 15, Phu and the main staff of the Second Army Corps pulled out by airplane to Nha Trang, giving the excuse that they were going to set up a forward command post to direct operations to retake Ban Me Thuot. So Phu did not die at Pleiku as he had promised. Specialized units retreating to Phu Bon took their families along. It was this that let the people see clearly we intended to abandon Pleiku. From then on, frightened officers and soldiers crowded into the airfield, struggling with each other to board airplanes, and causing a panic. Those who could not get into the airfield used all kinds of vehicles to flee toward Phu Bon. The road was clogged as soldiers fought with each other to get out, cursing and brawling, causing more scenes of panic along the road. At the same time, the 22nd ranger group was also withdrawing from Kontum. Then the Liberation Army caught up with the 25th group and ambushed them at Thanh An, causing heavy casualties.

"According to the plan, the Second Army Corps command and all combat units were to establish defense lines at Phu Bon and let the heavy mechanized units and specialized elements pass through ahead of them. When these forces reached Phu Bon on March 16, they were tired and fed up, so they stopped and wouldn't go any further. Not only were they in the town, but people and vehicles were scattered all over the roads around town. Transportation in town was clogged up because so many soldiers were piled up there, and meanwhile more vehicles kept crowding in. The soldiers began to destroy and loot the town, causing scenes of extreme panic.

"On March 16 the Liberation Army began to attack a unit of the 23rd ranger battalion in the Ban Blech Pass, inflicting heavy casualties. On March 17 the Liberation Army shelled the sector headquarters in Phu Bon, causing considerable casualties to the 23rd group. At this time the regional forces units attached to Phu Bon dispersed, on their own initiative breaking ranks and running, confusing the situation in town even more.

"The Liberation Army attacked again and blockaded the stretch of road from east of Phu Bon to the Tu Na Pass, leading to a quick collapse of the defenses in Phu Bon. On the afternoon of March 17 the 7th group called on the air force for support. A flight of A-37s came and dropped their bombs on the troops, and one battalion was practically wiped out. The next morning, when they were attacked again by the Liberation Army, this group took heavy casualties and only a very few made it past the blockade. The Liberation Army advanced and captured Phu Bon.

Phu ordered us to abandon all our heavy weapons and military equipment and flee Phu Bon. I ordered the troops to leave behind all vehicles and artillery, and circle around through the jungle, not go through the pass. The 3rd armored regiment also abandoned all their vehicles and fled into the jungle after being blocked off and attacked by the Liberation Army many times.

"The remnants had to evade the stretch of road from the Tu Na Pass to Son Hoa district town, slipping through the jungle. But the officers and soldiers had brought their families along, so hundreds and thousands of people stretched out behind them, making so much noise they revealed the target. The Liberation Army followed, attacking, close behind us, so we were scattered and took many casualties. The soldiers, exhausted and without commanders, left all their weapons and machines on the road and ran. The troops at Phu Tuc district town and all the local outposts deserted or broke ranks, and all those places were taken by the Liberation Army.

"The 6th ranger group was the rearguard, and had the mission of leading the remnants of all the other units to Son Hoa. On the morning of March 20, the Liberation Army unexpectedly began to attack the first units of the 6th group, causing considerable casualties. During the following days the group fled but was still being pursued and attacked all the time, and only a very few made it to Tuy Hoa. The quick movement of the Liberation Army to the east of Phu Bon town, blocking off the road up to Tu Na Pass, determined the defeat of the Saigon troops' flight from the Tay Nguyen."

So it was clear. The battle of Ban Me Thuot, followed by the attack that wiped out reinforcements from the 23rd division east of Ban Me Thuot so quickly and thoroughly, threw the enemy into panic and confusion, not only at the division and army corps level, but all the way to the top—to the quisling administration in Saigon. From tactical and campaign errors, the enemy went on to make strategic errors under our painful blows; the panicked

Saigon administration issued orders to flee from the Tay Nguyen and bring their troops to the plains in order to preserve their forces and hold onto their territory. But what troops had they brought anywhere, and what more territory could they hold! We had wiped them out along the route of their flight. After this strategic mistake, defeat in the war was certain; it was only a matter of time.

We had led the enemy to make those mistakes; we had known how to create and catch hold of opportunities, stimulate the process of the enemy's defeat, and create this turning point in the war. If we were still faster, still more resolved, still more daring, if we took the initiative still more, and took advantage of our victories to charge ahead, we would surely win.

9

Taking Advantage of Victory

When we opened fire on the Tay Nguyen front, our troops in Tri Thien also began coordinated operations, attacking the enemy both in the border zones and in the plains. Our armed forces encircled enemy bases over a broad area, wiped out and forced the evacuation of a number of outposts, and at the same time stepped up damaging attacks on the enemy's rear bases and storage areas, and cut communications routes. Forces of our Second Army Corps attacked along a line southwest of Hue in the Nui Bong—Nui Nghe region, wiping out a number of enemy bases and repeatedly hitting their counterattacks, nipping at the heels of their mechanized troops, and not allowing them to pull out of Tri Thien.

In the plains, seven of our regional force battalions along with one hundred armed special assignment squads thrust down deep into the enemy zone, and with the local armed forces and the people in eight districts they mounted a series of attacks, knocking out Mai Linh district town, destroying eleven of the thirty installations they attacked, and carrying out propaganda over a wide area including fifty-three villages with more than 20,000 people.

After the enemy's serious defeat in the Tay Nguyen, the Political Bureau and the Central Military Committee sent timely instructions to the Tri Thien front command and the Second Army Corps to recognize their opportunity clearly and change the thrust of their attacks. On March 18, anticipating that the enemy might pull out and abandon Hue, taking their 1st infantry division to Da Nang and organizing defenses south from the Hai Van Pass, the General Command directed the Tri Thien Zone, of which Brigadier-General Le Tu Dong was commander and political officer, and the Second Army Corps to send their forces in a daring thrust past the outer defense lines to cut off Route 1 and close in on Hue. The goal was first of all to knock out the 1st infantry division and prevent them from withdrawing to Da Nang, and then to liberate Hue and the whole of Tri Thien.

On March 19, Quang Tri's regional armed forces seized the opportunity to move onto the attack, to liberate the town and the whole province of Quang Tri. Big gaps were smashed through the enemy's northern defense lines, and they drew back to defense lines south of the My Chanh River.

At that time Ngo Quang Truong, the major-general who commanded Saigon's I Corps, came on Hue Radio with a great show of bravado, saying, "I will die in the streets of Hue. The Vietcong will enter this ancient capital only over my dead body." And Thieu boasted on Saigon Radio, "We have abandoned Kontum and Pleiku to preserve our forces, but we will hold Da Nang, Hue, III Corps, and IV Corps to the end."

Implementing the General Command's order of battle, on March 21 the forces of the Tri Thien Zone and our Second Army Corps mounted a series of attacks from the north, west, and south, leapfrogging enemy defense lines and forming into many spearheads to encircle Hue; they inflicted heavy casualties on Saigon's 1st infantry division and 147th marine brigade, and cut Hue off from Da Nang along the stretch of Route 1 from Mui Ne to Bai Son. Thousands of vehicles evacuating from Hue to Da Nang had to turn back amid scenes of panic. Our long-range artillery bore down on the Dong Da and Mang Ca bases and damaged Phu Bai airfield. The roads were cut. Air routes were blocked. The only escape route the enemy had left was to the sea via the Thuan An and Tu Hien estuaries. The Hue-Thuan An road was their last hope, but in fact it had turned into a road of death.

Our artillery forces, who fully grasped the enemy's intent to flee, blocked off the Thuan An estuary to keep enemy ships from coming in to pick up the retreating band, and at the same time concentrated fire on the enemy columns still bunched up at the Thuan An and Tu Hien estuaries, inflicting heavy casualties on them. Sapper troops also placed mines to blockade the Thuan An estuary. Tanks, armored cars, trucks, and tens of thousands of enemy soldiers—so thick you couldn't see the road—trampled each other to flee from our artillery, and shot each other to make room on the road.

On March 25, all wings of our troops got together in time to surround and wipe out or scatter what was left of the retreating enemy troops remaining at the Thuan An and Tu Hien estuaries, and at the same time our troops assaulted Hue from many directions. At exactly 10:30 A.M. the revolutionary flag was raised on the flag tower before the Ngo Mon Gate, the main gate of the old imperial city. Hue was completely liberated, and its people, after seven years of waiting, ever since Tet Mau Than [Year of the Monkey] in 1968, could again see the flag of the revolution flying proudly before the wind. As our soldiers were in the process of attacking, surrounding, cutting off and chasing down the enemy, the masses rose up and guided the soldiers, they pointed out roads on which the enemy had fled so our troops could pursue them, chasing down enemy who had gone into hiding, helping troops cross rivers, and killing or capturing Saigon thugs, causing the enemy to fall apart even faster.

Saigon's 1st infantry division, regarded by the Americans as an elite division, had been wiped out and scattered. In wiping out this division and liberating Hue and all of Tri Thien, we had struck a heavy blow against the enemy's strategic regroupment scheme, weakening and putting heavy pressure on their I Corps.

On the afternoon of March 26, I was in the command bunker reviewing the plan to implement the General Command's order to establish a Third Army Corps and to organize forces for the protection of the Tay Nguyen after liberation, thinking about how we should move the Tay Nguyen units ahead and preparing plans to shift logistics and reconnaissance units into eastern Nam Bo, when Nguyen Tuyen came to tell me the news that Hue had been completely liberated. I could not control my emotions. Hue had been liberated forever, not just come under our desperate control for twenty-five days and nights as had been the case at Tet Mau Than in 1968.

Tran Van Quang, Le Quang Dao, Tran Quy Hai, and all of our brothers in the Front Command, together with all the army units who had taken part in the general offensive and uprising on the Hue-Route 9-Khe Sanh-Quang Tri front in the spring of 1968 must also have been indescribably happy when they heard this news. I lit a cigarette. I had long ago "sworn off" tobacco, but whenever I solve some thorny problem, achieve a big victory, or receive news of some outstanding conquest, I enjoy a smoke.

In actions coordinated with the Tay Nguyen front, the armed forces of Zone 5, commanded by Lieutenant-General Chu Huy Man and Vo Chi Cong, political officer, besides using the 3rd division to attack the enemy and cut Route 19, had liberated Tien Phuoc and Phuoc Lam, and defeated counterattacking enemy troops. They also forced the evacuation of Son Ha and Tra Bong, liberated almost all of the border zone, and at the same time stepped up attacks against pacification efforts in the lowlands, especially in Quang Ngai and Binh Dinh.

After we won our big victory in the Tay Nguyen, Zone 5's party committee and its front command, in a sharp response to the new opportunity, abandoned their plans to advance to the south, and changed the thrust of their attacks to the north in order to establish conditions for the liberation of Da Nang. After March 18, the Central Military Committee and the General Command also instructed Zone 5 to quickly smash enemy defense lines along the border between the two zones, move down to cut off Route 1 between Da Nang and Tam Ky, and wipe out Saigon's 2nd infantry division, not letting them regroup toward Da Nang. They were ordered to organize the shelling of Da Nang, and make active and urgent preparations for the battle of Da Nang.

Carrying out those instructions, one regiment of our 2nd division captured Tuan Duong on March 21 and cut the road from Tam Ky up to Da Nang. They inflicted heavy casualties on the 5th regiment of Saigon's 2nd division, put pressure on Tam Ky, and drew Saigon's 2nd division out of Quang Ngai to wipe them out. Taking advantage of that opportunity they used another force in a quick thrust to liberate Quang Ngai. The Central Military Committee and the General Command, recognizing that the enemy were evacuating Hue, and that we could not discount the possibility that they would also abandon Da Nang, on March 22 directed Zone 5 to make concrete plans to attack Da Nang as planned.

With a clear understanding of these directives, and faced with the rapidly developing situation in Tri Thien, the standing committee of the Zone 5 party committee next day held an enlarged meeting and passed a new resolution: "Mobilize the whole party branch and the entire population in the zone to struggle enthusiastically and in the shortest possible time to liberate all of Zone 5." On March 24 and 25, the zone's 2nd division, in coordination with regional forces, wiped out and dispersed the 4th and 5th regiments of Saigon's 2nd division, and liberated Tam Ky and Tuan Duong. The Quang Ngai regional forces, in coordination with the masses, attacked and rose up to liberate the northern part of that province.

We moved on, attacking and capturing the base at Chu Lai, and at the same time Quang Ngai's armed and political forces continued attacks and uprisings to liberate all of Quang Ngai province. The liberation of Quang Ngai, Tam Ky, and Tuan Duong, and the destruction of enemy forces there, put more pressure on their southern defenses of Da Nang. In Saigon, Thieu vowed to "defend Da Nang to the death," and the United States and their quislings also intended, if they couldn't hold on, to mount a "delaying action" for a month or two. This would allow them to gain time to redeploy their strategic defensive positions that were falling apart in large chunks, and at the same time to evacuate a million people in order to exert an unfavorable political influence on us while they stepped up diplomatic activities to put pressure on us to halt the offensive. Saigon's Brigadier-General Nguyen Xuan Trang, deputy chief of general staff, received top priority orders to go to Da Nang to investigate the situation, and to transfer 20,000 guns from the Long Binh armory to Da Nang to supplement the armament there. The defense plan for Quang Nam and Da Nang which the enemy laid out was aimed at reducing the boundaries to be defended and concentrating the marines, the 3rd infantry division, and all the specialized arms and branches to try to defend Da Nang.

On March 25, the Central Military Committee and the General Command, concluding that after losing Hue, Tam Ky, Quang Ngai, and Chu Lai, the enemy could not hold Da Nang even if they tried, decided to open the offensive for Da Nang under these guiding principles: "in the best time, most rapidly, most daringly, most unexpectedly, and certain to win." They directed the Second Army Corps and Zone 5 to "act boldly and unexpectedly, so that the enemy cannot raise a hand in time; concentrate forces to destroy the large enemy force at Da Nang, most importantly their marine division and 3rd division; gain big victories in this decisive battle; and create conditions for a strategic victory later."

To direct this important battle, on March 25th the Political Bureau and the Central Military Committee decided

Hue–Da Nang Campaign
March 21–March 29, 1975

KEY 〰️➤ March 21-March 25   ➤ March 26-March 29

Dong Ha

9

QUANG TRI
3/19

1

14/
14

Thuan An Estuary

HUE
3/25

Phu Bai
3/25

Tri Thien
Military Zone

51

P.71

4

3

Tu Hien Estuary

15

Phu Loc
3/25

1

2
3/25
3/24

6

324

325

2

1

146H

AF

DA NANG
3/29

7MF
258
147

3

Laos

Dai Loc
3/28

Hoi An

10B

14

Duy Xuyen
3/29

Z6
304
2
02

2
01

2
07

1

Tam Ky
3/24

2
02

2
02

Tien Phuoc
3/15

5

1

Tra Bong

QUANG NGAI
3/25

Son Ha

to set up a Quang Da front command including Major-General Le Trong Tan as commander and Lieutenant-General Chu Huy Man as political officer. Le Trong Tan flew from Hanoi to Gio Linh. At that time Chu Huy Man was commanding a wing of troops a long way from there, between Quang Tin and Quang Ngai. To direct the attack on Da Nang they had to set up their headquarters west of Da Nang. Arriving at Quang Tri, Le Trong Tan immediately turned up to A Luoi along the route east of the Truong Son range, then circled around to the west of Da Nang. He used a telephone switching station along the route to make contact with all the wings of troops. Seeing that the situation was extremely urgent, he used the radio to work with Chu Huy Man, to agree on methods of combat operations. So the Quang Da front command and party committee had not yet met face to face.

During these days I was also very anxious about the situation in Zone 5. Far away and unable to get a concrete grasp of the situation, I cabled Hoang Van Thai, deputy chief of the General Staff, to direct the Second Army Corps, which included the 304th, 324th, and 325th divisions, to position their long-range artillery to bring Da Nang's seaports and airports under control, and join quickly with the forces of Zone 5 to wipe out the enemy units pulling in toward Da Nang. If that could be done, it would improve things for the fighting in Nam Bo in the next stage. And, I said, they should increase the command for this important battle.

After March 25, the city of Da Nang was in chaos. Our forces advanced quickly to put pressure on the city. The enemy had to abandon their plans to regroup in Da Nang, and began to use Boeing 727s and helicopters to evacuate the American advisers and a portion of the Saigon forces. They fought with each other to get on the planes, starting raucous brawls at the airport. Some were crushed on the runway by airplane wheels. Others were caught in the landing skids of helicopters. Puppet soldiers and officers and their families elbowed past each other to flee. The enemy marine division participated in many incidents of looting, shooting, and rape before they fled. Some 3,200 enemy recruits at the Hoa Cam training center rose up in struggle, deserted, and crossed over to the revolution or went home. Our big artillery began to fire on the Da Nang airport, the Hoa Khanh base where the command of Saigon's 3rd division was stationed, Son Tra port, and the division headquarters at Non Nuoc, terrifying the enemy in the city even more. Our brothers imprisoned by the enemy in the Non Nuoc prison arose, destroyed the prison, and escaped. The 2nd division from Zone 5, commanded by Colonel Nguyen Chon, Hero of the Army,* after liberating Tien Phuoc, Phuoc Lam, and Tam Ky, advanced against Da Nang from the south. On March 29, infantry and tanks attached to the Second Army Corps, along with armed forces from Zone 5, struck quickly from the north, northwest, southwest, and south, thrust straight into the city, and seized the Da Nang airport and other important positions, especially the Son Tra peninsula. At the same time, one of Zone 5's independent regiments attacked and captured Non Nuoc and the Nuoc Man airfield. Some members of our revolutionary infrastructure and special action troops in the city captured the Trinh Minh The bridge and raised the flag over city hall, and the home guard and the people guided soldiers in to seize enemy positions quickly and chase down enemy remnants. Within thirty-two hours we had destroyed and dispersed more than 100,000 enemy troops in Da Nang, taken over a strong combined forces base, and liberated Da Nang, the second largest city in the South. With the liberation of Da Nang we had completed the process of destroying and scattering all of Saigon's First Army Corps, wiped their I Corps off the map, and established conditions to encourage the rapid and complete collapse of their troops. Ngo Quang Truong, after escaping death in a meeting at the

---

* Hero of the Army is the highest award for combat exploits in the revolutionary army.

Son Tra navy base, took a helicopter out to a warship and fled straight for Saigon, where he entered Cong Hoa Hospital.

This big victory in the Hue-Da Nang campaign had an extremely important strategic meaning. Together with the Tay Nguyen victory it completely changed the strategic balance of forces to our advantage, having defeated the enemy's strategic regroupment scheme, weakened Saigon, and created conditions for us to concentrate the pressure of our forces on the final decisive battlefield.

We also received news of the Nam Bo battlefield in a letter from Tran Van Tra, commander of the Nam Bo forces and of Zone 6 (also known as B-2). After liberating Dinh Quan, Hoai Duc, and Gia Rai, we sent most of the 7th division, plus artillery and tanks, toward Long Khanh and Route 20, to attack and liberate Lam Dong.

The 7th division of our Fourth Army Corps for the first time used combined special branches advancing in formation, with armored cars in the lead, followed by tanks, infantry, artillery, and logistics. They fought the enemy wherever they met them, with a spirit never before seen. Groups of enemy soldiers standing along the road stared, terrified. Some fled; others ran up hills to watch our troops advance. The 7th division continued on rapidly and liberated Lam Dong province and the town of Bao Loc. Tran Van Tra was only sorry that he didn't have more forces, so that after he finished liberating Lam Dong he could move up to liberate Lien Khang, Drang, and Da Lat.

After wiping out the enemy in the Dau Tieng subsector and positions at Ben Cui, the Ong Hung stream, Cau Khoi, and the Dat Set crossroads on interprovincial road 26, we cut Route 22, isolated Tay Ninh, and drew Saigon's main-force troops out to destroy them, creating conditions for our troops to strike Tay Ninh and liberate it when the opportune moment came. Troops of our 5th and 3rd divisions finished opening the route to Zone 8 in the Mekong Delta and changed direction in order to knock out Saigon's

9th infantry division and 4th armored regiment at Moc Hoa. After that they would prepare to attack Moc Hoa sector headquarters. We had expanded our zone north of Cai Be (in My Tho province), into eastern Kien Phong, and along the Nguyen Van Tiep canal.

In Zone 9 in western Nam Bo, Vinh Long fought well, but Hau Giang still fought rather embarrassingly. In general the enemy still had large numbers of troops in Nam Bo. Their spirits had been influenced by the big defeats in I and II Corps. At the same time, we had not yet scored any earthshaking victories in their area, and so the enemy had not yet fallen apart. If we wanted to create an opportune moment, we would have to have some large battles of annihilation, unexpected blows that would shake the enemy severely and push them onto the road of dissolution, with nothing left to regroup and nowhere to fall back to. One of the basic rules of warfare is to wipe out the enemy's military forces, both men and materiel. The enemy had many kinds of troops, many kinds of forces. Only if we chose the correct opponent—struck down their most vital forces—would we make the enemy fall apart quickly, thereby changing the balance of forces in our favor and setting off a chain reaction that spread out wider each day. Now our main opposition was Saigon's main-force units, especially their command nerve centers. If they were smashed, the whole defense system and the quisling administration on every battlefield would dissolve. The enemy would not fall apart and flee if we did not deal them death blows, striking quickly, striking hard, striking repeatedly.

At the Tay Nguyen front command headquarters on March 18, while the enemy were fleeing the Tay Nguyen, we were discussing what our Tay Nguyen troops should do next. We carefully analyzed the enemy's situation and our own, concluding that our victory in the Tay Nguyen had strongly affected the enemy's strategic deployment and morale. Our heavy attacks and rapid moves caused them to fall apart quickly. To avoid isolation and encirclement with no possibility of supply, where sooner or later they would be completely wiped out, the enemy had to withdraw hastily from the Tay Nguyen. Their intention in pulling their forces back from the Tay Nguyen was to protect the neglected lowlands provinces of II Corps. In Binh Dinh they had the 22nd division, but all the rest of the provinces had only security forces and civil guards. Around Saigon the enemy still maintained the same forces as before, or had perhaps reinforced them. In all of the South the enemy's Second Army Corps was the corps which had had the greatest number of its forces knocked out. They had had to abandon the whole strategic area of the Tay Nguyen—five provinces. This was unprecedented in the history of warfare in Vietnam. Because Saigon's Second Army Corps was also the most dispirited corps, there was little chance their Second Army Corps would quickly organize any large counterattacks against the Tay Nguyen in general or Ban Me Thuot in particular. The defeats in the Tay Nguyen and other battlefields badly weakened the Thieu administration; more military defeats might lead to their collapse.

Our victory in the Tay Nguyen was tremendous, not only implementing but surpassing our plans. And we still had good conditions to exploit the victory. The enemy were in confusion and disorder, with us in close pursuit. Our forces were maturing increasingly through the fighting, their spirits many times stronger. Our logistics operations guaranteed that we had the amount of ammunition estimated in the plan, and that we could take a great deal more from the enemy. The strategic roads allowed our vehicles to run farther and faster than before. There was still about a month and a half of dry season weather for us to continue our activities. On all of our battlefields throughout the South we had coordinated actions well.

The immediate problem was which way to move the Tay Nguyen forces to assure the greatest continuity and speed, allow the greatest development of their strength, and leave the most time for action. This must aim to wipe out many of the enemy's forces, strategically divide the territory temporarily controlled by the Thieu administration in the South, both from military and administrative points of view, confuse the enemy's strategic deployment and strategic situation, and stimulate further military disintegration and political collapse for Thieu. If we stopped or attacked in a different direction, the enemy would regroup.

After heated discussions we agreed that the best direction for the Tay Nguyen forces to push the campaign was to the east. Specifically, we would move down to the coastal areas along with the Zone 5 forces, liberate Binh Dinh and Phu Yen provinces and part of Khanh Hoa, destroy many enemy forces, and liberate more than a million people. At this time our troops were clamoring to take advantage of their victories to advance quickly to the plains. And the people in the coastal areas were busily building and repairing roads, carrying rice and ammunition, and hoping to welcome the main-force troops back.

So we would take and hold the three strategic roads, Routes 7, 19, and 21, which joined the jungled mountains with the plains, the populous seacoast area of Zone 5 with the thinly populated Tay Nguyen. This advance to the plains would aim at finishing off Saigon's 22nd division, the only remaining force of their Second Army Corps, and the ranger and regional forces troops in Binh Dinh, Phu Yen, and Khanh Hoa provinces, staying ready to wipe out two or three enemy regiments from I Corps or III Corps if they should come in as reinforcements. If we could do this, we would basically have wiped out the enemy's Second Army Corps, liberated II Corps, cut their whole defense system in the South in two, and isolated their I Corps to the north. Later we added to these intentions so that after finishing the liberation of Khanh Duong, we would move along Route 21 down to the Mo Drac Pass and create conditions to liberate Ninh Hoa. Then we would proceed down to liberate Nha Trang and Cam Ranh.

At this time we had to solve two problems: first, that of

strengthening our army quickly, equipping all units with more weapons, and second, that of training them in fighting methods. We didn't worry about logistics because we had three strategic roads to the plains and could transport troops, weapons and ammunition, staples, and other food entirely by motorized vehicles. The General Political Office had sent many cadres down, not only to increase the fighting strength of our army, but to make an active contribution to developing grassroots governments in the newly liberated areas. The General Technical Office dispatched 300 more engineers and workers to the front to assemble and repair the hundreds of enemy tanks, trucks, and artillery pieces.

On March 19, I worked with Bui San and Nguyen Tuan Tai from the standing committee of the Zone 5 party committee, and Huynh Van Man, a member of the Zone 5 committee and also secretary of the Dar Lac provincial committee. The situation in town and in the surrounding areas was gradually settling down. Almost all of the people from town had stayed with the revolution. Markets were gathering and the hospital was back in operation. After two days, the town was being supplied with water. All classes of people were taking part in meetings to welcome the liberation of their homeland. Most enthusiastic were the circles of workers and of young people and students, many of whom volunteered to clean up the streets, repair the radio station, repair the electricity and water systems, and take part in maintaining order and security.

In all the meetings, townspeople raised many questions. How will people continue to make a living now? Can we go work in the fields all day and wait until evening to return? Can we go into the forests to cut wood? Can we withdraw money we have deposited in the banks? Will civil servants and teachers get their pay? Will the schools reopen, and what curriculum will they use? I discussed these questions with the local leaders and directed the Tay Nguyen command to help solve some of the big problems, such as building a grassroots government and regional armed forces, implementing economic, cultural, and educational policies, organizing supplies for the 100,000 people in and around Ban Me Thuot and the more than 50,000 refugees in the outlying areas, and correctly carrying out our policies toward the various ethnic groups, the bourgeoisie, and foreigners. The region was short of cadres and wanted the minority cadres studying at the Nationalities Institute in Hanoi to return immediately for assignments, and wanted cadres from the whole country to come help. As a first step, we set up a military region committee both to take care of military administrative duties and to lead the three provinces of the Tay Nguyen in all respects. The membership of the military region committee included military and civilian cadres, administrative and party cadres. This organization did not appear in public, but it directly guided the work of protecting, restoring, and building the Tay Nguyen economy. They hoped that within a few years they could exploit hundreds of thousands of additional hectares. One fighter said happily, "Going through Ban Me Thuot and seeing the land, my heavens, what a joy! With land like this we can't talk about being small and poor any longer."

The offensive moved on toward the central coastal plains from early March into early April 1975, following Routes 19, 7, and 21. Raising the curtain in strong spirits, the 968th division advanced into Binh Dinh along Route 19, and along with the 3rd division from Zone 5 wiped out and scattered Saigon's 22nd division at Phu Thong, Lai Nghi, and Phu Cat. The people in Qui Nhon town rose up and, along with the regional armed forces, liberated the town and the Phuoc Ly and Phuoc Hai peninsulas, and kept enemy ships from coming in to the coast to pick up their remnants. On the same day, we captured the Go Quanh airfield, along with 1,000 enemy soldiers, and confiscated thirty airplanes in perfect condition. So we had smashed the enemy's intentions of fleeing Qui Nhon and taking parts of the 41st and 42nd regiments down to reinforce the defenses of Nha Trang. On the beaches of Qui

Nhon, thousands of soldiers who had not been able to board ships in time were captured or deserted. The whole of Binh Dinh province was liberated.

On Route 7 the 320th division liberated Cung Son, then quickly advanced down to liberate the towns of Tuy Hoa, Tuy An, and Song Cau, and liberated all of Phu Yen province.

In the Nha Trang area Saigon's II Corps ranger command was directed to reorganize two groups at once, and as soon as the 72nd battalion was organized, it was ordered to reinforce the 3rd paratroop brigade at Khanh Duong. Remnant elements who had just landed at Cam Ranh in the morning got orders from Major-General Le Nguyen Khang, Saigon's deputy chief of staff, to arrange to go up to reinforce Khanh Duong, which was under heavy attack. General Pham Van Phu, commander of Saigon's II Corps, sounded off again about "defending Nha Trang to the death" at the very time that the U.S. consulate there was making plans to evacuate! Enemy officers and soldiers were trying to arrange for their wives and children to flee, and 3,000 enemy troops at the Lam Son Training Center, a school for noncommissioned officers, fled back to town, as did police guarding the detention camp. Two thousand Saigon soldiers imprisoned there escaped, stole guns, and went around shooting and looting wildly, panicking the town even more. At the same time, Vu Lang and Nguyen Hiep along with the 10th division chased the enemy toward the sea. Vu Lang was impatient to return to liberate Ninh Hoa where, twenty-nine years before, he had suffered and fought against the French invaders in the Southward March Army. But when he reached the Phuong Hoang Pass, he received orders to return to the headquarters of the General Command to receive a new assignment. The 10th division, after liberating Khanh Duong and Ninh Hoa, advanced into Nha Trang. Townspeople and a number of police came out on bicycles to greet our troops and lead them in to capture enemy military positions and administrative offices. Our troops rushed to Pham Van Phu's quarters. Trays of rice had just been set out; he hadn't had time to eat before he fled. A number of the enemy escaped Nha Trang and got to Cam Ranh, then kept on going to Phan Rang while, at 15:20 hours on April 2, Thieu was sending the II Corps command orders to "turn over the defense of Cam Ranh to the coastal command." Taking advantage of their victories, the 10th division fought on to enter and liberate Cam Ranh, a large, important military port, and thus liberated the whole of Khanh Hoa province.

Pham Van Phu fled to Phan Thiet where he met the deputy commander of III Corps, who told him, "Thieu is about to include the two southernmost provinces of II Corps, Ninh Thuan, and Binh Thuan, in III Corps, in order to form an outer defense line around Saigon." Thus Saigon's II Corps was erased from the map.

I should also say that when we saw that we still had a large number of reserve forces in the Tay Nguyen, we assigned one unit to attack and liberate Da Lat. This enabled us to open the road and send soldiers down to capture Thanh Son airfield (at Phan Rang), an important enemy airbase which blocked our troops' advance into Nam Bo from the east. We used a regiment of sappers for this mission. Da Lat was not just a famous place for vegetables, flowers, and fruit, but was also a resort city, and a cultural and scientific center. It had an atomic research facility as well as a number of schools and institutes. So we had to educate the soldiers attacking Da Lat in a spirit of discipline, and organize administrative continuity well, in order to preserve, protect, and administer all the equipment and resources, and all the installations. The 198th sapper regiment, commanded by Major Tran Kinh, equipped with motorized artillery, passed through Quang Duc province and the town of Gia Nghia, which had just been liberated by main-force troops from eastern Nam Bo, and joined troops from Zone 6 to move in and liberate Da Lat.

One staff cadre at the Front Command at the time

exclaimed, "I can't draw maps fast enough to keep up with our troops!"

All of the battlefields were surging forward to take advantage of our victories.

10

A New Opportune Moment, A New Strategic Decision

On March 20, while our Tay Nguyen forces were moving down to the plains along the three strategic routes, we received a telegram informing us that the Political Bureau and the Central Military Committee had just met so they could get a comprehensive view of the situation. Our recent tremendous victories had strategic significance, marking a new turning point in the war in the South, a very new development in the overall situation, and a new step toward the collapse of the Americans and their puppets. The enemy planned to carry out a large-scale strategic regroupment aimed at concentrating their forces in the Saigon region and part of the Mekong Delta, possibly in Da Nang and Cam Ranh as well, to establish a relatively firm position from which they could proceed to a political solution or coalition, or a division of the South. Thus we must save as much time as possible, operating absolutely unexpectedly as to time, direction, and forces, while at the same time assuring victory. In that spirit, the Political Bureau had weighed all aspects, and *had concluded that Saigon should be liberated sooner than had been foreseen.* The Political Bureau would appoint Le Duc Tho to come down on March 28 to meet with us in the Tay Nguyen to pass on the resolution in detail. At the same time, Hanoi had cabled Pham Hung and Tran Van Tra in

Nam Bo and Vo Chi Cong and Chu Huy Man in Zone 5 to immediately join me in the Tay Nguyen to hear the decision and debate plans for implementing it. A new situation had opened up. A new mission was taking shape based on the realities of the struggle and coming from the great mind of our party. A big opportunity had arrived. We waited impatiently for Le Duc Tho to arrive, and for the absolutely vital instructions of the Political Bureau.

On March 25 the Political Bureau met again, and that historic meeting decided: "Our general strategic offensive began with the Tay Nguyen campaign. A new strategic opportunity has come, and conditions allow an early completion of our resolution to liberate the South. We resolve to rapidly concentrate our forces, technological weapons, and materiel *to liberate Saigon before the rainy season*. Seize the opportunity of the enemy's strategic withdrawal and the destruction and dispersal of Saigon's First Army Corps and the bulk of their Second Army Corps, and do not allow them to withdraw and regroup around Saigon."

On the basis of a scientific analysis of the situation, responsive to its new features, the Political Bureau had discovered this opportune moment, and had passed the resolution to carry the general offensive to complete victory. As they had realized, the situation was changing very rapidly, by the hour, by the minute. The enemy were in confusion and disorder. With this opportunity we needed to act urgently, striking massively so they could not recover. If they were able to prolong their resistance until the rainy season, it would complicate the situation.

On March 25, the Political Bureau cabled to inform us that they had decided to concentrate three main-force divisions, and those units with the technological weapons taken on Route 7 and Route 21, in the Ban Me Thuot area for rapid reorganization, ready to move out and prepare to attack and liberate Saigon. All assignments were to be given out urgently so that within one month this decision could be implemented. The telegram continued: "Thus, we can still carry out the plan to liberate Saigon during the dry season, because there are nearly two months before the heavy rains, and once our forces have closed in on Saigon, even if we do run into the rainy season it will not be so great an obstacle. We must seek every means to overcome our difficulties. The situation is changing, and there must be new creative measures. . . . The situation now is developing very rapidly. This is a great leap. Saving time and grasping opportunities are decisive now."

The Political Bureau also decided to establish a Council to Support the Battlefield, with our beloved Prime Minister Pham Van Dong as chairman. Deputy Prime Minister Le Thanh Nghi was vice chairman, and Deputy Prime Minister Phan Trong Tue and a number of others were members.

On receiving the Political Bureau's telegram, we considered how best to implement it. Should the 320th and 10th divisions stop chasing down the enemy and shift immediately to Nam Bo? Or should we let them continue on into the lowlands, liberating Phu Yen and Khanh Hoa provinces, go on to Nha Trang and Cam Ranh, and then order the 320th division to return to the Tay Nguyen along Route 7 and the 10th division to move into Nam Bo along Route 20? If our army was not to spoil its opportunity, they should pursue the enemy to wipe out and scatter the maximum number of enemy troops, finish destroying the enemy troops in II Corps, and so create advantageous conditions for the next step, the decisive step of the war—liberating Saigon-Gia Dinh.

We carefully estimated the time for carrying out our mission, the resources and time needed to move the troops, transfer supplies, and prepare the battlefield, and how much dry season weather remained for the 320th division to finish liberating Phu Yen and the 10th division to finish capturing Cam Ranh without hampering our advance into Nam Bo on time. In the battles just past, the Tay Nguyen divisions had all attacked towns, won fast, and won big, and there had been no hesitation in any battle, so we had every confidence in these experienced troops. I reported these considerations to the Political Bureau and proposed that the Tay Nguyen units be allowed to fight on down toward the plains for a few days longer, because our troops had kept on the heels of the enemy and were full of the spirit of victory. The enemy were fleeing in confusion, enabling us to wipe them out and scatter them even more, and we could liberate a number of areas that were crucial both to avoid later disaster on the Nam Bo battlefield and to throw the enemy off our trail. We could still guarantee that we would meet the Political Bureau's schedule, so that the coming assignment could be carried out well.

We were immeasurably pleased when we received a telegram from the Political Bureau and the Central Military Committee approving this operational plan, with a reminder that even though their advances were to our advantage, the Tay Nguyen troops must afterward be concentrated and strengthened quickly to move into Nam Bo to strike the enemy's nerve centers in accordance with the new strategic decisions.

There were many new and quite complex tasks involved in organizing the advance toward the coast. First of all we had to consider helping the Tay Nguyen provinces to organize regional armed forces—to build up regional-force regiments and battalions with sufficient equipment and weapons to guard their newly liberated home provinces after the main-force troops pulled out. The 25th regiment was given increased artillery and antiaircraft guns to hold Route 21. The 29th regiment went down to protect Ban Me Thuot and to set up a regional-force regiment for Dar Lac which would also be stationed at Ban Me Thuot. The Tay Nguyen forces were given the responsibility of protecting Kontum and Pleiku, and a battalion of regional forces took responsibility for Phu Bon.

On March 27, faced with the new situation, and following instructions from the Political Bureau and the Central

Military Committee, we met with the Tay Nguyen front command at the headquarters which had just been moved west of Route 14, to pass on the spirit of the new directive. Everyone was most excited and in complete agreement, and resolved to carry it out strictly. We discussed the implementation of the two most important tasks: planning to bring the troops back in to strengthen and reorganize them, and organizing to send more than 50,000 troops and tens of thousands of tons of supplies from the Tay Nguyen into Nam Bo at once. In accordance with the decision of the General Command, I announced the formation of the Third Army Corps, including the 10th, 320th, and 316th divisions, with Brigadier-General Vu Lang as commander and Senior Colonel Nguyen Hiep as political officer. The 968th division and all the independent regiments in the Tay Nguyen were turned over to Zone 5. Hoang Minh Thao, originally deputy commander of Zone 5, had completed his responsibilities in the Tay Nguyen as headquarters commander for the campaign, and now returned to Zone 5 to command the wing of troops that included the 968th division and the 3rd division in the plains. This wing was to push into Cam Ranh and relieve the divisions from the Tay Nguyen so they could carry out other assignments. We organized a light command section with communications equipment so Hoang Minh Thao could maintain direct contact with us.

As we shook hands and embraced Hoang Minh Thao after our big victories on the Tay Nguyen front, it was very difficult for us to part. We wished each other continued good health to secure complete victory.

Our Third Army Corps came into being as the war was approaching a turning point. The establishment of the Third Army Corps while attacks were still continuing signaled a new feature: that we were growing stronger as we fought in the process of a campaign as well as in the process of the strategic offensive. In the past, after each round of fighting or after each campaign we had a period of time to rest and strengthen our army, consolidate our experiences, prepare the battlefield, prepare our logistics, and so on. When we sent our troops out on the next campaign, they were usually stronger than in the campaign before. But within the bounds of a single campaign we had never before put into practice the slogan of growing stronger as we fought. In the campaign to counterattack on Route 9 in 1971, after forty-three days of combat operations we had to stop and could not continue on toward Khe Sanh, even though the opportunity was still there. In the 1972 spring-summer campaign in Tri Thien, after liberating Quang Tri we only pushed our attacks forward as far as the My Chanh River and then had to halt. But in 1975 the situation was different. As we fought a number of campaigns in succession, we were clearly growing stronger the more we fought. The Tay Nguyen forces were at first only a collection of regiments and divisions, and after less than a month of fighting they had been organized into a strong mobile army corps with a full complement of specialized technological branches. Our armed forces in Tri Thien, Zone 5, and Nam Bo were also developing and maturing, both in material forces and in spirit, in their level of fighting ability and in command organization. And for the first time in the history of building the Tay Nguyen forces, each of our battalions was complete with over 400 soldiers, and every division had greater firepower than the enemy.

The opportunity for liberating Saigon was ripening daily. Our Political Bureau, with a thoroughly revolutionary spirit and the concept of active attack, analyzed the task scientifically, with far-seeing eyes, and applied this analysis to new developments. Determined to seize every opportunity to push our attacks forward, they responded promptly to problems which were being posed at a seething pace. At this time to hesitate, to waver, to be sluggish was to commit a serious error.

On March 28, General Weyand, U.S. army chief of staff—the man who had furled the American flag to withdraw from South Vietnam with the last American unit two years before—came to Saigon to outline defense plans directly to the puppets. After our troops had liberated everything from Cam Ranh Bay north, and the Saigon regime's First and Second Army Corps had been destroyed and scattered, Weyand hastily urged the Saigon troops to build a strong defense line at Phan Rang to stop our troops at a distance. Weyand cabled back to the United States to ask them to send urgent aid to the puppet administration. President Ford set up an airlift to carry arms from Bangkok, Thailand, to Saigon, and used huge C-5 Galaxie transport aircraft to move hundreds of artillery pieces and great amounts of weapons and munitions from the United States to Tan Son Nhat. He sent four big LST transport ships along with the aircraft carrier *Hancock*, fifteen large helicopters, and 300 marines to sit bobbing in the East Sea.

At this time the United States and Saigon thought that after we had liberated all the provinces of I Corps and II Corps, we would have to leave behind several army units to hold these areas—at least one regiment per province. Thus the maximum force we would be able to dispatch to reinforce eastern Nam Bo would be one army corps, and it would take us at least two months to move them there. Even they, with all their airplanes, transport ships, and trucks, would take a month to move such a force.

In their hour of agony, the enemy were still very subjective, and were completely mistaken in their assessment of us. Naturally it was no longer any surprise to them that we were mounting sustained attacks throughout South Vietnam, but clearly they did not yet know the direction or timing of our actions, the forces we would use, our manner of fighting, our strategic intentions, or the extraordinary efforts we would make to seize this new opportune moment. If the enemy were completely surprised in the Tay Nguyen, and surprised again at Hue and Da Nang, they would be even more surprised in Saigon-Gia Dinh.

On April 2, Cao Van Vien, chief of staff of the Saigon forces, blustered that he was "determined to hold on to our remaining territory, and to try to defend from Phan Rang southward," and set up a III Corps front command headquartered at Phan Rang with Nguyen Vinh Nghi, the puppet major-general, in command.

Dong Van Khuyen told a meeting of Saigon's General Staff: "According to Mr. Thieu's orders we must, whatever the cost, attempt to defend from Ninh Thuan province down, and if necessary we will send all our forces to fight to the finish there." Saigon's commanders reinforced the Phan Rang front with a brigade of paratroops, a ranger group, and a number of armored and artillery units. Off the coast they stationed a group of warships to give fire support when needed, and their air force gave priority to bombing missions in support of efforts to hold Phan Rang. On April 3, Nguyen Vinh Nghi met with the topranking commanders of the Saigon air force, paratroops, and rangers, and commanders in the Ninh Thuan sector, to explain defense plans for Phan Rang and stress the importance of defending Phan Rang, Saigon's distant line of defense.

The enemy ordered all fronts to try to hold on until the rainy season, until the beginning of June 1975. Then we would be unable to act, and they would be better prepared; their recruit training centers would turn out a considerable number of troops on May 15 so they could re-form a number of their divisions which had been wiped out. Saigon's General Staff planned to: 1) recruit more soldiers and integrate remnant soldiers into the units of III Corps to form four ranger divisions, and most immediately move the 101st and 106th divisions into position; 2) organize eight more armored regiments by accelerating training; 3) reconstruct three infantry and marine divisions; 4) deploy their air force divisions and naval units to prevent us from using the ports, and increase the coastal fleet from Nha Trang down for priority fire support from naval artillery for the Ninh Thuan, Binh Thuan, and Binh Tuy sectors. They also decided to graduate all their training classes early and requested the United States to rush more artillery, tanks, and armor.

Since the beginning of the campaign our troops had won wherever they had fought, especially from the thunderbolt strike against Ban Me Thuot until the attacks on the enemy as they fell apart in I Corps and II Corps, so spirits rose higher and higher, and victories were as easy as splitting bamboo. But if we thought that the enemy would fall apart and collapse so easily in the remaining areas of III Corps and IV Corps—the center of the American lackeys' ruling apparatus—and that we could attack without thorough preparations or attack without superior forces, that would be very wrong. Saigon was the enemy's final lair, the last big place they could regroup their forces, the final defense for an absolutely obstinate and reactionary enemy. This would be the final battlefield and the final battle which would determine the victor in this struggle between revolution and counter-revolution, between our people and U.S. imperialism. This decisive test of strength required our most objective analysis; the victories that we had recently amassed must not allow us to become intoxicated, or to think of the enemy simply as they were when they were fleeing in disorder.

We proposed to the Political Bureau and the Central Military Committee that they dispatch one or two additional divisions, including a full complement of specialized units, to come down and, in coordination with the forces in Zone 5, wait along Route 1 and Route 20 as strategic reserves for the campaign. The enemy fighter planes at Thanh Son airfield in Phan Rang had a range of only 400 kilometers, and thus could not reach Da Nang or Kontum, so we should boldly use transport planes and ships to transfer troops and all kinds of materiel to Da Nang and Pleiku. The General Command should send its additional troops down to the decisive Saigon front, and need not detach any for Tri Thien and Zone 5, where they could mobilize forces on the spot.

We went to visit Ban Me Thuot, Phu Bon, and Buon Ho to inspect the old enemy positions and our troops' routes of advance in the recent campaign. The Tay Nguyen front, where this turning point in the war had opened up, was today completely peaceful. Looking at the old battlefield with the enemy's whole defense system collapsing and our troops' victory flags now flying, we understood more each day about this enemy that we would have to deal with in the days to come. We were overflowing with pride in the clearsighted, active, determined, timely leadership of the Political Bureau and the Central Military Committee, in the level of organization of our cadres at all levels for strict and creative battlefield implementation of their orders, and in the perfect revolutionary heroism of our people's armed forces. We were urgently studying the statements of enemy officers captured in the Tay Nguyen and enemy military documents so we could use this information for the battle to come.

We went to visit Ban Me Thuot prison, where Nguyen Chi Thanh, Nguyen Chanh, and To Huu, among so many others, had been detained and persecuted, but had retained their cheerful revolutionary optimism. Ban Me Thuot. It was on this very front that, twenty-five years ago, a number of my comrades from that first graduating class of our army school had heroically sacrificed their lives when French troops captured this place.

We had a meeting place ready for Le Duc Tho to present the Political Bureau's resolution to the cadres in charge down here. It consisted of bamboo and thatch buildings temporarily set up at Chu Leo, beside Route 14, west of Thuan Man. Seeing how rapidly the situation was changing, and especially that the whole length of Central Trung Bo had been liberated, we cabled the Political Bureau suggesting that we not meet in the Tay Nguyen, but go straight to Nam Bo and wait for Le Duc Tho to come all the way down there. Le Duc Tho left Hanoi on March 28 and flew down to Dong Hoi. He traveled with his heart as happy as if he were at a festival, and the first night as he rested in Quang Binh he wrote a few lines of poetry for Le Duan:

> You warned: go out, and come back in victory.
> In such moving moments what could I say?
> Your words are those of the whole land;
> What obstacle is the thousand-mile Truong Son
>   range?
> Such good news on the road to the front!
> Glad cries of victory are everywhere,
> Urging haste to my steps on the long road;
> The time of opportunity has arrived . . .

On March 31, both Le Duc Tho, who was on his way down the Truong Son range, and I, in Ban Me Thuot, received flash telegrams from Le Duan:

WE MUST SAVE TIME AND ACT URGENTLY. THEREFORE BROTHER TUAN SHOULD GO TO NAM BO IMMEDIATELY TO MEET BROTHER BAY CUONG [PHAM HUNG]. BROTHER SAU [LE DUC THO] WILL COME ALL THE WAY DOWN THERE FOR THE MEETING. BROTHER BAY CUONG AND BROTHER TU NGUYEN [TRAN VAN TRA] ARE NO LONGER COMING TO THE TAY NGUYEN.

Both Vo Chi Cong and Chu Huy Man in Zone 5 also received cabled announcements from the Political Bureau that they should not come up to the Tay Nguyen for the meeting.

In fact, Vo Chi Cong came up to Kontum from Zone 5 just after the Tay Nguyen had been liberated, and seeing the big changes in the situation and that in the lowlands of Zone 5 they had the opportunity to press on quickly, he turned back at once so as to be able to give directions in time. When he got back to Zone 5, he received the cable saying never mind coming to the Tay Nguyen to meet Le Duc Tho. Bui San, after working with me at Ban Me Thuot, hurried back up to Kontum to meet Vo Chi Cong. They only worked together for a very short time before parting, because the situation was so urgent and things were piling up. Right after that, Le Duc Tho met Vo Chi Cong at Ben Giang in western Quang Nam on his way to Nam Bo and passed on the Political Bureau's resolution to liberate the South before the rainy season. Vo Chi Cong and Nguyen Xuan Huu (Bay Huu) promised on behalf of the Zone 5 party committee and the whole Zone 5 party branch to do everything in their power to continue the liberation of the remaining provinces in Zone 5, and to stand ready to respond to every request from the decisive final Saigon-Gia Dinh front. At the leadership level, every comrade saw that we must take full advantage of this new opportunity. Moreover, the entire party and army and all the people were extremely excited and enthusiastic, and all were prepared to bring their strength and their intelligence to strive to complete whatever task they might be assigned.

The slogan, "All for the front, all for victory!" had become a reality in this high point of the final phase of the resistance against the United States to save the country. The great rear area, the socialist North, rapidly marshaled all its human and material strength for the battlefield, for the great front lines of the South. Night and day our troops roared forward, advancing into Nam Bo at lightning speed, in high spirits, and confident of victory.

11

At Lightning Speed

If the individual activity of warfare is a desperate life-and-death struggle, then the final strategically decisive battle is always the high point in the test of strength between the two sides. It is the supreme effort of the two sides, from the giving of directions to actions implementing those directions.

On the morning of March 31, the Political Bureau met to hear the Central Military Committee report on the developing situation of our troops' attacks during the past three weeks, especially in recent days. The Political Bureau unanimously recognized that following our victory in Zone 9 and eastern Nam Bo in liberating Phuoc Long province, and with the tremendous victory on the Tay Nguyen battlefield, our general strategic offensive had in fact begun, and within a very short time had gained extremely large victories. We had wiped out and scattered more than 35 percent of the enemy's forces and had for the first time killed and put out of action two enemy army corps. More than 40 percent of their modern technological weapons had been lost. We had captured and destroyed more than 40 percent of the Saigon troops' material and logistics infrastructure, liberated twelve provinces, and brought the total population of the liberated zones up to nearly 8 million.

131

One noteworthy thing was that in the battle of Da Nang, coordination between military attacks and uprisings by the masses had clearly begun, in a situation where popular resentment against the enemy was high and people were just waiting for a chance to rise up. Most of the enemy officers and troops had lost their fighting spirit. And so in just over thirty hours from the time we opened fire, with a force much smaller than that of the enemy, our army and people had daringly knocked out one of Saigon's firstranking large-scale combined military bases in the South.

Our armed forces had grown larger and stronger by leaps and bounds in the fighting; the number of our soldiers who sacrificed their lives or were wounded was very small compared to the victories we had gained; and we had expended little in weapons and munitions. Using our strategic position and the military and political forces at our command, we had the strength to put pressure on the enemy troops and topple them. The strategic initiative lay completely in the hands of our army and people, while the enemy were passive and awkward; having reached a serious deadend both strategically and tactically, they were confused and vacillating. The United States appeared completely impotent, and even if they increased their aid they would not be able to rescue their puppets from the impending collapse.

So the March 31 meeting of the Political Bureau concluded: "Not only has the revolutionary war in the South entered a period of developing by leaps and bounds, but the time is ripe for carrying the general offensive and general uprising to the enemy's lair. From this moment, the final decisive battle of our army and people has begun; its aim is to complete the people's national democratic revolution in the South and bring peace and the reunification of the Fatherland.

"The tempo of revolution in our country is so ebullient that one day is like twenty years. Thus the Political Bureau has decided to seize the strategic opportunity even more firmly, with the guiding concepts of lightning speed, daring, surprise, and certain victory, and carry out the general offensive and general uprising at the earliest possible time—best of all in April. It must not be postponed.

"To ensure certain victory and keep the element of surprise, it is essential to save time, to attack the enemy while they are confused and collapsing, and to concentrate our forces on the essential objectives.

"We must firmly grasp the content of our strategy, which is to develop the strength of three strategic blows by coordinating offensives and uprisings, striking from the outside in and from the inside out. In every direction and at every time we must concentrate our forces to pressure and topple the enemy troops, quickly creating new opportunities and taking advantage of them to continue piling up victories.

"We must increase our forces west of Saigon, cut Saigon off from the west, and set up a strategic encirclement, then close in on Saigon and choke off Route 4. At the same time we must concentrate forces to the east to capture important objectives and complete the encirclement, isolating Saigon completely from Ba Ria and O Cap. The main forces, including technological weapons, should stand ready so that when the opportune moment appears, we can strike directly at the most vital and important objectives in the very center of Saigon city."

Looking at the actual situation at that time, anyone could see two major, nearly contradictory characteristics emerging—the extreme urgency of the new strategic opportunity, and the need to prepare a strong, multifaceted force for the final decisive battle, which would be on a large scale and over a broad area, and would employ a new and unique method of attack. While the first characteristic demanded that we complete preparations in the shortest possible time, the second demanded a relatively long time to achieve good results, both quantitative and qualitative. Meanwhile, the United States and their puppets were seeking every way to take advantage of the situation to block us, to force us to prolong our preparations for the strike on Saigon-Gia Dinh.

The Political Bureau decided to concentrate both leadership and troops to achieve victory in this historic decisive battle. All military zones, all local areas, and all levels of government throughout the country were ordered to give first priority to the needs of this critical battlefield. Every service of the General Command worked day and night, both to direct the work of administering the newly liberated areas, and to prepare for the coming battle.

Our party, our people, and our armed forces devoted their strength to transforming this new strategic decision of the Political Bureau into reality. Beginning in early April 1975, on all the nation's thoroughfares—highways, rivers, sea lanes, railways, and air lanes—our people lived through the most stirring and tumultuous of days. The whole nation was on a pilgrimage in this historic spring. The whole nation sent out its army under the slogan, "Lightning speed, daring, surprise, certain victory." The troops moved like flowing water, and trucks rode as if there were only one direction—to the South. From the North all manner of vehicles rushed day and night, nose to tail, jumping past the way stations to carry men and supplies to the front. When they got to Dong Ha, one branch went up to the east and west of the Truong Son range, and one branch followed Route 1 south past Hue, Da Nang, Quang Ngai, and Qui Nhon, following the advancing footsteps of our troops.

Along the red-earth Truong Son route, blinded by the dust in the brief remaining days of the dry season, the lines of vehicles poured south without cease, past Duc Lap and Bu Gia Map, down to Dong Xoai and Loc Ninh, then spreading out into the rubber forests of Dau Tieng, into War Zone D, along the shores of the Saigon River, the River Be, and the eastern Vam Co River. Seeing this torrent of revolutionary soldiers flowing past their homes all through the day and into the night, seeing how young and healthy and cheerful our soldiers were, seeing our large artillery, our antiaircraft guns and missiles, our units of tanks and armored cars, and our amphibious vehicles, the newly liberated compatriots of the Tay Nguyen ethnic groups along Route 14 were overjoyed, and could not conceal their surprise. Because of the distortion and deceit of the United States and Saigon propaganda which they had heard for so long, they had never before been able to imagine that Uncle Ho's soldiers would have so many vehicles and artillery pieces, or that they would be so young and handsome, so kind and cheerful. When they saw the trucks carrying rockets go past, they called the rockets "airplanes without wings."

Hundreds of thousands of vehicles ran bumper to bumper day and night. There were stretches of road where the dust was so blinding that they could not see each other clearly, and had to turn on their lights and sound their horns continuously. The swirling dust spread out, and before it had time to settle to the road, they were gone—past the dense jungles of the Tay Nguyen, past the deep green hills of Bu Prang, and on past the bamboo forests of Bu Gia Map.

And day and night, at one high pass where the eastern and western Truong Son routes met, Phung The Tai, deputy chief of staff, along with construction and transport cadres and military police, urged the advancing units on, directing them along the correct routes at set times, quickly resolving pileups and road blocks and assigning priorities to each unit, each kind of vehicle, each specialized branch. He and those cadres worked like this for weeks on end, beside a signboard with big letters saying, "Lightning speed, lightning speed, daring, and more daring"; together they pulled and shoved and drove on tens of thousands of vehicles carrying hundreds of thousands of tons of goods and thousands of kinds of war materiel down to the battlefield in time to meet the plan, trying to finish before the rainy season poured down on the Tay Nguyen.

Some of the fighters driving trucks, who did not know

that this was Phung The Tai but saw only a comrade who
was very devoted and determined, severely reprimanding
them and urging them on whenever vehicles were blocked
or piled up, made up a verse as a warning to each other:

> Listen, when you meet Mr. Lightning Speed
> Out supervising operations,
> You'd better get your legs moving
> If you don't want a hard time . . .

And it was from that that all the fighters on the front called
him Mr. Lightning Speed and Mr. Operations Supervisor.

Along Route 1, besides our own military vehicles and
those we had taken from the enemy, there were also buses
and trucks belonging to the state and to the people,
which had been mobilized and sent down from the North
and from the provinces and the cities and towns just liberated. As a timely service to this last battlefield, Zone 5
organized a special convoy to carry the most essential
kinds of guns and ammunition they had just captured
from the enemy, as well as those their soldiers had not
used up in liberating Da Nang and the provinces to the
south. This convoy, directly commanded by Brigadier-
General Vo Thu, deputy commander of Zone 5, drove from
the lowlands of Zone 5 up into the Tay Nguyen and then
down into eastern Nam Bo.

The Gia Lam, Vinh Phu, Dong Hoi, Phu Bai, Da Nang,
and Kontum airfields were unusually busy. All manner of
heavy and light helicopters, all kinds of transport planes,
and even our special passenger planes were mobilized;
not just to carry people, munitions, weapons, books, news-
papers, films, drawings, sheet music, etc., but also to
carry tons of maps of Saigon-Gia Dinh, just printed at the
General Staff map service in Hanoi.

The docks on the Red River, the Gianh River, the River
Ma, the River Han, and the ports of Hai Phong, Cua Hoi,
Thuan An, and Da Nang were also bustling day and night.
All kinds of goods were loaded in time for the convoys of

ships from the Ministry of Transport and ships from the People's Navy to take them down, with the sea lanes extended to newly liberated ports like Quy Nhon and Cam Ranh. It took all of these routes and all of this equipment to give us the strength to carry this large quantity of soldiers and materiel, unprecedented in our country's revolution, to the front quickly enough.

All of the suffering and hardship borne by our people, their thrift and frugality, all of our patient preparation of forces for so many years, were like tens of thousands of small streams which today were coming together in a great roaring waterfall—pouring down to wash away the last ramparts of neocolonialism in our land. Vietnam, this Phu Dong of 1975,* stretching its shoulders and arising, had the power to shake the heavens and rock the earth, and to vault onto its horse and fly off at once at full gallop, because it understood that an opportune moment is priceless, and that time is strength.

The General Staff stayed on top of action plans and forces on the battlefield, and also kept up to date on the status of each munitions storage site in the country, directing and supervising the rapid transport of all kinds of munitions to respond completely and promptly to every request from all troops on the Saigon front. It particularly concentrated on sending enough munitions to the First Army Corps and the 232nd force, which included all the independent divisions and regiments from the area and from Zone 8 combined under the command of Major-General Le Duc Anh and Brigadier-General Le Van Tuong

---

* Phu Dong was a mythical Vietnamese hero from the time of the Hung kings, nearly 4,000 years ago. Until he was three years old, he could neither talk nor sit up. But when the country was threatened by an invasion from the An dynasty to the north, he suddenly spoke, ordering the king's emissary to have a gigantic iron horse and other implements of war cast for him. When they were done, he grew magically into a giant, mounted the horse which came to life under him, and rode off to raise an army and defeat the invaders.

(Le Chan), political officer. At that time the big concerns of the whole front were artillery shells, rounds for recoilless guns, mortar shells, and antiaircraft ammunition. The engineering troops and the people of Nam Bo quickly repaired and widened the roads from Dong Xoai to Cay Gao and Ben Bau, and repaired the Nha Bich bridge and the Ma Da and Ben Bau tunnels, thus preparing routes for our artillery units to close in on Saigon, and routes to move the mechanized infantry forces deep into the center of the city.

On March 25, the First Army Corps, commanded by Brigadier-General Nguyen Hoa and Brigadier-General Hoang Minh Thi, political officer, which was building dikes in Ninh Binh, was ordered to make a high-speed motorized advance to the South to take part in the fighting. The army corps leapt past Route 9 and followed Routes 12, 15, and 14 through Pleiku and Ban Me Thuot, traversing 1,700 kilometers and arriving in Nam Bo by the third week in April.

The Second Army Corps, under the command of Brigadier-General Nguyen Huu An and Brigadier-General Le Linh, political officer, began to quickly move its troops out of Da Nang along the coastal route into eastern Nam Bo. Many bridges had been destroyed along their 900-kilometer route; six bridges were down on the Da Nang-Quang Ngai stretch alone. And they had to fight the enemy at Phan Rang and Phan Thiet on the way down. But their orders from above clearly stipulated that within eighteen days they must arrive at Bien Hoa and Ba Ria. Getting the corps' 2,000 vehicles across six big rivers, to say nothing of having to fight along the way, was a complex organization and command assignment. In 1962, when the 308th division was on maneuvers with only 400 vehicles, they piled up along the road until it was impossible to move. This time, the troops were organized into columns for the advance: engineers went first, to repair damaged bridges and roads at once, and tanks followed them to fight wherever they found the enemy. Each advancing column had an antiaircraft regiment for protection, with infantry and artillery behind them. The corps carried a quantity of rice and other food sufficient for one month's rations, and a supply of munitions so it could begin fighting as soon as it arrived. The General Command appointed Major-General Le Trong Tan and Major-General Le Quang Hoa to command this "coastal" wing. Many cadres from agencies of the General Command, went ahead of the army corps to investigate the battlefield along with local leaders along the route, and to prepare supplies of gasoline and oil, additional rice, salt, and other foodstuffs for the corps. Alongside the road many old aunts and uncles, many mothers and children stood waiting for a long time to bring tea, coconuts, and sugarcane to give the soldiers. But the soldiers in their trucks, with the slogan, "Lightning speed and daring," affixed to their helmets, could not stop even a minute to talk with the people. They only had time to wave as they sped singlemindedly toward the front.

On April 13, the corps arrived next to Phan Rang, the place the enemy were shouting about "defending to the death." The following day, the 3rd infantry division from Zone 5, reinforced by the Tay Nguyen's 25th infantry regiment, opened fire on this advance defense outpost of Saigon's Third Army Corps.

After two days of heavy fighting, our troops had only been able to capture a few outlying positions. The enemy bombarded us fiercely from airplanes, and relied on positions prepared in advance to mount a desperate resistance. Faced with this situation, Le Trong Tan and Le Quang Hoa decided to throw one section of the Second Army Corps into the fight to increase their assault strength. Brigadier-General Nam Long, deputy director of the Military Academy, along with a number of political and logistics staff cadres from the General Command, were also sent to reinforce the command of this wing of troops. In the early morning hours of April 16, with strong fire support from our artillery, a force of the 325th division of the Second Army Corps, reinforced by tanks and armored cars, advanced along with the 3rd division and the 25th regiment into the center of Phan Rang and Thanh Son airfield from three directions.

In the face of the heavy pressure from our artillery and the daring deep strikes by our combined armor and infantry units, the enemy troops panicked and fled. The result was that we wiped out the advance command of their Third Army Corps, capturing its commander, Major-General Nguyen Vinh Nghi, as well as the command of their 6th air force division, capturing its commander, Candidate-General Pham Ngoc Sang, and the command of their 2nd infantry division. We also knocked out the 2nd paratroop brigade, the 31st ranger group, and one newly re-formed regiment of the 2nd division, captured many other highranking officers, and seized nearly forty airplanes in perfect condition.

When the enemy discovered our Second Army Corps advancing south along Route 1, they tried every means to halt them, sending flight after flight of airplanes to bomb their route of advance. Enemy warships fired in from the sea, and a special forces company landed from the sea in Tuy Phong district north of Phan Thiet. Immediately, infantry troops from the Second Army Corps and reconnaissance troops chased them down, and just two hours later the whole band had been rounded up. Then our artillery units set up their guns beside the road, aimed them toward the sea, and set an enemy warship ablaze with their fire. Taking advantage of its victories, the Second Army Corps coordinated with Zone 6 forces to attack Phan Thiet, and fought on to liberate Ham Tan as well.

We left the Tay Nguyen on the way to eastern Nam Bo at noon on April 2, 1975. Before that I had gone to visit the 316th division and meet with the division commanders. Senior Colonel Dam Van Nguy, Hero of the Army and division commander, had gone to inspect his troops that day, so Colonel Ha Quoc Toan, the political officer, and Colonel Hai Bang, deputy commander of the division, reported on the preparations for their new mission. This division would set out first, along with a light command section from the Third Army Corps command. Hearing the division commanders report on the situation and meeting the units directly, looking at all of the division's equipment, and seeing how quickly the unit had grown and strengthened set my mind at ease. I gave directions for a number of things that needed to be done quickly before they moved out. It was in this division, too, that some had been worried before they moved into the Tay Nguyen campaign, thinking, this is a strange new battlefield, the first time we have fought in big combined units with all kinds of modern weapons, and against a big town. They didn't know whether they would be able to fight well. Events had shown that the division could fight and had carried out its mission well. Today, as they prepared to set out for eastern Nam Bo, the division's spirits were surging. Their determination was high and they were confident of victory, equipped with plenty of all essential weapons. They had matured quite rapidly.

The route of advance for the 316th division was from Ban Me Thuot along Route 14 toward Saigon from the northwest. The 320th division, under the command of Senior Colonel Kim Tuan and Colonel Bui Huy Bong, political officer, was ordered to turn back along Route 7, after liberating Tuy Hoa and all of Phu Yen province, then follow Route 14 into eastern Nam Bo.

Only for the 10th division, commanded by Senior Colonel Ho De and Senior Colonel La Ngoc Chau, political officer, was the road down to Nam Bo extremely difficult. After liberating Phuong Hoang Pass and Mo Drac, then advancing to attack Nah Trang and Cam Ranh, the division followed interprovincial road 2 to Route 20, then went down to Saigon from the northwest. The road was bad, and an engineering unit had to go ahead to repair it and throw up hasty bridges. Meanwhile, the enemy had discovered the 10th division's movements and tried every means to stop them. Enemy planes bombed the whole

length of the road fiercely, and artillery on enemy warships fired up to halt them. The 10th division had to fight
to open the road as it went.

Dinh Duc Thien was busy day and night with the work
of organizing logistics for the Third Army Corps' advance,
especially to guarantee supplies for the new campaign. He
wore a "ba-ba" suit, like the peasants in the South, as he
went to inspect and supervise all our storage areas and
units. Coming into a truck park near Duc Lap, he saw two
sloppily dressed drivers repairing their truck and asked,
"Say, what unit are you from? Don't you think that's a
ridiculous, inappropriate way for victorious troops to
dress?" The drivers answered, "Sir, we're POWs!"

At this time over the whole battlefield, and in all units,
our soldiers were using people who had previously been in
Saigon's armed forces to drive and repair all kinds of vehicles. Our fighters had competed to research and investigate and study the use of all kinds of American weapons
and modern means of war. In our advancing columns
American M-113 armored cars, M-48 and M-41 tanks,
105mm and 155mm artillery pieces, and PRC-25 tactical
radios began gradually to make their appearance. And
especially there were the A-37 and F-5 fighter planes
taken from the enemy which our fighter pilots had been
sent down to practice using. Our possibilities for taking
enemy supplies to fight the enemy had never before been
so rich as in this campaign. Because of that tremendous
potential, our firepower bore down more and more terribly
on the enemy, and the tempo of our advance kept increasing.

Since the Tay Nguyen victory, there were many
changes in the route to eastern Nam Bo. It was possible to
take Route 14 through Ban Me Thuot, Duc Lap, Bu Prang,
and Bu Gia Map to Loc Ninh. The stretch from Bu Prang
and Bu Gia Map was quite good and all kinds of vehicles
could run on it. It was called Route 14A. After the liberation of Gia Nghia and all of Quang Duc province, all kinds
of vehicles could go from Duc Lap through Kien Duc and

down to Don Luan, meeting Route 13 at Chon Thanh. It took just over a day for small vehicles to get to Loc Ninh from Ban Me Thuot.

In the first years of fighting against the United States, our troops moving out through this region endured great suffering. The enemy were always firing artillery, B-52 airplanes dropped bombs according to map coordinates, and special forces spread various kinds of mines. This stretch of road was also short of water and infested with dangerous mosquitoes which spread malaria. Seeing the bomb craters all along both sides of the road, and the twisted skeletons of trucks and barrels of artillery pieces bearing American insignia, and piles of rust-stained barbed wire lying smashed atop the old bases, we thought back to the "search and destroy" and "cross-border" operations by the Americans and their allies which had been defeated by our troops in 1965, 1968, and 1970.

On a number of sunlit hilltops and along the margins of tall, dry forests there were still some high earthen mounds, the final resting places for some of our comrades. On this remote and cruel corner of suffering earth who knows how many comrades, how many of our beloved cadres and fighters went ahead to open the way, and sacrificed their lives here to contribute to the creation of this vast, broad road for the march to Nam Bo, cleared of all the enemy's outposts, so that today we could move toward that final, strategically decisive battle. Their exploits and their spirit were shining examples to us as we plunged toward the impending battle, and a challenge to us to score victories befitting the memory of our fallen comrades.

Spring was noisily returning to the grassy hills and sun-drenched mountains. The rubber forests that stretched as far as the eye could see were putting out new leaves. Orchids were blooming on ancient jungle trees. The rubber forests on both sides of the road were excellent fields for billeting troops. Trucks, tanks, and cars pulling artillery could hide securely under the umbrella of their leaves. Along the banks of all the streams, Hoang Cam kitchens* were in operation. Orderly rows of hammocks hung heavily; our fighters were sleeping after a tiring night on the march.

To hide the technological weapons and decrease the density of vehicles on the road, each stretch of road had stations to regulate and inspect vehicles, remind them of their formations for the operation and methods of camouflage, and warn them of enemy aircraft. At every crossroad there were whole "forests" of signs pointing the way for all the units and services, and all the wings of troops—signs of all sizes and shapes, all manner of letters, and in every color. An outsider standing at some fork in the road would have had a hard time trying to tell where those signs were leading, or for whom they had meaning. Strands of telephone wire strung hastily through the forests ran alongside the road. Who knows how many secrets about this strategically decisive battle there were on those wires?

The scenes of trucks and artillery bustling along the road and bivouacked along both sides of the road leading down to Nam Bo made me think back to the years of the resistance against the French colonialist troops, in the zone behind the enemy's backs in the Bac Bo delta. Back then, along with the other fighters in the Delta Brigade, I wore a brown peasant shirt and conical palm-leaf hat, a walking stick in my hand, poking each toe into the muddy sections of road as we "snaked" along, drawn out in single-file formation along the paddy dikes and bamboo hedgerows of the Ha Nam-Ninh Binh region. I remembered sitting at night in a bamboo boat as we passed through French "controlled villages" on the plains of Thai Binh and Nam Dinh, under the light of parachute flares and random salvoes of enemy shells, amid the sound of waves slapping and gurgling in the fields. In the daytime,

* Hoang Cam kitchens used a network of underground flues to lead smoke away from the cooking fires, to guard against detection from the air. They were named after a fighter who developed them during the anti-French resistance.

we split up into small units and went into villages which had a resistance network. We sunk our boats under the water to hide them, and organized to be ready to fight if necessary. Guerilla brothers and sisters stood guard and mothers took care of rice and water so we soldiers could rest. Then at night we continued our operations.

In the past thirty years our people had witnessed and taken part in who knows how many operations for the independence and freedom of our Fatherland. There had not yet been a day when our people and our army had halted their operations. From South to North, from North to South, our fighters and people went the whole length of the land, going wherever the Fatherland needed them. "Wherever the enemy are, we will go." In the spring of 1975, in the formation of vehicles and artillery advancing to the Saigon front, just as in every village, on every dock, in every trench in the South, it was impossible to distinguish southerners from northerners. There were only Vietnamese, charging toward the final battle against U.S. imperialism and its lackeys, to win back complete independence, freedom, peace, and unity. The whole land was on the march at top speed. The whole land was going to the front. The spring of earth and heaven and the spring of our nation clung fast together in this historic April of 1975.

12

The Campaign Bearing Uncle Ho's Name

At noon on April 3, about fifty kilometers north of Bu Gia Map, we met Colonel Mai Van Phuc (Tu Phuc), deputy chief of the regional logistics office for eastern Nam Bo, who had come up to meet us. Standing atop a hill with many scars from the furious battles of the U.S. "border crossing" of 1970 scattered all around, we shook hands, joy shining in our eyes. We were moved because this was the first time we had stood on the earth of Nam Bo, this firm ground, this heroic front line so far from the center in Hanoi. Uncle Ho always remembered this part of the land with affection, and had directed the party, the army, and the people to contribute everything for the liberation of the South. We stood looking at the scenes about us. Our respectful greetings to the South, first to set out and last to return, this long-suffering battlefield of the Fatherland. Our respectful greetings to all the fighters and compatriots of Nam Bo who had held fast with courage of gold and steel through decade after decade, successively fighting off the richest and most cruel of enemies, holding aloft an example of indomitability, of revolutionary optimism, and of continuous attack.

We went in to take a noon rest at the 770th force compound, a way station of the regional logistics office. The

146

road to the way station was well concealed, with no tire tracks. The houses were strong and well hidden, with rows of vegetables, a banana orchard, flower beds, displays of blooming orchids, and even a flock of animals. Around the house were communications trenches, hidden bunkers, and guard posts. Although everything here was on a small scale, it was representative of the spirit of clinging fast to the earth, holding on to their territory, the spirit of self-reliance in daily life and readiness for battle of the services and units of eastern Nam Bo, one of the most long-suffering and one of the firmest base areas of the South.

That afternoon as we went to the office of the regional command, we passed rubber forests with many patches destroyed by enemy airplanes, through orchards of pepper and durian, and saw light-skinned jack fruit and rows of newly planted coconuts.

There before our eyes was Loc Ninh town. The town still bore the scars of war, but we could see many features had changed after three years of liberation. The roads were being widened, newly built thatch houses ran along both sides of the road, fields of manioc and rice were turning a healthy green, and in the rubber forests workers were cultivating the trees, cutting grass, and collecting sap. Loc Ninh, liberated in 1972, along with the whole province of Phuoc Long, liberated at the first of this year, had become an important base for us, and now gave us a great advantage for the coming attack on Saigon.

On the road we met many convoys of cheerful soldiers on their way to the front. The men and women guerillas of Loc Ninh stood guard at every fork in the road, carefully checking every vehicle coming to the base area. We salute you, comrades, resolute fighters. In the years of cruel fighting, your exploits, known far and wide, aroused our admiration and pride. Looking out at the large fields, the rubber forests, the orchards of fruit, and the red-earth hills of Loc Ninh, I remembered part of To Huu's poem, "This Thousand-Mile Land."

Oh, Binh Long, here in our Nam Bo,
This morning for the first time I meet you face to
     face.
Holding a clod of your red earth in my hand,
My heart chokes as if intoxicated with strong wine.
As I clasp you, liberation brother, to my heart,
I dream of running all the way to the fields of Ca
     Mau.

It was nearly night on April 3 when we returned to the
office of the regional command west of Loc Ninh. Most of
our comrades from the Central Office for South Vietnam
(COSVN) had arrived. Dinh Duc Thien went straight to
the office of the logistics section, while I went to see Pham
Hung, secretary of the southern party branch, in a house
on the far side of a clump of trees. Looking into the house,
under the light of a blacked-out lamp, I saw him sitting
beside a table, his shirt open to the chest, with a
parachute-cloth fan in his hand. When he saw me coming,
he stood up cheerfully: "We've been waiting for you." We
shook hands and embraced, immeasurably happy as I told
him that our victories had come in such rapid leaps that I
had got here sooner than I had expected when we met in
Hanoi. Saigon would surely be liberated within the time
limit set by the Political Bureau. I told him about the
victories in the Tay Nguyen and the coastal plains of Zone
5, and about the situation of our main-force units on their
way to this front. After that, we discussed the agenda for
the days ahead, before Le Duc Tho arrived.

The office of the regional command was arranged in
front of the living and working places of the A-75 force. A
number of wooden buildings covered with leaves had been
set up quickly. More air-raid bunkers had been dug. A
number of tents had been set up all around in preparation
for the cadres who would be coming later. As night fell,
the forest grew busy as the noise of generators and the
motors of all kinds of vehicles running back and forth
blended gradually with the sound of radios in all the huts.

THỐNG NHẤT

Top. Liberation forces units move into Da Nang, March 1975. *Bottom.* A villager waves the liberation flag.

Top. Officers and soldiers of the liberation forces in Da Nang. *Bottom.* At Front Command headquarters. Left to right: Tran Van Tra, Le Duc Tho, Van Tien Dung, Phan Hung, and Dinh Duc Thien.

Top. Local population greets liberation army soldiers on Phu Quoc, prison island, May. *Bottom.* Southern civilians meet soldiers from the north in Da Nang, March.

Top. Villagers assist the liberation forces during the Tay Nguyen campaign, March. *Bottom*. Soldier daughter being greeted by family and friends.

Top. Liberation forces move south on Route 1, April. *Bottom.* Lines of liberation troops, April.

Top. Soldiers and peasants cross the Trang Tien bridge over the Perfume River in Hue, March. *Bottom, left.* A soldier instructs local security forces in Hue in the use of weapons, April.

Center. Vehicles abandoned by the Saigon forces in retreat toward Thuan An, April. *Right.* In anticipation of liberation, a woman in Da Nang sews the new flag.

Top. Camouflaged vehicles on the Ho Chi Minh trail. *Bottom, left.* General Van Tien Dung crossing a quickly built bridge on the way to the battlefield. *Right.* Ethnic minorities in the Tay Nguyen celebrate their victory.

Top. Civilians in Qui Nhon support the liberation forces, April. *Bottom.* Students in Pleiku join security forces and patrol the city, April.

Top. A military representative describes the new situation to recently liberated ethnic minorities along Route 19 in Kontum province. *Bottom.* At the headquarters for the Ho Chi Minh campaign in late April. Seated, left to right, Van Tien Dung, Le Duc Tho, and Phan Hung.

Top. The fifty-five-day campaign ends as troops move onto the grounds of Independence Palace on the morning of April 30. *Bottom.* Destroying a "strategic hamlet" in Chou Thanh in Ben Tre province in order to rebuild homes.

Top. Victorious soldiers drive through the streets of Saigon, May 1. *Bottom, left.* Woman soldier guides troops to Tan Son Nhat airport, May 3. *Right.* The U.S. embassy in Saigon.

Top. Saigon teenagers meet "the enemy." *Bottom.* Captain Nguyen Thanh Trung and fellow army pilots return from bombing Independence Palace on April 8, having joined the revolutionary forces.

Top. Saigon army guards at Independence Palace surrender to the liberation forces. *Bottom.* Fireworks over the old imperial city of Hue celebrate final victory, May 15.

Top. Women political prisoners released from Con Son Island tiger cages arrive on the mainland. *Bottom.* Saigon forces surrender.

Without the cold and
Bleakness of winter
The warmth and splendor
of spring
Could never be.

Misfortunes have steeled
and tempered me,
And further
Strengthened
My resolve.   –Ho Chi Minh

Van Tien Dung and Vo Nguyen Giap at the end of the Ho Chi Minh campaign.

This was our first night to sleep on the land of eastern Nam Bo.

Tran Van Tra, who had gone down to visit the Fourth Army Corps to inspect their plans for attacking Xuan Loc, returned that night and as soon as it was light, he came over to where I was staying. We happily told each other tales of recent battles on each battlefield, and discussed in a general way how to organize the work between the A-75 force and the regional staff. Early on the morning of April 4, we contacted Hanoi by telephone, which required a big effort by the communications battalion just arrived from the Tay Nguyen, with the close cooperation of regional communications units. As soon as this communications battalion had been organized in early 1975, they had set out for the Tay Nguyen to guarantee communications for command work throughout the time of the campaign to liberate the Tay Nguyen, and had carried out every assignment well. All the cadres and fighters had then been ordered to set out for Nam Bo to serve in this final battle in coordination with the other communications units and resources of the region. Colonel Hoang Niem, deputy commander of the communication troops, was busy day and night, organizing communications for the headquarters and training communications fighters who had just arrived on the battlefield.

Motorcycles, a unique means of transportation here, operated continuously day and night. The drivers carried us around to the various offices attached to the regional headquarters, which were scattered over a broad area as a precaution against enemy air attacks. When we were still in the Tay Nguyen, the B-2 command (which covered Nam Bo and Zone 6) had sent a unit of motorcycles on special assignment to come up and help us, and now they had returned to eastern Nam Bo with our convoy. The drivers, with colorful scarves around their necks and folding-stock automatic rifles slung from their shoulders, stuck with our convoy to show us the way, now dashing ahead at high speed to make contact with the leading vehicle, now dropping back to look for slow or lost vehicles. Every night they carried telegrams along the bumpy, winding jungle roads to the radio-communications truck, which usually worked at night because it was on the road during the day. It always stopped far from us to guarantee security and secrecy for the commanders and for the radio system, and to evade electronic reconnaissance by enemy airplanes and special forces.

Those from COSVN and the regional military committee who had worked for many years on the Nam Bo battlefield and had a deep understanding of the enemy and of us, as well as of the situation in Saigon, helped us get a quick understanding of the battlefield situation in Nam Bo in general and of the situation in Saigon-Gia Dinh in particular.

After several days of reports from comrades from the regional staff, we met on April 7 with COSVN and the regional military committee, along with Pham Hung, Nguyen Van Linh (Muoi Cuc), Tran Nam Trung, Tran Van Tra, Phan Van Dang (Hai Van), Vo Van Kiet (Sau Dan), Nguyen Van Xo (Hai Xo), plus Major-General Le Duc Anh, deputy commander and chief of staff of the regional headquarters, Brigadier-General Le Van Tuong (Hai Le), deputy political officer of the regional headquarters, Brigadier-General Dong Van Cong, deputy commander of the region, Brigadier-General Le Ngoc Hien, Senior Colonel Luong Van Nho, and a number of staff, political, and logistics cadres. Major-General Dinh Duc Thien also took part in the meeting.

Pham Hung, secretary of COSVN, and all of the others always had a simple style of behavior, an ebullient optimism, and an iron determination to win. The meeting room was always filled with relaxed, spontaneous laughter. The conference carefully considered the situation in Nam Bo, and especially the situation in Saigon, following our victorious rout of two enemy army corps and the liberation of all the provinces, towns and cities in the enemy's I Corps and II Corps. The conference studied the directives of the Political Bureau and the Central Military Committee and discussed measures to implement them. It was necessary to step up military and political activities to gain new victories and create the right conditions for the general offensive and uprising to liberate Saigon and the entire Mekong Delta.

When we discussed the problem of ensuring logistics, Pham Hung asked what preparations we had already made for munitions, and Dinh Duc Thien brought out a statistics chart showing the amounts of munitions received and the amounts that had arrived at or were on the way to various places, and said, "Let me report to you that we can fire enough munitions at them to scare them for three generations." Then each time we were discussing something that needed to be gotten ready for the campaign, if there were almost enough of something, or if we were still far short of something, Pham Hung would give instructions for measures to overcome the problem, sometimes echoing Dinh Duc Thien's words—make sure we have enough, and have it quickly enough, to "strike fear into them for three generations," sending everyone in the -meeting into gales of laughter.

COSVN and the regional military committee met in the atmosphere of ebullience and excitement that characterized the whole region. All the districts and provinces in Zones 8 and 9 were continually reporting on their combat and construction accomplishments in the first days of April 1975. Tra Vinh informed us that before they had had only two regional forces battalions, and now they had already increased them to five battalions. In one day Rach Gia had mobilized 200 recruits to form an additional provincial battalion, and every village had a company of guerillas. The regional forces in Zone 9 had captured the Cai Von outpost at Cho Gao in Long An and were rapidly expanding the liberated zone.

On the afternoon of April 7, as we were meeting, a motorcycle drove up into the yard carrying a tall, lean man wearing a sky blue shirt, khaki slacks, and a soldier's hard helmet, with a big black leather satchel slung from his shoulder. We recognized him immediately as Le Duc Tho. The whole room was excited and happy, and everyone stood up. We all embraced him, overjoyed. This was Le Duc Tho's third mission to Nam Bo over the past thirty years, since Nam Bo entered the resistance against France and then against the United States. At times he had gone on foot, crossing dangerous jungle trails carrying rice balls and dry rations. This time he had traveled by airplane, car, and even motorcycle on his way here.

Le Duc Tho told us cheerfully of events in the country, of world public reaction to our victories, of the rear area, the socialist North, and of things that had happened along the road. He said that before he had set out, the Political Bureau and Uncle Ton [President Ton Duc Thang] had cautioned, "When you leave, you can't come back without victory."

On April 8, in a full meeting of COSVN, the regional military committee, and the B-2 command, plus additional cadres from the General Command, Le Duc Tho passed on the resolution of the March 25 meeting of the Political Bureau in Hanoi. He talked about the Political Bureau's perception of the enemy's situation on the battlefield and our own, and of the schemes of the Americans and the Saigon quislings in the face of their recent defeats and the threat of their impending collapse. After that, he spoke in detail about the Political Bureau's strategic resolution, emphasizing the guiding concepts for successfully carrying it out. At the end of the meeting, he informed us of the Political Bureau's decision to set up a headquarters for the campaign to liberate Saigon-Gia Dinh, with myself as commander, Pham Hung as political officer, and Tran Van Tra and Le Duc Anh as deputy commanders. Le Duc Anh was also given the responsibility for commanding the wing of troops to the southwest of Saigon—the 232nd force. Major-General Le Trong Tan, who was commanding the eastern wing of troops, was also designated a deputy commander in the headquarters for the campaign to liberate Saigon. Dinh Duc Thien was deputy commander in charge of logistics, to help Brigadier-General Bui Phung, head of the regional logistics section. Major-General Le Quang Hoa, who was serving as secretary of the technical section for the eastern wing of troops, was reassigned as deputy political officer and campaign headquarters political director. Le Ngoc Hien was assigned as acting chief of staff with special responsibility for combat operations.

The campaign headquarters drew upon the staff, political, and logistics offices which the region already had for its work, reinforcing them with a number of cadres from the A-75 force who had just arrived from the Tay Nguyen, and some detached from the General Staff, including Brigadier-General Doan Tue, artillery commander, Senior Colonel Nguyen Chi Diem, commander of the special elite troops, Senior Colonel Le Quang Vu, deputy head of the military intelligence section, Senior Colonel Nguyen Quang Hung, deputy commander of the air defense-air force troops, Colonel Truong Dinh Mau, deputy head of the troop training section, Colonel Le Xuan Kien, deputy commander of the tank troops, and so on. Thus the Central Office for South Vietnam and the regional military committee and headquarters continued in their previous responsibilities for the whole region. Only a few of their staff were taking part directly in the campaign headquarters for the liberation of Saigon.

In this final strategically decisive battle for the liberation of Saigon, three members of the party's Central Political Bureau were appointed to take direct responsibility for leadership at the front, and to receive direct instructions from the Political Bureau. From April 8 until about April 20, the Political Bureau and the Central Military Committee as well as those of us at the front followed the progress of each infantry division, each logistics convoy, each artillery regiment or antiaircraft battalion toward its assembly point hour by hour and day by day. In our daily discussions such questions came up as: Where is this division? How many transport vehicles does it have? How many artillery pieces is that regiment pulling? What road are they taking? How many 130mm artillery shells do we have? How many loads of 100mm tank shells have been brought in so far?

For all the roads involved in the operation groups of cadres had been selected to supervise the advancing un-units, meet logistics vehicles and guide them to the predetermined storage areas, and guide units of fresh troops coming to reinforce various units before they entered the campaign.

When the first rains of the season fell on the forests of Loc Ninh, Le Duc Tho wrote a poem that captured the mood and the feelings of us all at the time.

> I hear the cuckoo calling.
> It's morning in the Loc Ninh forest.
> All night long I couldn't sleep,
> Lying, counting drops of falling rain.
> Worried for our army brothers
> Mired along the flooded roads;
> First come tanks and then come cannons,
> Hoping to see no least trace of steam.
> The battlefield awaits each minute.
> Oh rain, please rain no more!
> Let the road dry off quickly
> So our trucks can reach their places.
> In this final historic battle,
> The sound of guns has already begun.

We worried in particular about the 10th division, which was still in the Cam Ranh area and still faced enemy troops along their route into eastern Nam Bo. With the long, difficult route they had to travel, we did not know if they would be able to get down within the appointed time period. We cabled Hoang Minh Thao in Zone 5 to send troops to Cam Ranh quickly to relieve the 10th division, and sent a cable directly to the 10th division command to request that they report three times a day on their formation on the march, their progress each day and estimate for the following day, and the circumstances they had to deal with along the road. We cabled Dong Si Nguyen to send more transport vehicles down so that all of the 10th division could be transported quickly, and if they were short of vehicles to propose that the Zone 5 command find some way to dispatch some of its vehicles or borrow some from the people to help the 10th division.

Time urged us on. The Political Bureau had directed us to work most urgently so that we could begin the general offensive on Saigon as soon as possible. After reviewing the situation, however, and seeing that all the main-force divisions could not get down within that time period, and wanting the offensive to have both sufficient strength from the outset and sufficient reserves to continue the attack until victory, the Political Bureau gave us more time to prepare and determined that we must *begin the general offensive on Saigon at the very latest by the final week of April 1975.*

In following enemy activities at this time, we paid special attention to internal political developments within the Thieu administration and in the United States, both daily and hourly. Naturally we continued to stay on top of the enemy's military activities, not only within Saigon but throughout Nam Bo and Southeast Asia, especially Thailand and the Philippines. We followed military developments on the Cambodian battlefield in the first days of April 1975 in minute detail, and though no promises were made, we maintained close coordination, at strategic and campaign levels, with our friends.

The Political Bureau sent another cable.

THE OVERALL ATTACK PLAN MUST GUARANTEE THAT ONCE THE ACTION BEGINS THERE WILL BE POWERFUL, CONTINUOUS ATTACKS, ONE ON TOP OF THE OTHER, UNTIL COMPLETE VICTORY. IT MUST CARRY OUT THE PRINCIPLE OF FIGHTING FROM THE INSIDE OUT AND FROM THE OUTSIDE IN—INITIATING ATTACKS IN THE OUTLYING AREAS AND KEEPING

FORCES PREPARED TO SEIZE THE OPPORTUNITY TO STRIKE
DEEP INTO THE CENTER OF SAIGON FROM MANY DIRECTIONS.
IT MUST ALSO PLAN HOW TO CREATE CONDITIONS FOR AN
UPRISING BY OUR COMPATRIOTS. IN THE CURRENT SITUA-
TION THIS IS HOW YOU WILL ACHIEVE LIGHTNING SPEED,
DARING, AND SURPRISE. THIS IS THE FUNDAMENTAL DIREC-
TION, AND THE ONE MOST CERTAIN TO WIN. YOU MUST HAVE
THE FORESIGHT AND MAKE THE NECESSARY PREPARATIONS
TO DEAL WITH A BATTLE WHICH MAY LAST FOR SOME TIME.

One after another, the commands of the various
branches, specialized services, and army corps came to
campaign headquarters to receive their assignments. In
the case of the Fourth Army Corps, the Second Army
Corps, and the 3rd division from Zone 5, who were engaged in combat on the eastern flank at a considerable
distance from headquarters, we appointed Senior Colonel
Luong Van Nho (Hai Nha), who was at the time our deputy chief of staff, to take them their assignments. He took
a copy of the order of battle, signed by myself and Pham
Hung, to give directly to Le Trong Tan. The order clearly
stated that all units in the eastern wing were placed under
the command of Le Trong Tan, operating in accordance
with the unified plan of the campaign headquarters.

The assignment for the southwest wing (the 232nd
force) was received directly by Le Duc Anh after it had
been debated and decided at campaign headquarters. Vu
Lang, commander, and Nguyen Hiep, political officer, of
the Third Army Corps, came to campaign headquarters on
April 12 to receive their assignment. Two days later
Nguyen Hoa, commander, and Hoang Minh Thi, political
officer, of the First Army Corps also arrived to receive
their assignments, after a telegram had summoned them
to a meeting. They reported that the First Army Corps
received its orders to take part in the campaign on March
25. On April 2 the 320th division set out first, and all the
branches attached to the corps followed one after the
other. At the latest, the final unit should have moved out

by April 7, and they were counting on all of them arriving
at the assembly area by April 25.

After mentioning the special characteristics of the
enemy and the aspects that would have to be overcome on
this new battlefield, and after giving assignments to each
army corps, I emphasized again that all the commanders
must rapidly move their units in by the designated day,
organize their command and communications, and maintain the secrecy of every action of their units until the day
they opened fire. They must pay particular attention to
educating their troops on the decisive significance of this
campaign to guarantee victory in the war, and the need to
maintain tight discipline and strictly implement all our
policies when they entered the city.

In a sincere and affectionate tone, Pham Hung spoke to
the commanders of the army corps before they returned to
their units to lay out the plans. "When those of us here at
B-2 saw we had won big in the Tay Nguyen and in Central
Trung Bo, we were very happy, comrades. And we saw
that the opportune moment for liberating the whole South
would come this very year. When we liberate the South
and then go on to reunify the country, the U.S. imperialists will never ever be able to return again. You will,
along with us, COSVN, and the regional military committee, and with the army and the people of the South, carry
out our mission to complete the popular national democratic revolution throughout the country. This is the most
glorious hour of history since the founding of our party. In
the past, Quang Trung also attacked invading troops at
lightning speed, but he stopped.* Today, with all the troop
units that have come down from the North, to coordinate
with all the forces already in the South, we will not stop
anywhere. Wherever we fight, we will win. We will strike
fast and win big. The strength of our party, of our patriotic
people, and of our people's armed forces is immense. Our

* Quang Trung, also known as Nguyen Hue, led Vietnamese troops to
victory over invading Chinese armies in the late eighteenth century.

party has a tradition of unity, our people and army have a
tradition of unity, North and South are one family, and
Vietnam is one country. This is the foundation that
guarantees our victory.

"We welcome your recent victories, welcome your
timely presence on the southern battlefield, and welcome
your readiness to take part in this historic, strategically
decisive battle, striking into the last bastion of neocolonialism in our country. Let me wish us all complete victory!"

In a voice deeply moved, Pham Hung reminded
everyone, "Let us be sure that this time we celebrate
Uncle Ho's birthday in Saigon."*

Le Duc Tho then cautioned all the army corps: "The
center has given the southern party branch and all of our
armed forces the responsibility for completely liberating
the South. Army corps are powerful forces, fighting with
large, coordinated special branches with modern equipment, with the cooperation of all the forces on the spot,
and the support of all the other specialized branches. You
must carry out your missions well. We are striking Saigon
at a time when the enemy are falling apart and are no
longer in a strong position. But this is their final lair. They
have no way to flee. They will regroup and respond. They
have five divisions; we have fifteen divisions, not to mention our other strategic reserve forces. Thus we can only
fight to win. That is how the center looks at it, too; when I
left, our comrades on the Political Bureau said, 'You must
win. You cannot come back until you do.' That is the
resolution of the Political Bureau."

After analyzing the situation, he declared, "The U.S.
imperialists absolutely do not have the ability to return. At
present all the news which we have received from the
United States confirms this, and even if they risked intervention they could not possibly turn the situation around.
They could only suffer a heavier defeat. We are certain to

---

* This is on May 19.

win. In the past ten years and more of fighting, our people have taught them some well-deserved lessons. The situation is very much to our advantage. The possibilities are abundant. We must seize the opportunity, do it quickly, and do it with certainty."

Le Duc Tho also cautioned the army corps to carefully research the topography, because the corps had just arrived and were not familiar with the battlefield, and to investigate the complex layout of the buildings in Saigon, methods of organizing communications during operations, methods of organizing antiaircraft defenses for advancing and bivouacked troops, and so on. He emphasized the element of surprise, and warned all units to try to create many surprises for the enemy, and aim to strike directly at the critical points, the enemy nerve centers. He spoke with animation, calling forth images of the two sides fighting, saying even if the enemy were still strong, if we struck unexpected knockout blows they would topple immediately.

He did not forget to remind the corps that the people of Saigon had their own political movements and had a tradition of revolutionary struggle, and that even though they were temporarily held down, they had great potential to rise up if they had the support of quick, powerful, successive attacks from military forces on the outside. As for the timing, he reminded them that the rainy season was about to start, and that they must complete their mission quickly and victoriously before it began, and that if they completed it during the month of May it would be even more meaningful.

The jungle base at Loc Ninh was filled with the resounding roar of convoys of tanks and trucks pulling artillery down the road, with the ringing of dozens of telephone bells, and with the sound of discussions in all the staff, political, and logistics offices. At night as we lay thinking, we remembered the teachings of Uncle Ho when he was still alive, and remembered clearly the sacred admonitions in his testament. Remembering his life, in which he had sacrificed everything for the revolution, and recalling that Uncle Ho's name had been given to the city of Saigon, the campaign headquarters unanimously agreed to send a telegram to the Political Bureau proposing that this largest, most significant campaign of our war of national liberation be given the name *Ho Chi Minh campaign*.

At 19:00 hours on April 14, 1975, the Political Bureau sent telegram no. 37/TK to the front:

AGREE SAIGON CAMPAIGN BE NAMED HO CHI MINH CAMPAIGN.

Below the message was the signature of Le Duan, the beloved first secretary of the party's Central Executive Committee.

13

Battle Positions Take Shape

Saigon-Gia Dinh was a large city with 3.5 million people, covering 1,845 square kilometers when the suburban districts are included, with many tall, solidly constructed buildings and a quite complex architectural layout. Here the nerve centers of the quisling army and government, along with their important storage areas and rear bases, were concentrated; it was an important political, military, and economic center for the enemy— their final lair.

Saigon's surrounding terrain is quite complex. South of the city rivers and streams run everywhere, and marshy areas abound. The southwest also has many marshes, but close to the outskirts of the city the land is high and good for movement. North and northwest, and especially east of the city, many large bridges lead into the city, including the Bong, Sang, Binh Phuoc, Binh Trieu, and Ghenh bridges, the Dong Nai River highway bridge, and the Saigon River highway bridge. We had information that the enemy planned to mine all of these important bridges, ready to drop the spans to halt our troops' advance. If we couldn't capture these bridges quickly, our tank and artillery troops and all our heavy technological weapons would have a hard time getting into Saigon. The rainy season would begin here in mid-May, and the large troop units would run into many obstacles if they went off the major roads then.

Having lived for more than a hundred years under the French colonialists and after that under the American neocolonialists, Saigon had enjoyed independence and freedom under the regime of the Democratic Republic of Vietnam for less than one month. Since the United States imperialists had sent their troops in to invade the South directly, they had turned Saigon and the whole South of our country into a neocolony. Through their actions and policies, cynical yet subtle, pragmatic yet treacherous, they poured in weapons and dollars, trying to enslave the people of Saigon ideologically, politically, and culturally. The Americans and the various Saigon regimes destroyed the ancient foundations and good morals of our people. "Skag," narcotics, prostitution, gambling, delinquency, theft, and murder spread out in waves. Almost every family included someone who had been swept up through deception or force either directly or indirectly into the machinery of war, repression, and bondage. They flung in money and goods to create a class of comprador bourgeoisie and militarist officials grown wealthy and bloated on the blood and bones of the people, creating an economy and a consumer society completely dependent on the dollar and a foreign country. The apparatus of the CIA and their psychological warfare machinery engaged day and night in distortion, deception, and terror, trying to make the people oppose or at least fear the revolution and the resistance.

But the people of Saigon-Gia Dinh have a tradition of patriotism, of opposition to imperialists and their flunkies. The streets and lanes, the rivers and streams of Saigon-Gia Dinh still record many glorious exploits, many heroic tales of people from every walk of life. The Saigon party branch operated on a fierce battlefield. The enemy were always trying to scour out the infrastructure of the movement. Now, still standing firm, it was a precious resource, and indeed quite a feat, for our party. The leaders of the movement from Saigon whom we were able to meet symbolized Saigon's long-suffering but glorious struggle. In their eyes and in their voices they bore the aspirations of a people who wanted to rise up and smash the Americans' savage lackey regime, to recover peace, independence, and freedom. Saigon-Gia Dinh, firm and indomitable, courageous and loyal in the illustrious struggle against the imperialists, was now to take on the historic responsibility in coordination with the main-force troops of the whole country of writing the final radiant chapter of this epic. At campaign headquarters we occasionally watched the farces the Americans and the Saigon regime were presenting—and the miserable scenes of the people—on the television screen, and grew all the more anxious to hasten the day we opened fire to begin the battle.

In a new directive from the Political Bureau and the Central Military Committee, Le Duan cautioned our headquarters to extend our preparations for a few more days, until the arrival of the bulk of the Third Army Corps and the First Army Corps, including both infantry and technological weapons units, and then begin the large attacks. From now until the full-scale offensive was launched, we should issue orders to the western and southwestern wings to step up their activities, cut Route 4, force the enemy to spread out their forces to respond to us and make it difficult for them to guess our intentions, and increase the enemy's disorder and confusion inside Saigon. At the same time, we should send our sappers and special action forces into the city quickly, and should carry out stronger actions in all directions to establish good conditions for the big offensive.

As all the big units from the North, from the Tay Nguyen, and from Central Trung Bo advanced one after the other into Nam Bo, vast quantities of materiel and supplies were being transported day and night to storage areas and to all the units, preparing for the decisive attack on Saigon. Southern combat units took this new opportune moment and began a seething upsurge in activities with a new sense of excitement, using our new experiences and calling forth great efforts.

The units of Zone 8 and Zone 9, as well as the sapper units and special action squads on the outskirts and inside the city, mounted continuous attacks on the enemy, causing them considerable losses in men and materiel. They liberated a number of important areas, linking up our scattered bases behind enemy lines in Long An, Go Cong, Ben Tre, and My Tho, and opening up continuous corridors from eastern Nam Bo through the Plain of Reeds into western Nam Bo. They took control of important communications routes along canals and rivers in the border zones and used them to bring more forces and technological weapons down as reinforcements. Every province was engaged in both fighting and building their forces. A number of provinces and districts stepped up recruitment of new soldiers at the local level, and formed additional province-level regional-force battalions and district-level regional-force companies. Villages developed platoons of guerillas, and some villages even had full companies. With additional weapons and munitions sent down from the regional level and a large number taken from the enemy, the newly established units were all equipped in time. These continuous activities tied down and drew off a number of enemy main-force units in IV Corps, and diverted some of the enemy's air force and naval activities.

The Fourth Army Corps, our main-force unit for the region, had mounted a string of attacks since March 10, in close coordination with those in the Tay Nguyen. They had wiped out many of the enemy, liberated Dau Tieng subsector, An Loc town, and Chon Thanh, enlarged a very advantageous area north of Saigon, tied down the enemy's 25th division in the Trang Lon-Tay Ninh area, and even put pressure on the enemy's 5th division, which was defending the Lai Khe-Ben Cat area. From the last week of March until early April, our Fourth Army Corps rapidly transferred its forces from north and northwest of Saigon to positions east of Dinh Quan, liberated Lam Dong-Di

Linh, then concentrated their forces and opened a big attack on the enemy's 18th division at Xuan Loc in Long Khanh province.

On April 5, Thieu ordered the urgent strengthening of the Phan Rang defense line, and reprimanded those of his generals who favored an early regroupment around Saigon-Gia Dinh for being defeatists. At this time the enemy's defensive deployments in III Corps still took the form of many lines from the outside moving in. Their infantry divisions had been reinforced. Their armored cars and artillery held the key defense zones, reinforced by mines, barbed wire, and antitank barricades. All of this was coordinated with a system of security and self-defense-force outposts in a thick web. They hoped our troops would have to shove their way through one step at a time, and would be exhausted by the time they reached the outskirts of the city.

In the early days of April 1975, the town of Xuan Loc turned into a crucial enemy defense zone for III Corps, as it protected Saigon from the east; this was one strong point in the U.S.-Saigon distant defense line. The enemy tried to hold Xuan Loc to block two of the routes our troops could use to advance into Saigon—Route 1 and Route 20. At that time our troops on Route 1 had advanced nearly to Phan Rang, and on Route 20, after liberating Lam Dong, Da Lat, and Tuyen Duc, our troops had advanced down close to Kiem Tan. The enemy tried to hold Route 15 from Saigon to Vung Tau to bring in American aid coming to Saigon by sea, and that was one of the very routes they later used in flight.

If they could hold Xuan Loc and Long Khanh, then the Bien Hoa-Nhan Trach-Ba Ria-Vung Tau line would not come under direct pressure, and the airfields at Bien Hoa and Tan Son Nhat could still operate. So, they were trying to hold this zone at whatever cost. Their Third Army Corps, and in particular their 18th division, were still intact and had not yet been hit hard. The Saigon quislings and the United States gathered all their strength to support Xuan Loc—with the sole hope of prolonging their days of agony. They hoped they might be able to hold out there and not lose everything, not collapse completely, not be defeated absolutely.

On April 9 our Fourth Army Corps, including the 7th division, the 341st division, the 6th division, and the Zone 7 forces, with Brigadier-General Hoang Cam as commander and Brigadier-General Hoang The Thien as political officer, opened fire on Xuan Loc. The units of the Fourth Army Corps, with all their experience in combat, were for the first time confronting an enemy who had reached the end of the road and were ready to risk their lives.

The enemy dispatched all the forces of their 18th division, reinforced by the 3rd cavalry brigade; one element of the 5th division, which was defending Route 13, and the artillery battalions directly attached to them; the ranger groups from III Corps; and the crippled ranger groups from I Corps and II Corps which had not yet had time to reorganize, and flung them pell-mell into Xuan Loc. It was a test of troops and a test of generals by the Americans and Saigon as they faced the danger of collapse.

That was not yet enough. The enemy also sent the 1st paratroop brigade to the Xuan Loc front, and mobilized their remaining air forces from Bien Hoa, Tan Son Nhat, and Can Tho at the highest possible level, in order to postpone their day of doom. But that was not enough, either. The United States and Saigon mobilized a propaganda and psychological warfare apparatus, both within the country and from the Western world, to come to Saigon and to Xuan Loc to "buck up the spirits" of their soldiers and commanders. Candidate-General Le Minh Dao, commander of Saigon's 18th division, proclaimed, "We will fight a noble battle for the world to see, and so America will give us more aid." He was suddenly transformed into a "heroic personage," a savior of the Thieu regime, under the pens of reporters who, respecting dollars more than honor, signed their names to articles in various inconsequential rags.

The battle for Xuan Loc was fierce and cruel from the very first days. Our 7th, 6th, and 341st divisions had to organize many assaults into town, striking and striking again to destroy each target, and had to repel many enemy counterattacks. The enemy's 43rd regiment was seriously crippled. Our campaign artillery and the artillery units with our divisions had to use extra quantities of shells. A number of our tanks and armored cars were damaged, and others had to return to their staging areas for more fuel and ammunition.

The Fourth Army Corps' initial plans for the assault on Xuan Loc had not been able to calculate the complex developments in the situation, or to evaluate the stubbornness of the enemy. The fierce tug-of-war battle was not just over Xuan Loc and Long Khanh, but reflected the life-and-death struggle of the quisling administration to prolong their dying days. We could no longer organize, command, and carry out battles as we had in the past. Our method of fighting had to change to fit the situation.

During the days that the Fourth Army Corps was assaulting Xuan Loc, we urgently had to develop plans for the attack on Saigon as well as direct the regional headquarters and the Fourth Army Corps command to change their fighting style. We also reinforced the Fourth Army Corps with the 95th regiment and sent them additional materiel.

Tran Van Tra went down to the Fourth Army Corps from Loc Ninh again to tell them about the new style of fighting and supervise its implementation. We advised that once the enemy had amassed troops to try to save Xuan Loc, we need not concentrate our forces and continue attacking them head on. We should shift our forces to strike counterattacking enemy units in the outer perimeter, where they had insufficient defense works and were not in close coordination with each other, before they could get their feet on the ground. We should use our long-range artillery to destroy the Bien Hoa airbase and keep it under control so enemy fighter planes could not take off.

After capturing Tuc Trung and Kiem Tan and wiping out the 52nd regiment of Saigon's 18th division, we continued along Route 20 to the Dau Giay intersection and set up a firm blockade of a section of Route 1, knocking out one tank and beating back the enemy's 3rd cavalry brigade coming up from Bien Hoa as reinforcements. Xuan Loc had been cut off from Saigon. The town and the headquarters of their 48th regiment were still under artillery fire, and at Bau Ca their 3rd cavalry brigade was still blocked and couldn't move a muscle. The Fourth Army Corps used artillery to choke off the enemy artillery positions gradually, and to wipe out each element of the 48th regiment and 1st paratroop brigade, which had just arrived as reinforcements.

On April 19, the eastern wing of our troops rushed forward and along with the Zone 6 troops, liberated Phan Thiet. The next day the leading troops on Route 1 reached Rung La near Xuan Loc. That night, April 20, all the enemy forces at Xuan Loc, faced with the danger of being surrounded and annihilated, were forced to abandon the city and flee in confusion along interprovincial road 2 toward Ba Ria. Cut off and attacked along the road, they abandoned large numbers of vehicles and artillery pieces, plus large quantities of guns and ammunition. Some Western journalists had to cable their editors to drop articles they had just sent that very evening, in order to "conform to the situation." Saigon's military radio station shamelessly kept up its efforts to boost the morale of the remnants of the 18th division hiding out in forests in the Ba Ria area. Saigon Major-General Nguyen Van Toan, commander of III Corps, went to Cu Chi to discuss trying to defend the Cu Chi line to the west while dispatching forces to the east to hold on to the Bien Hoa-Long Binh-Long Thanh line.

Xuan Loc was liberated. The eastern gateway to Saigon was open, ready to welcome the forces of the Second and Fourth Army Corps and the 3rd division from Zone 5 to the final strategically decisive battle. The 3rd division prepared to advance toward Ba Ria and Vung Tau. Thus before the date for launching the general offensive on Saigon-Gia Dinh, the eastern wing of troops had established a most advantageous attack position.

Southwest of Saigon we had dispatched a force down to the Ben Luc region in Long An province to open up corridors from Tay Ninh and Kien Tuong, finish opening the areas of Ben Cau, Ben Soi, and Queo Ba, take control of part of the western Vam Co River, and continue their advance to the Tan An-Thu Thua region. They were then to close in on Route 4 and attack traffic, wipe out the surrounding small outposts, and open up a liberated zone to serve as a springboard for the forces of the 232nd force to attack Saigon from the southwest. Tanks, amphibious vehicles, 85mm low-trajectory artillery, cat-tracked 122mm self-propelled artillery, and even 130mm artillery, along with antiaircraft battalions, the 5th, 3rd, 9th, and 8th infantry divisions, the 16th, 88th, and 24th independent regiments, and hundreds of tons of ammunition and fuel had arrived at their appointed places. Rocket and mortar positions were quickly prepared around the Can Tho airfield, awaiting the day to attack what would be the enemy's last airbase once Tan Son Nhat and Bien Hoa were closed down.

Setting up positions southwest of Saigon was a real exploit for the army and people in western Nam Bo, because the geography here made it difficult to deploy a large force, especially their heavy technological weapons. We would need to use tens of thousands of artillery shells, but they had to be borne on shoulders or carried in small boats. There were few roads for motorized artillery; in fact, it could be said that the sole route was across exposed marshlands. Artillery positions had to be set up along the sides of the roads. The only means of communication from campaign headquarters down to the southwestern wing was radio. As time grew shorter the task of establishing positions for the southwestern wing became ever more urgent. The preparation of bridges and ferries and roads, the transportation of supplies, and so on, had to be completely secret, to preserve a big surprise for the enemy from this direction.

Northwest of Saigon, the enemy's 25th division still held fast to Tay Ninh. Indeed they were in a position where if they held it they would die, and if they abandoned it they would die, too. The police and all offices of the quisling administration in Tay Ninh burned all kinds of papers and files and fled to Saigon. We did not attack to finish off Tay Ninh, but had to pin it down, to keep the forces of Saigon's 25th division spread out there and not let them pull back gradually to the area around Saigon. Our Third Army Corps used one regiment of the 316th division to cross the Saigon River and cut off a stretch of road from Tra Vo and Bau Nau to Go Dau Ha, not letting the enemy move up or down. Our regional forces in Tay Ninh and Binh Duong provinces encircled and knocked out the outposts of the security forces and civil guards, and shelled Trang Lon, blowing up 20,000 105mm shells and nearly 5,000 175mm shells at one time. The enemy's 25th division was stretched out along Route 1 and Route 22.

Special action and sapper units deployed in the city and suburbs closed in on Saigon and secretly took up their predetermined positions. Meanwhile, the Bien Hoa airbase was being hit without a day's rest by our sappers and our mortars and long-range artillery, obliging the enemy to take the planes from Bien Hoa back to Tan Son Nhat at night to avoid the shellings. We thus gradually paralyzed the Bien Hoa airbase. Then we quickly readied our firepower to strike the enemy's last two remaining airfields, Tan Son Nhat and Can Tho, to cut down on the fighting ability of their air force, depress their morale, counter their "refugee" plans, and help establish favorable conditions for the attack on Saigon-Gia Dinh.

On the morning of April 8 we were at work when we got the news that a patriotic officer piloting one of the enemy air force's F-5E planes had just bombed "Independence Palace," then flown to the liberated zone and landed safely at Phuoc Long airfield. This was Air Force First Lieutenant Nguyen Thanh Trung of Ben Tre, one of our party members who had been working secretly in the Saigon air force for a long time. He was the son of a district party committee member who had sacrificed his life in the revolutionary struggle.

According to Nguyen Thanh Trung, the Saigon air force had only 120 A-37s and 70 F-5s left, and their normal mission capability was only two-thirds of that. Mobilizing as many planes as they could, they could still fly only 120 sorties a day. He said that in shelling the Bien Hoa airbase, there was no need to fire continuously; one salvo every half hour would be enough, because after an artillery salvo exploded, it took half an hour for the pilots to get out of their bunkers and to their planes. That way, we could achieve good results and still economize on shells. We had an idea, and proposed that the General Command allow us to send Nguyen Thanh Trung to Da Nang at once to train a number of our fighter pilots to fly the American A-37s, of which we had captured so many, and form an A-37 squadron to use if we needed it.

The sapper units on the Saigon front—intelligent, shrewd, and courageous fighters whose exploits had echoed throughout the land—were reorganized into six groups under a unified command before going into the campaign. Group 10 was at Nha Be and Long Tau to attack ships and cut the enemy's river route from Long Tau to the sea. Group 116 was at Nuoc Trong and Long Binh. Group 113 was in charge of the Bien Hoa area. Group 115 was at Lai Thieu and Quan Tre awaiting orders to enter Saigon. Group 117 was at Vuon Thom and Ba Vu waiting for the order to attack Saigon from the west. Group 429 prepared to attack the artillery positions in ward 8 and ward 9.

Saigon's long-famous special action fighters, fighting silently and courageously, had so many times terrified the Americans and quislings. They had attacked American hotels in Saigon, such as the Caravel, the Brinks, the

Victoria, and the Metropole, had attacked Saigon's
Directorate-General of Police and the American embassy,
sunk ships in the Saigon River, and had often shelled
"Independence Palace," Tan Son Nhat airfield, and the
quislings' "National Day" celebrations. Today their bigger
and stronger forces were in firm positions both inside and
outside the city. Outside, there were four battalions and
many special action squads, and inside we had 60 special
action cells, 300 armed civilians, and a large force of
people organized and directed by the special action troops.
The armed forces of Saigon-Gia Dinh's municipal unit
were also quite strong. In Nha Be, South Binh Chanh,
North Binh Chanh, Tan Binh, Hoc Mon, Go Vap, and
other districts, each place had previously had one platoon,
but going into this campaign had increased their forces to
one or two companies. Thu Duc had a battalion; Cu Chi
was even stronger. And the municipal units also included
main-force regiments that had been positioned in advance
in Gia Dinh. That was without mentioning our cadres and
fighters on special assignments who had operated for
many years in the city, working inside enemy offices, supplying timely information and hoping for the day our big
units would move in.

The Saigon-Gia Dinh municipal party committee
printed and passed out hundreds of thousands of leaflets
and formed vanguard propaganda units. The seething
spirit of the masses made the enemy's already confused
spirits still more confused and wavering, and the enemy's
machinery of control at the grassroots loosened one more
notch. Within a few days we had sent hundreds of additional cadres and armed unit members into the city center. Inside Saigon there were dozens of members of the
municipal party committee and cadres of equivalent rank,
members of special ward committees, hundreds of party
members, thousands of members of various mass organizations, and tens of thousands of people who could be
mobilized to take to the streets. Our political infrastructure existed in every section of town, holding a number of

large and small print shops, preparing hundreds of loudspeaker cars, and taking tens of thousands of meters of cloth to tailor shops to be sewn into flags. Cadres who were preparing to continue the administration of the city moved in right next to the city's suburbs.

To carry out the directive of the Political Bureau, COSVN and the regional military committee discussed and approved plans for the general offensive and preparations for an uprising for all of B-2. At the same time, Vo Van Kiet was appointed to work directly as secretary of the Saigon-Gia Dinh municipal party committee with special concern for organizing and directing plans for a mass uprising coordinated with the attack on the city by our main-force units.

Thus, before the first guns of the general offensive on Saigon were fired, we had established battlefield positions around the city from every direction. To the east, we had completely cut Route 1, and closed in on Trang Bom, and were ready to cut off Route 15 and the Long Tau River and keep Vung Tau under control. We were also paralyzing the Bien Hoa airfield. To the west and southwest, the Zone 9 forces had closed in on Cai Von and to the south of Can Tho. Most important of all, they had closed in on Route 4, the lifeline from Saigon to the Mekong Delta. Units attached to Zone 8 had expanded their activities in southern Long An, preparing to cut Route 4 and the Cho Gao canal.

The large units in the campaign had also gradually moved in and taken up their positions. The Fourth Army Corps, after taking Xuan Loc, moved in close to Trang Bom, and the Second Army Corps had closed in on Long Thanh, Vung Tau, Nuoc Trong, and Ba Ria in the southeast. The 232nd force had moved in close to the line along the eastern Vam Co River and Hau Nghia. The 5th division and the 8th division were next to Route 4 between Tan An and Cai Lay, in close to My Tho, and in particular, two infantry regiments were stationed in Can Duoc and Can Giuoc south of Saigon's 8th ward.

To the northwest and the north, we had an expanded

liberated zone running continuously from Loc Ninh to
Phuoc Long. The First Army Corps had moved into as-
sembly areas south of the Be River, and the Third Army
Corps into the Dau Tieng area.

Corridors between each of the wings in every direction
were completely open. Campaign and strategic routes
were linked tight, without a break, guaranteeing that all
kinds of vehicles could move at high speed. It was also the
first time in the decades of resistance in Nam Bo that
trucks of the regional logistics section and the logistics
departments of all the zones could come down from the
east all the way to interprovincial road 26 north of Cu Chi,
drive all the way to Binh Co and Binh My north of Tan
Uyen, or drive straight through to Long Khanh and Ba
Ria.

The leading forces of the party and the revolutionary
government had reached the outskirts of the city, and
some elements had entered the city to prepare for the
mass uprising and for the continued administration of the
city. Our people stayed on top of the situation in Saigon
and reported it to campaign headquarters daily.

One group of cadres and fighters remained right in Tan
Son Nhat throughout these days of tumult in the South.
This was our military delegation to the Two-Party Joint
Military Commission, headed by Brigadier-General Ho
Xuan Anh (Hoang Anh Tuan). They kept up their regular
daily reports of information, and in those days they also
guessed that we must be about to strike Saigon, even
though we had not cabled them about our plans. They had
lived surrounded by enemy troops for nearly three years,
holding firmly to their position of struggle, not yielding to
the enemy. They had quickly and strictly carried out all
directives from their superiors, and had made timely reports to us on the news and public sentiment among all
circles of the people, as well as information on the enemy
which they could get in a number of ways, including reconnaissance with their own eyes. When they saw so
many enemy airplanes coming back to Tan Son Nhat from

everywhere, and parking right next to the delegation's living quarters, they sent a telegram suggesting that we shell the airfield. In one part of the telegram they wrote:

WE WILL DIG BUNKERS AND HOLD FAST TO OUR FIGHTING POSITIONS HERE. IF THE ENEMY ARE OBSTINATE, HAVE OUR ARTILLERY FIRE REALLY HEAVILY, AND DON'T WORRY ABOUT US IN HERE. WE ARE PREPARED TO ACCEPT THAT SACRIFICE FOR THE TOTAL VICTORY OF THE CAMPAIGN, FOR THE TOTAL VICTORY OF THE REVOLUTION. WE WOULD CON-SIDER IT AN HONOR.

Their housing compound, set up by the Saigon ad-ministration, had sheet metal roofs, dirt floors, and wooden walls, and was "decorated" all around by barbed wire fences. In such circumstances it was hard to dig individual foxholes, then develop them into both com-munications trenches and combat trenches. They had to dig their bunkers at night. They had no shovels or hoes, and had to use fenceposts and knives to dig with. The earth they dug up they pressed down on the floors of their quarters or put in carrying bags and wrapped up in clothes and put in their storehouse. When we had an opportunity provided by the turning over of a number of employees of the Joint Military Commission who were trapped the day we struck Ban Me Thuot, we decided to bring out some comrades who were really essential to the campaign. The rest of them remained, including the delegation head. And when we drew up plans for shelling Tan Son Nhat, we repeatedly warned those responsible about the location of the compound our delegation was in, to guarantee their security.

In the overall field position that was taking shape in preparation for the Ho Chi Minh campaign, our comrades at Tan Son Nhat had their own particular position, stand-ing proudly and publicly amidst the enemy. That position not only symbolized the revolution and its political cause, but also helped the party better understand the feelings of the people about liberation, and helped us understand the enemy during the days of their death throes. Surely in those turbulent days and nights, those comrades awaited our troops more anxiously than anyone else.

After our offensive against Saigon during Tet Mau Than in 1968, the enemy had ridiculed us and blustered, "The Vietcong will never again have the strength to attack Saigon." Today, as we looked at the field positions we had set up, with the close coordination between our troops inside and outside Saigon, and saw the firm operational areas we had captured, as we determined the objectives we would strike right from the outset, calculated the time, and completed our final tasks before "H" hour—the final "H" hour of the war, and also the biggest "H" hour in the history of our people for more than a hundred years—we were pleased, happy, and proud.

14

Daring, Surprise, Certain Victory

In the days when we were still in the Tay Nguyen, when we learned that the Political Bureau had resolved to strike Saigon before the rainy season, we began to think about methods of attacking Saigon. At that time, we did not yet have a really concrete grasp of the enemy's situation, of the topography, or of the revolutionary organizations and movements in the city. Still, based on the mission, which we knew, the principal lessons we had drawn from our experiences so far, and the enemy's strategic confusion and collapsing morale, we tried to imagine whether the style of attack might resemble that at Ban Me Thuot, though surely in these new conditions the situation would be more complex, and the campaign would be on a larger scale, demanding a higher level of organization. Because of the decisive role this campaign would play in the revolutionary war, because of the change in the balance of forces between us and the enemy, and because of new critical elements which had appeared, preparations would have to be made on many fronts with the greatest urgency, especially the work of organizing the command and organizing truly tight coordination among all forces taking part in the offensive, to guarantee certain victory. Naturally this attack on Saigon could not be a simple mechanical copy of a model. Our craft would have to be more developed, more creative. But to decide how it should be creative, how it should develop, how it should be organized, we would have to rely on the concrete details of the situation.

These questions, these thoughts, had stuck with us, especially since the day we got a map of Saigon from the enemy's map supplies in Ban Me Thuot. We recalled the weekly and monthly reports from the regional command and the Saigon municipal party committee on the military, political, and economic situation, and on the situation of the struggle by all classes of people for welfare and democracy, for peaceful reunification. We reviewed the reports of the units that had attacked Saigon in 1968 and the recent one from Colonel Vu Long, a cadre of the regional command, who had come up to the Tay Nguyen to report on the regional headquarters' plans for their spring-summer campaign. Thanks to these, we had a better basis for understanding Saigon, so we could gradually continue forming plans in our minds for its liberation.

On the road down to B-2, sitting in the car and thinking about the method of attack, whenever I came to something I couldn't remember I turned straight to Hoang Dung to ask him—for example, how wide and deep the rivers around Saigon were, whether the population had risen to 4 million yet, or who the general commanding Saigon's 25th division was—and reminded him to cable Zone 6 right away to send someone to the Geographic Service in Da Lat to get maps of Saigon and send them as quickly as possible to B-2 for the A-75 force.

When we reached B-2, after listening to three days of quite detailed reports by the regional staff on all aspects of the situation in Saigon, and especially after meeting with COSVN and the regional military committee and hearing their all-around, in-depth analysis of the special characteristics of Saigon, we had a firmer basis for discussing plans for the general offensive.

During our discussions in the conference room with people at headquarters and cadres in charge of various branches, and when we were working alone, before we went to sleep, when we woke up in the middle of the night, the topography of Saigon-Gia Dinh was constantly in our minds. The image of Saigon-Gia Dinh, with its network of roads, rivers, canals, bridges, supply depots, and the locations of all the military and civilian offices of the quisling army and administration, gradually imprinted itself in our memories. There were many of us at headquarters, myself included, who had never once set foot in Saigon. But through a period of much listening and looking and after many days with our eyes glued to maps of Saigon-Gia Dinh—even those printed up for sale to tourists—we had memorized the names of many streets, all the bridges, the areas with multistoried buildings, warehouses, and docks, and although we didn't yet know the landscape, the colors, the features of the roads, or the specific architecture, we could still remember the distances, widths, areas, and so on, of those places. We could talk and work together on the situation in Saigon without always spreading out maps as we had when we first got to B-2.

As we researched the enemy defensive deployments in the Saigon zone on the maps, and combined this with the daily reports by staff and military intelligence personnel, I became obsessed with names of the enemy infantry divisions, like the 5th, 25th, 7th, 18th, and 22nd (this one had just been re-formed after its great defeat in Binh Dinh), the paratroop brigades, the 468th marine brigade, the 3rd armored cavalry brigade, and by the locations of the enemy General Staff headquarters, the Special Capital Zone headquarters, Tan Son Nhat airfield, and so on, even though they were nothing but green and black symbols on the map. As they gradually grew clearer, I could imagine pictures of the enemy, and the state of the enemy's morale, and even came to know the biographies and the temperament of Saigon's generals and field officers commanding those units.

Discussing and deciding the plan of attack on Saigon was a process of intense mental labor for our campaign headquarters, because the remaining time was short, the situation was changing rapidly, and there were many problems which were not simply military but were related to many political, diplomatic, economic, cultural, psychological, and other such aspects, which had to be thought through carefully, and weighed and calculated most thoroughly.

The two problems in the overall plan for the attack on Saigon which stood out most were how to attack and what targets to attack. The Political Bureau also cabled us about those two problems, and those of us near Saigon who were responsible to the Central Political Bureau of the party thought day and night about them. We knew that in Saigon-Gia Dinh more than 3.5 million of our compatriots were living smothered under the tyrannical U.S.-Thieu regime, hoping and waiting for the day of liberation. Some, if not many, of them had been influenced by life under the neocolonial regime. Some of them had loved ones in the ranks of Saigon's army and government, and were worried and anxious as they faced the present situation, thinking a great deal about their own fate and that of their loved ones as the quisling regime shuddered and fell apart. And also, because the Americans and quislings had put out such distorted, deceitful propaganda and had concealed so much from them, they could not tell what was true and what was not. They worried whether they and their families would live, and could not yet understand the revolution and the correct policies of the revolution, which the U.S. and Saigon leaders had done all they could to distort in the days of their regime's collapse, with statements about "bloodbaths," "reprisals," "hard labor camps," and "brainwashing."

How should we attack Saigon so we could do it fast and be certain of victory, make the whole reactionary regime collapse, smash the quisling army and administration's entire system of organization from the center all the way to the lowest levels, smash the lackeys' war machine, which was by nature reactionary, hawkish, and obstinate, and overwhelm the U.S. imperialists' aggressive will?

And how should we do this in such a way that the city would not suffer much destruction, so that we could liberate these millions of compatriots without making them endure any great loss of life or property, and so that their lives could return to normal?

Another problem was that the hundreds of thousands of Saigon soldiers were all Vietnamese. They were youths and students, workers, peasants, and artisans, most of them sons of working families. They had their own families and their own lives, but because the reactionary leaders had deceived or coerced them, the great majority of them had been swept along the wrong path, taking up guns against their compatriots and against the revolution. They wanted peace, and wanted to escape their situation as mercenaries, dying for hire. They wanted to return to their families, be reunited with their loved ones, and continue their studies and production.

When he was still alive, Uncle Ho had said, "The puppet soldiers are also sons of Vietnam, but have unwisely taken the wrong road, so the government and I are prepared to forgive those who are early to realize their error and turn back to the great family of the resistance." So how should we attack to make the organization of this tremendous unit of enemy troops dissolve and their morale collapse, so that they would no longer be capable of following orders to oppose the revolution issued by their desperate band of leaders? We must be determined to wipe out their obstinate leadership, who intended to oppose the revolution until the end, without regret. But for the great masses of enemy troops, we should open a path to life, and not destroy their lives once they laid down their weapons, surrendered, and escaped the grip of their leaders, those hirelings of the Americans. We were completely confident that they would recognize our just cause and accept the education of the party and the revolutionary government, and that those hundreds of thousands of soldiers would return to their homes and their families, return to become citizens of an independent and unified Vietnam, and contribute their labor to the common task of building a strong, rich land and ensuring personal happiness for themselves and their families.

This time there was nothing strong enough to halt our forces in their attack on Saigon-Gia Dinh. For this attack we mobilized five well-trained main-force army corps with hundreds of thousands of troops, and that was without mentioning the other strategic reserve forces and the Nam Bo regional forces, which were bigger and stronger than ever before, and without mentioning the divisions, brigades, and regiments attached to the specialized branches with their many modern weapons and high technical level, their tactical expertise, their thousands of artillery pieces and mortars of all calibers, their thousands of antiaircraft weapons, both artillery and machine guns, their hundreds of tanks and armored cars, and tens of thousands of tons of artillery and mortar rounds. And even that did not yet take into account the large quantity of bombs and rockets of the air defense-air force troops, or all the weapons of the naval forces taking part in the campaign. Our cadres and fighters, the most precious children of the people, the most beloved children of the people, had passed through hundreds of battles already, letting no hardship or danger slow their pace, and were now taking part in this historic campaign bearing our beloved Uncle Ho's name, a campaign which we all realized would conclude the war so we could return to a life of independence, freedom, and peace, to build up our land. All of us from top to bottom were prepared to complete this glorious mission without thought or hesitation, ready to sacrifice our own lives for the revolution, for the day of our nation's total victory.

Given that spiritual strength and that material capability, we had to choose the directions and objectives to topple the enemy rapidly. We had to decide how to use our forces appropriately, what fighting methods to use, how to organize our command and coordination, how to guaran-

tee organization of every aspect to develop to the fullest
our overall strength, to keep our casualties to a minimum
in the final days of the war, and still gain the fastest and
biggest victory.

Choosing the manner of fighting and confirming the
targets were also related to the problems of the opportune
moment and the deadlines for beginning the attacks and
concluding the campaign. If our style of attack was not
unexpected, not daring, not appropriate, then the time
would drag out, the field positions would be tugged around
here and there, and the rainy season would come. And we
could see the political entanglements of the Americans
and their protégés both within the country and around the
world. They would put pressure here, make arrangements
there, and put sand in the gears, "open a way for the stag
to flee," pull out all the stops, using dollars or rank. They
would put forward some sort of measures to rescue the
regime of the reactionary Nguyen Van Thieu which the
United States had set in place, but which was now
shaken to its very roots. But with the most appropriate
means of attack, with the most complete preparations,
then once we launched the general offensive, we would
pile up successive victories and conclude them rapidly.
This would be appropriate for the military opportunity,
and well suited to the tempo of political and diplomatic
developments.

Actually, by the middle of April, when all of the Tay
Nguyen and Central Vietnam had been liberated and our
troops had fought their way into Xuan Loc and closed in
around Saigon, the enemy had discovered a number of our
main-force divisions which had just reached eastern Nam
Bo or were on their way there. They knew that our offensive would be against Saigon. Even a number of foreign
correspondents in South Vietnam during those days made
predictions—more accurate than those of Saigon's General Staff—about our forces and the thrust of our offensive. Although the surprise about the thrust of our offen-

sive and the attacking forces had thus lessened, we would create other surprises, more important surprises: the *manner of attack* and the *time of attack.*

In the process of debating the campaign plans which Le Ngoc Hien presented, Le Duc Tho, Pham Hung, Tran Van Tra, Le Duc Anh and the others all thoroughly analyzed those problems, going deep into each concrete aspect and weighing things in an all-around manner. It was a collective mental labor, full of excitement but also very difficult and intense, because the situation was developing very urgently, the preparations were very complex, and the opportune moment was rapidly appearing.

In all of Saigon-Gia Dinh, the largest city in Vietnam, with hundreds of thousands of enemy troops deployed in inner and outer rings of defensive positions, we chose only five of the largest objectives for certain capture. Those were the quisling General Staff headquarters, "Independence Palace," the Special Capital Zone headquarters, the Directorate-General of Police, and Tan Son Nhat airfield.

These targets were the most important nerve centers of the Saigon army and the quisling administration, the primary elements in the machinery of war and oppression of the people, which the Americans directed. These were the places which most completely concentrated the essence of the lackey leadership's antinationalism and the harm they brought the people, the places where they plotted to continue the war, continue repression of the patriotic, revolutionary and progressive masses, continue their "anticommunism" to the end, and continue wholehearted service, through this neocolonial war, to the U.S. imperialists' schemes and their fundamental stance of aggression in Vietnam. Tan Son Nhat was the enemy's final big air link with the outside.

If we struck straight at those five targets, the whole quisling regime would be shaken. Those were the most important "vital points" in the collapsing organism of the U.S.-Thieu regime. If we smashed those five objectives, the Saigon army and administration would be like a snake without a head. What remained of their system of defense and repression would fall apart, the masses would rise up, and there would be no force, no "great man" who could halt it, whatever scheme he might use. The strategically decisive battle would be concluded rapidly, and Saigon would quickly be liberated. And if we attacked only these five targets, then the lives of the more than 3.5 million of our compatriots who lived in Saigon-Gia Dinh would be protected, and economic, cultural, and social establishments would not be damaged.

Having chosen the five objectives to attack, how should we strike to capture those objectives, when the enemy had five divisions deployed in an outer circle directly confronting our main-force units, with plans ready to pull back farther and farther along those defense lines, regrouping toward Saigon to "defend it to the death"?

When we attacked Ban Me Thuot, we had diverted the enemy's large main-force units toward Kontum and Pleiku, and set up campaign positions cutting off the rescue routes so that Ban Me Thuot would be neglected and isolated. Then we evaded the forces deployed in the outer circle, most of them security and civil guard forces, to strike unexpectedly straight at their two nerve centers deep inside the town. Only when we finished the attack inside did we turn back around to finish off the positions in the outer circle. But now, in the attack on Saigon, the enemy's strong main-force units were in the outer circle, wanting primarily to halt us thirty to fifty kilometers from the center of the city when we attacked, and the enemy both inside and outside were prepared. It would be hard to carry off a plan to evade the enemy forces on the outside, not attacking them, but unexpectedly thrusting straight in with large combined units. Or if we could get in, then those five enemy infantry divisions would pull back to go to the rescue, and the field positions would seesaw back and forth. But if we concentrated our forces to wipe out the enemy's five infantry divisions in the outer circle before attacking the five targets inside the city, it would certainly drag the time out. And thus it was certain to cost more blood and bones and to use up more materiel, and it would be hard to avoid loss of life and the destruction of the people's property. So if we let the enemy divisions pull back inside the city, destroy the big bridges on the Dong Nai and Saigon rivers and all the other bridges, and take over tall buildings or crowded areas to make a stand, then damage, destruction, and death would be hard to avoid.

If we wanted to create surprise about our method of attack, we had to be extremely daring. One comrade put it in an easy-to-remember phrase: "Only daring will bring surprise." And the more surprising we could be, the more certain would be our victory. That daring had to be based on the revolutionary concept of active offensive, and on an analysis that was truly scientific, correctly working out the relationships and contradictions that had arisen in the actual situation in order to achieve surprise and certain victory. After all, daring, in the final analysis, is also fervor, an enthusiastic heart, high determination, and endurance, whatever the hardship or danger. But to achieve certain victory, we would have to hold fast to the objective laws of the developing situation and stimulate them to our advantage. Fervor alone was not enough.

Our forms and methods of fighting and style of attack bore the spirit of the rules of revolutionary warfare in the South. The history of the Vietnamese revolution over the past forty-five years under the leadership of the party is a history extremely rich in methods of revolution, in the use of revolutionary forces and revolutionary armed forces, in unique methods of fighting with no battle the same as any other, and no campaign the same as any other. In these tempestuous hours, the revolutionary inventiveness of the masses of people was richer than ever before in developing forms and methods of revolution, in mobilizing forces, and in their style of attack.

This was a step forward in the ripening final period of this whole anti-United States resistance to save the country. It drew on the experiences and traditions of our forebears fighting long ago, of the August Revolution in 1945, and more recently of the victorious resistance against the French colonialists and the many years fighting against the United States to save the country, and developed those experiences further. It resulted from the mobilization of all our forces and all our strength for this final battle right in the enemy's lair, creating a strong position and a mighty force to overwhelm enemy troops and gain complete victory. We needed the most effective style of attack to develop the full strength of all our forces. Naturally, the essential blow to end the war would have to be a military blow.

In view of the condition of the enemy, the terrain, and the nature of the mission, relying on our superior forces in terms of quality, numbers, spirit, and command, and on the basis of the demands of the final decisive battle and new developments in the objective situation, the campaign headquarters agreed that the method of attack for this historic campaign would be to *use whatever forces necessary from each direction to encircle enemy forces, isolating them and preventing them from pulling back to Saigon; to wipe out and disperse the enemy main-force infantry divisions in the outer defense perimeter right on the spot; and to save the greatest number of our forces to thrust in quickly and capture key positions in the outskirts. This would open the way for mechanized and tightly organized assault units to advance rapidly along the main roads and strike directly at the five chosen objectives inside the city.* To coordinate with those assault units and enable them to move quickly to their targets, the city's sappers, special action units, armed security forces, and self-defense units, and the mass political forces of Saigon-Gia Dinh, would capture bridges and springboards ahead of time, guide those units in, neutralize traitors, and mobilize the masses for an uprising.

All of the campaign's firepower would be concentrated to strike the essential military objectives, like Tan Son Nhat airfield and Saigon's General Staff headquarters,

drawing on the air force when necessary to bomb Tan Son
Nhat airfield. Antiaircraft artillery and missiles would be
arrayed in an air-defense network around Saigon to control the skies and protect the campaign formations. This
style of attack was clearly most appropriate. We could not
allow the enemy to halt or slow down our advance at the
outer perimeter, nor would we allow them to pull back and
regroup in Saigon to continue their resistance along with
forces inside the city. By concentrating our attack on the
primary objectives, and wiping out the enemy in the outer
perimeter, we would keep the enemy troops on the inside
and outside from rescuing each other, and keep the enemy
from spreading their defenses out into residential areas,
bringing death to the people in the process. And the main
thing, the most important thing about this style of attack
was that it aimed to achieve the highest goal of the campaign bearing Uncle Ho's name in the quickest and most
certain way: liberate Saigon-Gia Dinh, topple the central
quisling administration, and then liberate the entire
South, in accordance with the Political Bureau's guiding
principles of daring, surprise, and certain victory. We
would carry out Uncle Ho's teaching to fight until the
Americans quit, fight until the puppets topple, liberate the
South and reunify the Fatherland.

As we worked out plans for the general offensive on
Saigon-Gia Dinh, our campaign headquarters also developed plans for uprisings by the masses, coordinated
closely with the military attacks and uprisings by political
forces. In the actual situation in Saigon-Gia Dinh at the
time, preparations for a mass uprising had to be calculated carefully and carried out urgently while at the same
time maintaining absolute secrecy. A plan had to be
passed all the way down to the neighborhood level, to all
members of our political and popular mobilization infrastructure in the city. We knew that the Saigon administration's machinery of repression was immeasurably cruel
and dangerous. The enemy's foreign and domestic secret
service and intelligence organizations hired tens of

thousands of thugs and informers with American dollars. They were dressed in the clothing of all classes of people and mingled with many sectors day and night, spying on, arresting, and beating to death patriotic and progressive compatriots throughout the South in general, and Saigon-Gia Dinh in particular. And that was without mentioning the tens of thousands of police, combat police, and military police, including a number who were forced by circumstances to earn their portion of rice and clothing by taking up guns and clubs and carrying out the orders of their cruel leaders to oppose the people and oppose the revolution.

Our compatriots in Saigon-Gia Dinh who had lived for so long in that harsh, tricky situation were thinking a great deal about the recent developments and about how what was about to happen related to each individual and each family, to the present and the future, to spiritual and material life. We firmly believed that with their tradition of struggle from the past through the present, and with the indignation and resentment toward the United States and Thieu that they already felt, that when they had a convenient opportunity and the leadership of strong-willed compatriots and firm comrades, they would rise up and join the struggle when our troops attacked Saigon. That did not yet take into account the hundreds of thousands of people recently piled into Saigon from the provinces, who were just waiting for the collapse so they could return to their liberated home villages.

The U.S.-quisling machinery of repression and their psychological warfare apparatus were still trying with all their might to rescue their rotten regime, and in those days the most reactionary, hawkish leadership along with their obstinate retainers might, for their selfish class interests, commit even more crimes.

We had to take into account this real possibility, and guide the form and timing of the uprising appropriately; we needed to mobilize mass forces to rush out before the enemy guns, in time to help the campaign gain rapid victory, yet in such a way that the military attacks would be the decisive blow, going one step ahead to create conditions for the masses to rise up. Nguyen Van Linh was assigned to direct this work, working day and night with the Saigon-Gia Dinh municipal committee and other related offices.

The job of mobilizing Saigon soldiers and administrative personnel was also laid out before the opening shots of the general offensive. Our comrades who had responsibility for this work in Saigon and the outlying areas had always been extremely determined and wise, enduring every hardship. Faced with this new situation, they acted all the more positively and urgently, and were very brave. They were in direct contact with the enemy, showing them the way to save themselves and save their suffering families, the way to bring those who had taken the wrong road back to the just cause, back to the nation. A number of our comrades were arrested and killed, but their spirit of sacrifice for the revolution awakened and converted who knows how many people who had taken up arms for the enemy. Now they were awaiting the opportune moment. So in our general offensive on Saigon, we had to create conditions for these large numbers of soldiers and police and quisling administration office workers who stood with the revolution and with the people to strike back at the obstinate leading group. The policies of the revolutionary government toward prisoners of war and soldiers who surrendered had to be publicized quickly, before and during the general offensive.

The task of continuing the administration of Saigon-Gia Dinh was an all-encompassing one, which demanded considerable forces and rapid deployment. COSVN assigned one comrade to take direct charge of this work. The center also appointed Nguyen Van Tran, secretary of the party's Central Committee, to come down to reinforce us, and, detached many cadres and technical personnel from all ministries and branches to come down quickly so they would be in time for the general offensive on Saigon-Gia

Dinh. This job was not simply an administrative and technical one, but included military, political, diplomatic, cultural, and social aspects, and demanded tight and timely leadership and thorough education among all the forces advancing into the city. A series of party and revolutionary government policies on religion, the bourgeoisie, and foreigners, on Saigon troops and administrative workers had to be publicized in time among all strata of the people.

After much discussion, with guidance from the Political Bureau and additional cadres sent down from the central level, Le Duc Tho and Pham Hung took direct charge of the preparations for continuing the administration of the city of Saigon-Gia Dinh. The Central Military Committee also selected Brigadier-General Giap Van Cuong, deputy chief of staff, to lead a delegation of military cadres and technical personnel to come down in time to meet with us before the general offensive began, to receive assignments for organizing the continued administration of the military structure.

During these days, Tran Van Tra, Dong Van Cong, Le Ngoc Hien, and I concentrated on dealing with the problems of combined organization, and approving the plans of action and support for each thrust, each zone, each unit, each specialized branch, as well as on organizing the supervisory work. The campaign headquarters was really full of activity. "Guests" came to headquarters from every direction to receive their assignments, report on the situation, or coordinate their plans.

Every comrade wanted to make his own and his unit's best, greatest, and most timely contribution to the victory of this historic campaign. They sought to overcome whatever difficulties they encountered, and demonstrated a high degree of unity of will, thought, and action between higher and lower levels, and among the various arms and specialized branches. When we met Doan Tue and Colonel Nguyen Tam, head of the artillery section for Zone 7, to give assignments to the artillery, we saw that the positions for 130mm artillery to fire on Tan Son Nhat and other selected targets in the city could not yet be used. They proposed using an infantry division to fight down to Binh Duong and liberate an area there ahead of time, then bring the long-range artillery in there before we began the general offensive. We could surely have fought our way down, and the artillery positions would have proved most useful. But looking at the overall field position and the demands of the campaign, we had to "sacrifice" the individual daring and surprise of the artillery, even though that proposal was very attractive as well as very daring.

On the day we were checking preparations to ensure mobility for all the thrusts, Phan Khac Hy, deputy commander of the 559th force, informed us that they had repaired all of the bridges the enemy had destroyed on Route 1 and Route 20. But there was the Nha Bich bridge on Route 14 between Dong Xoai and Chon Thanh, which was very important to the mobility of units advancing on Saigon from the north and east as well as to ensure logistics support for the whole campaign. The river was deep and the banks were steep, but the enemy were using their air force, determined to destroy the bridge, so repairs had not yet been completed and it remained a great obstacle to us. So we increased the antiaircraft units there and assigned Phan Khac Hy to take direct command of repairing this bridge.

We also had to take into account the enemy's plan to destroy bridges across the Saigon River and the Dong Nai River and all the other bridges when we advanced on Saigon. So while we were working with Colonel Tran Ba Tong, political officer of the region's engineering corps, on plans to repair damaged bridges, set up temporary bridges, and use ferries, we also figured on mobilizing ships, boats, and barges along those rivers to move part of our troops in along the Saigon River or to take troops and technological weapons across the rivers. Our comrades in COSVN, especially Nguyen Van Xo, took a very active part in guaranteeing the success of this plan.

The deployment of antiaircraft missiles in the Ho Chi Minh campaign called for big efforts by the air defense troops. These units, all of which had participated in the Tay Nguyen campaign, were now in the columns of the Ho Chi Minh campaign. Our success in maintaining mobility and guaranteeing the technology of those units as they traveled the Truong Son highway into Nam Bo was already a victory. After we worked with Quang Hung and Colonel Pham Xa, deputy political officer of the regional air defense units, before we shook hands in farewell and wished them victory, we joked that the enemy air force was almost out of resources to fling at us, and we had all kinds of antiaircraft guns stationed closer to Saigon than those rockets, so if the rocket crews didn't have quick hands and quick eyes, they would find themselves "unemployed."

The day we worked with Tran Van Danh (Ba Tran) on assignments for the sapper troops, we also discussed another quite special plan: when we attacked Tan Son Nhat airfield, we would send one sapper force to advance quickly to the area called "Camp Davis," where our military delegations were living, to link up with our comrades there and bring them out.

The final days of preparations for the general offensive were extremely urgent and tense. Many groups of cadres had gone in every direction, to every wing of troops, every force, and every specialized branch to inspect all aspects of the preparations. Also, thanks to the fact that the campaign communications system was growing more stable and getting through more completely, and because the communications and cryptographic cadres and fighters had a very good spirit of service, we could stay on top of the situation in all directions, and could work regularly every day with Hanoi. Senior Colonel Nguyen Xuan Thang, commander and political officer for communications forces in the region, along with Hoang Niem, had carried out all aspects of the communications work with the greatest urgency.

The logistics work, which made up the first and also the

final stage of every battle and campaign—often said to be
first out and last to return—was most closely supervised,
received the most urgent demands, and also had its requests most completely filled by the rear area of the North.
Those in charge of logistics for the campaign, reporting
that all their preparations were complete, said happily:
"B-2 has never before been so happily crowded or so rich
as now. Never before have we had the honor of receiving a
'visiting delegation' of hundreds of thousands like this.
But these 'guests' are traveling by car and plane and ship,
bringing all kinds of things with them, so the 'host' has
much less to worry about than before."

The stories told by our comrades who had just come
down from Hanoi gave us a picture of the entire socialist
North both building and fighting, continuing to overcome
the serious after-effects of the war of destruction which the
United States had carried on nearly continuously from
1965 to 1972, and in only a short time had organized and
mobilized a massive amount of human and material
strength for victory at the front.

The Council to Support the Battlefield had worked urgently since the day it was founded, with no thought of
sleep, to resolve many important problems, and the members of the Political Bureau and the Central Secretariat of
the party often came to contribute their opinions to the
Council on how to step up support work for the battlefield.
We knew that in recent days the responsible officials in all
party and state offices in cities and provinces in the North
had worked day and night to respond completely, rapidly,
and with the highest priority to requests from the Ho Chi
Minh campaign. We were very moved when we received
news that the ethnic groups in the Tay Bac and Viet Bac
autonomous zones had proposed that the center take over
the transportation scheduled to bring rice and salt to their
regions, reserving those truck units and their precious
cargoes to send to Nam Bo in time for the general offensive. It was also moving to hear of the many work projects,
factories, and services which had pulled 30 to 50 percent

of their people out of their organizations to take part in all kinds of work to guarantee the success of the Ho Chi Minh campaign.

The troops and people of Zone 5 also wholeheartedly supported the Saigon front with all their strength. A Council to Support the Front was founded in Zone 5 with Vo Chi Cong as chairman. Vo Chi Cong's directive to the whole zone was: "All for the Saigon front," "All to serve the Ho Chi Minh campaign." Zone 5 also organized a front line section including Major-General Hoang Minh Thao, Brigadier-General Vo Thu, and Brigadier-General Lu Giang, to give special attention to serving the eastern and western wings of troops for the campaign, to concentrate the largest part of the zone's forces and material resources to serve the units moving toward the front, and mobilized vehicles for nearly 2,000 journeys to transport troops and 4,000 tons of supplies to the Saigon front.

The newly liberated zone from Tri Thien to Phan Thiet was gradually being stabilized, and the newly liberated people were also trying to contribute their efforts and their possessions to the Ho Chi Minh campaign. Health, commerce, culture, education, and training sections from the North had come down to those zones to help overcome the material and spiritual problems left behind by the enemy. In particular, many security force troops from the North, along with Minister Tran Quoc Hoan, were stationed along Route 1 going south to provide timely reinforcements. Along with local troops and security forces, they did a good job of protecting order and security, overpowering surviving groups of holdouts, and thus not only guaranteeing a peaceful life for the population, but also establishing conditions for our armed forces to advance safely to liberate Saigon. The rear area had been extended from the socialist North into the large, newly liberated area of the South, giving added strength to the front lines.

We were clearly aware of the great efforts and labors of our compatriots and comrades in the rear, working with a spirit of one person doing the work not just of two, but of even more, to replace those of us who had the honor of being dispatched to the front. We were sure that many of them would also have liked a chance to come to the front lines during these historic hours. As for those of us cadres, fighters, and workers in the agencies of the General Staff, who had worked side by side for over twenty years through two wars, we could imagine in the clearest detail the bustle and tension, the spirit of exactness and perfection in their work which all our comrades, especially those in the combat operations, military intelligence, and cryptographic sections, and in the communications command, would show as they kept on top of the situation, so they could report in time and submit their ideas to the Central Military Committee and the Political Bureau.

Under the leadership, tutelage, and organization of the party, the entire heroic nation and army had become like some great factory running at full tempo, at the highest number of revolutions, with the highest productivity, so that in the shortest possible time it could create the most beautiful product of the age: *the Ho Chi Minh campaign.*

15

The Enemy's Final Hours

During the process of the strategic general offensive, our party followed the enemy's decline very closely, discovering evidence of their disintegration in time to take positive steps to capitalize on it. Striking just at the opportune moment, a small force would have great power, and a large force would have much greater power. Indeed, the opportune moment itself is force and power.

The changing balance of military forces and the political circumstances had led to a turning point entirely to the enemy's disadvantage. Rockefeller, the United States vice president, had been forced to recognize this on April 2, saying, "It is far too late for us to do anything to reverse the situation." But obstinacy and cunning had always been fundamental characteristics of the U.S. imperialists and their flunkies. The war-crazed American and Saigon governments continued their efforts to plot something that could rescue the situation, to prevent a "second Waterloo" which could bury the prestige of the ringleaders of U.S. imperialism.

As time passed, the battlefield narrowed. Enemy soldiers and commanders, defeated in battle, fled to Saigon and made those who remained all the more nervous and fearful. Ford and Kissinger were at the same time pathetic and touching as they told Thieu and his retinue, "We share

your unhappiness and regret over these necessary with-
drawals," and made stirring promises: "America will
stand firmly behind the Republic of Viet Nam." Ford
and Kissinger tried to coerce the U.S. Congress into increasing the amount of emergency aid to $722 million,
and requested authority to use armed forces for what was
called "an evacuation and protection of the evacuation."

With their guiding mandarins breathing encourage-
ment, the Thieu crew issued orders to try to defend the
remaining land from Phan Rang on down. Until their day
of doom, they continued to nurture the illusion that the
U.S. imperialists were a reliable master, ready to extend a
hand to lift them out of their quagmire. United States
"Ambassador" Martin, like a medicine man sitting beside
his gravely ill child, Thieu, kept Thieu alive with that
illusion.

But Saigon's troops admitted to themselves that they
hadn't "much time to implement plans for a defense to the
death, or to stabilize a defensive perimeter for the third of
South Vietnam still left." Our general strategic offensive,
which was developing at very high speed, was approaching
a new high point.

Meanwhile, the Cambodian liberation troops had closed
in on Phnom Penh. Lon Nol abandoned Phnom Penh itself, with time to take only a small shoulder bag as he fled
with his American masters. The Pentagon mounted operation "Eagle Pull"—their withdrawal. While John Dean,
U.S. "Ambassador" in Phnom Penh, boarded an airplane
and fled to Thailand, carrying a plastic bag containing the
American flag he had just lowered at the embassy, the
band of advisers and their lackey leaders raced with each
other to get out of Phnom Penh. On April 17, the Liberation Army entered the city and the Cambodian quislings
surrendered unconditionally. The United States appeared
totally unable to reenter the war to save its hirelings, not
because they lacked the forces, but because they saw that
no amount of money or weapons would be enough. Even if
they risked using military forces to invade Cambodia and

South Vietnam again, it still could not turn the situation around, but would only bring them greater defeat. Public opinion around the world said that the U.S. withdrawal from Cambodia was a practice run for pulling out of South Vietnam.

The liberation of Phnom Penh, the liberation of Cambodia, was a great victory, an epic of the Cambodian army and people. That fact showed the pitiful weakness of the U.S. imperialists on the Indochinese peninsula, and foretold the total defeat they and their lackeys would suffer in South Vietnam. The Saigon administration watched the situation in Cambodia in obvious fear and confusion, suspicious of their American masters.

The situation of the Lao revolution was developing well, too, stimulating our cadres and fighters at the front even more. The Lao ultrarightist reactionaries were being denounced and punished by the Lao people in many places. The masses were turning toward the revolution, toward the Lao People's Revolutionary Party and the Lao Patriotic Front, and demanding the formation of a people's democratic government.

The Americans and their protégés, trapped on their deadend street, outwardly continued to shout about defending to the death, but inwardly they wavered and panicked. Thieu's "Independence Palace" turned into a defensive fortress reinforced three times over what it had been before, with a small blockhouse every thirty to forty meters, the barrel of a machine gun pointing out. Right in front of the palace a helicopter waited on the lawn, ready to go, while tanks were deployed under the trees on the palace grounds. In an April 18 report, after he had inspected a number of the defense positions, Saigon's defense minister, Tran Van Don, said tragically, "The country is in a truly perilous situation. We can calculate its continued existence only by the day or week; we cannot calculate it by the month."

Martin, the U.S. "ambassador," sent a secret report to Washington on April 19 on the desperate situation saying that "the adversary's units are converging simultaneously on the Saigon region from every direction, with a reserve force much larger than the government forces. They have the capability of encircling and isolating this city in one or two weeks more. Although the government can possibly reinforce one or two fronts by pulling forces out of the Can Tho or My Tho regions in the Mekong Delta, this could do nothing more than prolong the survival of Saigon for about one week, because the adversary's troops will almost immediately be able to counter these reinforcements with a force of their own twice that size."

In Da Nang, Quy Nhon, Nha Trang, and elsewhere, the Americans had fled sooner and faster than their protégés. Arriving at this black hour, the American guiding mandarins hastened to develop this "specialty." The Ford-Kissinger administration carried who knows how many ambitions in their heads, but there was no other way around it, because whatever risk they took, they could not rescue the situation. They could only turn around and stick their heads back into the tunnel with no exit, and their defeat would be yet bigger. Of thirty-six strategies, the best strategy was to "beat it."*

On April 18, Ford and Kissinger issued orders for the immediate evacuation of Americans in Saigon, and put Dean Brown in charge of a special task force, under their guidance, to direct the evacuation. A large U.S. air and naval force, including thirty-five warships with four aircraft carriers, nearly a third of the American total, and hundreds of aircraft of all kinds, worked at fever pitch in a panic withdrawal operation beginning on April 21. In the whirlwind confusion of the evacuation, which in its final days was dubbed an operation for "high-risk individuals," U.S. helicopters swooped nervously through the Saigon skies, alighting on the helicopter pad of the U.S. embassy and a number of other helicopter pads in the city to pluck

---

* This is a traditional Vietnamese expression used to refer to someone who has reached an absolute impasse.

up Americans, clustered and waiting on the roofs of buildings. The puppet soldiers grew desperate as they watched these scenes of the American flight. There was no longer any imposing parade of "search and destroy" operations, only the historic "high-risk" flight of the U.S. imperialists.

Before they were up and away, the Americans caused our people who knows how many more tragic scenes filled with blood and tears. They kidnapped thousands of children to take to the United States and other foreign countries, with the immediate goal of arousing public opinion and getting more aid for Saigon, and the longer term goal of making these children forget their homeland and oppose it. These tiny souls, victims of a large U.S.-puppet con game, had to leave their families and their homeland amid heartrending cries. Hundreds of children died when an airplane that had just left the airfield was damaged and crashed to earth. The savagery of the U.S. imperialists only made those of us on the battlefield more indignant and more determined to win as quickly and thoroughly as possible.

They evacuated and fled, but still used psychological warfare to deceive, distort, and terrify, to drive tens of thousands of so-called refugees after them. These were immeasurably treacherous crimes, slashing deep wounds of division in who knows how many families. The evacuation which the Americans advocated aimed to make propaganda about how the people were not following the revolution, make use of the "gray matter" of a number of intellectuals and technical personnel, and use some people to work for them in later dark plots. How pitiful were those who were deceived, and how angry we were at those who intentionally followed the Americans, forgetting all the principles of the Vietnamese people, and abandoning their Fatherland.

The Saigon army's paper, *Tien Tuyen*, ran an eight-column headline: "Republic of Vietnam Will Never Surrender to Communists." But on April 21, Weyand moaned, "The military situation is desperate." And in a speech at a

university in New Orleans on April 23, Ford said sorrow-
fully, "The war is finished as far as America is concerned.
We cannot help the Vietnamese any more. They must
confront whatever fate awaits them."

The internal affairs of the guiding mandarins were
tragic and confused; and the internal affairs of their protégés in Saigon were also about to enter an extremely
serious crisis. United States neocolonialism usually operated by way of many horses. In ordinary situations, this
policy was useful because the various flunkies would keep
each other in check, creating a facade of counterfeit
democracy to deceive the masses and to conceal the U.S.
rule. In a time of disaster, however, this policy bred confusion. The various cliques of lackeys did not simply act in
concert to shout "anticommunism" and prevent defeat,
but used the defeat as a weapon one against the other,
settled accounts with each other, and vied with each other
to be the Americans' "thoroughbred," weakening the quisling administrative apparatus still more. In the face of
Thieu's impotence, Tran Thien Khiem, who had long been
at odds with Thieu, mobilized a "conference of leading
generals" to issue a resolution forcing Thieu to resign.
Nguyen Cao Ky, the cowboy general, who had long before
been cheated by Thieu, also jumped in along with Cao
Van Vien, intending to topple Thieu in a coup. The contradictions within the leadership affected the already collapsing and dissolving morale of Saigon's generals, field
officers, and soldiers. They shot and killed each other, as
when Saigon Major-General Nguyen Van Toan, commander of their Third Army Corps, shot his deputy commander, Brigadier-General Nguyen Van Hieu, dead, and
said, "I will not accept any order other than an order to
evacuate."

We paid the closest attention to the enemy's situation,
especially news of the U.S. evacuation. Just as Le Duc
Tho, Pham Hung, and I had finished meeting to make our
final check of preparations for the Ho Chi Minh campaign,
on the afternoon of April 21 a tearful Nguyen Van Thieu

announced that he was withdrawing from the so-called presidency of the Republic of Vietnam.

Thus ended the vile political career of an absolutely miserable traitor to the Vietnamese nation, who had been a vassal of the Americans, and had committed who knows how many bloody crimes against our compatriots throughout the land. He complained of his fate, railed at his masters, and cursed his servants in the tone of a French legionnaire. What he regretted most was that he did not get enough aid, that he did not get U.S. intervention to prolong the war, and he challenged the Americans to come in again to fight the "Vietcong" if they were smart.

Thieu's fall represented the unraveling of an American illusion; their scheme was to use the Thieu crew as an instrument to continue the policy of "Vietnamizing" the war. Thieu's fall came not because it was the Year of the Cat and he was born in the Year of the Rat; nor did it come because lightning struck the knifelike rock next to the magnificent pagoda he had built halfway up Dao Mountain at Phan Rang. (He had used a battalion of the engineering corps to build this pagoda and a company of security troops to guard it at all times, so his mother could live there as a "nun accumulating merit.") He fell because the U.S. imperialists' policy of aggression ran directly counter to the people's will for independence and freedom and had been completely defeated.

The United States put up Tran Van Huong, another able American lackey, to replace Thieu. The difference between Thieu and Huong was only that between a savage militarist traitor and a very crafty civilian traitor. They were both obstinate, committed to continuing the war, opposed to the Fatherland and opposed to the people. The Huong administration was just a Thieu administration without Thieu.

Everyone knew that the Americans had flung Thieu on the garbage heap, but the Thieu group still held power in Saigon, and Thieu still sat in Saigon behind Huong's back to direct his "little brothers." This crew tried to keep each other's spirits up by saying, "The stories about ten or so Vietcong divisions encircling Saigon are just bugaboos fabricated by the opposition," or, "How could ten or more Vietcong divisions have reached Saigon? And even if they are there, our air force is strong enough to flatten them all. We have a cluster bomb unit (CBU) with the strength to wipe out a whole division at once." One of Thieu's retainers in the scarecrow national assembly blustered, "I will definitely not hand power over to a government of surrender."

It was April 26, when Thieu and his family took sixteen tons of gold and silver, dollars, and belongings and fled to Taiwan, before they finally awoke from their dream and one after another followed Thieu in flight. Many of the Americans' thugs and retainers, many of those who owed blood debts to the people, gathered up their possessions and fled, not forgetting to take along the certificates, diplomas, and awards the Americans had issued to them. All the bank branches in Saigon were packed with people demanding to withdraw their money, and within forty-eight hours they had withdrawn as much as 40 billion piasters, in other words about $60 million. Almost all of the international airlines had canceled their flights to Saigon. So many people were calling each other to inquire about the situation that Saigon's central telephone exchange was overloaded. A number of enemy airplanes took off and fled to Thailand, or the pilots impulsively flew to the countryside to get away.

United States "Ambassador" Martin and other Western diplomatic figures worked feverishly in the wings of the Saigon political stage. Pressure was strong, even from the United States, for Tran Van Huong to resign and be replaced by someone who could "more easily make contact with the National Liberation Front." Huong wanted to yield the throne only to someone from Thieu's group, and Huong tried to cling to the "presidential" chair so all the "little brothers" would have plenty of time to sell permits to flee abroad for high prices, then have time to get their own affairs in order. We knew that there was one new card peeking out from behind the curtain, waiting for the day to come out and replace Huong. There were many diplomatic activities sprouting up noisily on all sides. The Americans, using every kind of maneuver—some of them shrewd diplomatic maneuvers—wanted to halt our advancing troops and save themselves from total defeat.

The American CIA in Saigon, like a poisonous snake, always slipping around and spying, with its many diabolical schemes, spread rumors that, "Huong will only be president temporarily, and is ready to reach an accommodation. The United States is awaiting a response," and the like. Meanwhile, General Vanuxem, who was Thieu's teacher as well as the teacher of many corporals from the old French red-sash units who were now topranking officers in the Saigon army, came hurriedly from France to Saigon. During the Indochina War he had commanded the 3rd mobile group, and escaped death in many battles. He came to Saigon to beat the drums for the quislings in their hour of greatest danger. He thought an "opportunity" was coming for him. The whole lot of them were nothing but a bunch of sleepwalking ignoramuses!

The situation had developed just as the Political Bureau perceived it would in their January 1975 meeting. The United States had clearly weakened and no longer had the ability to save the Saigon administration from total collapse. All the news we received showed that the United States was publicly stepping up the evacuation of Americans, and abandoning their hirelings in South Vietnam just as they had abandoned them in Cambodia. This situation shook the quislings' strategy and forced them to deal with the situation in some new way. Perhaps they calculated the possibilities: one, to regroup their forces to hold Saigon; a second, if they could not hold Saigon, to pull their forces together to hold IV Corps. We received information from within enemy ranks that they were desperately preparing to pull back to try to defend Can Tho (in IV

Corps) if we liberated Saigon. They thought that there were so many rivers and streams around Can Tho that we could not use tanks, armored cars, and heavy artillery, and that it would be hard for us to resupply.

On April 21, General Wilson, U.S. military attaché in Saigon, went with a number of U.S air force advisers all the way to the Binh Thuy airfield, along with the commander of Saigon's 4th air force division, to investigate it as a place to evacuate airplanes from Bien Hoa and Tan Son Nhat. They augmented its equipment so it could be used to support Saigon in the event that the Bien Hoa airfield was paralyzed. They also considered a situation where they might have to move the air force command to Binh Thuy to serve a long-term plan of support if they had to pull back and try to make their defense at Can Tho.

But we knew that when we struck our most powerful, most decisive blow to liberate Saigon-Gia Dinh, then all the remaining enemy troops in the Mekong Delta must sooner or later lay down their arms and surrender.

During this time, when we went back to our huts to sleep after discussions at headquarters, when we awoke in the night, or when we were listening to the latest news about the enemy, memories and images appeared one after the other, as well as many tasks. We remembered Nguyen Chi Thanh, a member of the Political Bureau, who had been selected more than ten years ago by Uncle Ho and the party's Central Political Bureau to come down to Nam Bo and lead the resistance against the United States along with the others in COSVN. At that time, faced with the danger of defeat in their "special war," with their lackeys wavering in confusion, the U.S. imperialists poured American and satellite troops into the South, and at the same time waged destruction in the North with their air force and navy. They sought out the most obedient and loyal lackeys in order to carry out these policies, resulting in a succession of servants, as they were continually changing horses in midstream within the collection of their protégés in the South.

Day and night Nguyen Chi Thanh experienced the
hardships of the southern battlefield, getting a clear,
firsthand view of the position of the enemy and our own
position, and thinking carefully about the way to fight the
Americans. When he came up to Hanoi to report to President Ho and the Political Bureau about the overall situation in the South, he had promised, on behalf of the southern party branch, the armed forces of the South, and all
our compatriots in the South, that they were determined to
fight against the U.S. "limited war" and win. With his
keenness, depth, and breadth of vision, with his boundless
confidence in the advancing position of the revolution, in
the unlimited potential of the revolutionary masses, and
in the vast support of the socialist North, he presented the
proposed strategic plan to the Political Bureau. The
domestic affairs section of the Resolution of the Ninth
Conference of the Party Central Committee declared
eleven years ago that the U.S. imperialists, no matter how
many troops they sent to Vietnam, no matter how savage a
war of aggression they mounted, would be defeated in the
end.

Speaking at a class studying this resolution at the
Nguyen Ai Quoc School* in September 1964, Thanh
explained, "We have a saying that if one horse falls sick,
the whole stable stops grazing. That's real horses. But
with this herd of men in the South, the more fodder their
American masters give them—they eat dollars, not
grass—the more heatedly they fight among themselves
for it. So as you can all see, now that the Americans have
just arrived, they are fighting among themselves to get to
the trough, smashing each other around—dozens of coups
in just over a year. Later, when we have struck powerfully
and won big victories, they will gallop off—retreating, that
is. Then it won't just be the horses biting and kicking each

---

* The Nguyen Ai Quoc School is a training center for party cadres.
Nguyen Ai Quoc (Nguyen the Patriot) was one of Ho Chi Minh's earlier
and more famous names.

other. Even the owners and their stable of thoroughbreds
will be confused and shouting noisily, breaking from their
stalls and running, not racing toward the finish line, but
fleeing before the punishing blows of the revolution."

At times when we were working together, Thanh often
confided, "It is Uncle Ho's aspiration and the desire of
people in the South to liberate the South and reunify the
Fatherland so that Uncle Ho can come South to meet the
people and party comrades. He has often wanted to go,
and has practiced his hiking. But the party's Central Political Bureau does not want him to go at this time. So we
must do what it takes, fight truly well, and defeat the
Americans if we want to make Uncle Ho happy.

> Uncle Ho misses the South as he misses his own
>   home,
> The South awaits Uncle Ho as if waiting for its
>   own father."

Today Uncle Ho and comrade Nguyen Chi Thanh are no
more. But Uncle Ho's greatest desire, the confidential
words of Nguyen Chi Thanh, and the aspirations of more
than 20 million southern compatriots were now being
brought to pass with the highest determination. We were
following Uncle's instructions and continuing the footsteps Nguyen Chi Thanh had left in the jungled zones of
Tri Thien and the Tay Nguyen, in the rubber plantations
of Loc Ninh, Dau Tieng, and Chon Thanh.

As we marched into Nam Bo, we hung our hammocks in
the forests where our comrade had once lain thinking of
ways to fight the Americans. In only a few days, we would
surely enter Saigon, the place where in 1911 Uncle Ho had
gone out to seek the road to national salvation, and the
place where eleven years ago Nguyen Chi Thanh had
worn the pants and shirt of a Nam Bo peasant, wound a
colorful scarf around his neck, put a conical palm-leaf hat
on his head, and gone by sampan to meet with the comrades of the Saigon municipal committee, right beside an

enemy base, surrounded by a thick web of police and secret agents.

From the very first day we confronted the U.S. imperialists, our party evaluated the schemes, nature, and the ability of the Americans correctly, and resolved to defeat the United States' war of aggression. Our party knew how to begin and how to carry forward this war for independence and freedom. And now the time had come, and our party knew how to bring the long revolutionary war to a victorious conclusion. The Americans had quit; the puppets had to fall. Our Fatherland would be completely independent and free. Our land would be reunified, and North and South joined together again as one family. Our people would together build socialism in the whole country.

On April 22, Le Duan cabled us on behalf of the Central Political Bureau:

THE MILITARY AND POLITICAL OPPORTUNITY FOR LAUNCHING THE GENERAL OFFENSIVE ON SAIGON IS RIPE. WE MUST MAKE THE BEST USE OF EACH DAY AND LAUNCH THE ATTACK AGAINST THE ENEMY FROM EVERY DIRECTION IN TIME, WITHOUT DELAY. IF WE DELAY, IT WILL NOT BE TO OUR ADVANTAGE EITHER POLITICALLY OR MILITARILY. TO ACT IN TIME NOW IS TO GUARANTEE WITH THE GREATEST CERTAINTY THAT WE WILL GAIN TOTAL VICTORY. YOU MUST IMMEDIATELY DIRECT OUR FORCES IN EVERY DIRECTION TO ACT IN TIME, AND PAY ATTENTION TO COORDINATING THE MILITARY OFFENSIVE WITH UPRISINGS BY THE MASSES. AS THE ACTION PROGRESSES, THE VARIOUS THRUSTS SHOULD BE COORDINATED WITH EACH OTHER, AND THE OFFENSIVE COORDINATED WITH THE MASS UPRISINGS. THE PRESENT OPPORTUNITY SPURS US TO ACT AS QUICKLY AS POSSIBLE. IF WE GRASP THIS GREAT OPPORTUNITY FIRMLY, OUR TOTAL VICTORY IS SURE.

On April 22, the campaign headquarters rechecked the official plan for the Ho Chi Minh campaign one final time, and spread out the campaign resolution, a map with fresh red markings indicating the directions of all our units' attacks on Saigon-Gia Dinh. In the presence of Le Duc Tho, representative of the Central Political Bureau of our party at the front, and the others in the campaign headquarters, Pham Hung, as political officer, and I, as campaign commander, signed the map.

We were extremely honored to be representing all of our beloved compatriots and comrades on this front, and greatly honored to accept the mission which the Political Bureau had given us in this campaign. That resolution was the resolution of the heroic Vietnamese nation, of the glorious Vietnam Workers' Party, of the People's Army of Vietnam, victorious in hundreds of battles. That resolution sealed the fate of Nguyen Van Thieu and his crew of reactionary traitors, and of the U.S. imperialist aggressors.

Over 4,000 years of building and protecting the country, especially since we had had the leadership of our party, the Vietnamese people had won the experience and the ability to distinguish clearly between those two categories of people, and had a traditional ability to deal with and take charge of them. The first category, who took on many forms and employed many schemes, and who had great strength, could not vanquish the Vietnamese nation no matter how savage they might be, no matter what opportunities they might have. The U.S. imperialists, the strongest, richest, and most bellicose in the capitalist world today, had for the past twenty years and more gone from this principle to that doctrine, had escalated from one rung to another. They had sent in the bulk of America's own military forces and dragged along troops from their satellites, and after smelling the odor of defeat long enough, had quietly furled their flag and fled back home clutching their so-called peace with honor. The United States also had to bear the consequences of its unsuccessful aggression against Vietnam, which had weakened it on every front for a long time to come. The fate of those who would steal our country from us was clearly sealed. It was indeed sad, ironic, and bitter.

In the second category were those who would sell out their own country, sell themselves for dollars, sell their souls to foreigners. In the past there had been those like Tran Ich Tac and Le Chieu Thong, and modern times had seen the likes of Ngo Dinh Diem, Nguyen Van Thieu, and Nguyen Cao Ky.* Their fate was all the more shameful and vile. Some had changed masters as many as three times, and in the end had been killed by those very masters. There were those who killed each other off in their "plots against the prince" and their competition for dollars. There were also some, exceedingly stubborn in the face of the punishing blows of the people, who finally had to surrender or flee.

They had no Fatherland, and acted not for the Fatherland or for any ideal, but only for dollars. All the things they had ever done were crimes against the people: bringing the United States in, offering plots of our precious southern soil to the United States, bringing millions of our youth to the Americans as cannon fodder, offering up tens of thousands of our sisters as playthings for the Americans, bringing disaster to southern society on many fronts in place of its former good morals, pride in our national traditions, and sense of the glory of our history and civilization. Everything they had said had been deception and falsehood, demagoguery, and reaction. They were the criminals, not the victims. The hour for their regime to bow out had arrived.

---

* Tran Ich Tac was a prince of the Tran house who served the interests of Kublai Khan's invading Mongol armies in the late thirteenth century. Le Chieu Thong was heir to the throne of the feudal Le dynasty in the late eighteenth century. He tried unsuccessfully to restore the old feudal order after it had been overthrown by the Tay Son peasant rebellion.

16

The Advance Into Saigon

After completing all the organizational work for coordination among all the thrusts of the attack, and among all the specialized arms and branches, we reorganized the campaign headquarters into two sections: Tran Van Tra and I went with the advance headquarters down close to the main-thrust troops so we could keep in close touch with the situation and command the attack more conveniently; Le Duc Tho and Pham Hung remained at the base headquarters to follow the overall military, political, and diplomatic issues related to the campaign, and to solve any general problems on the B-2 battlefield.

At this time one problem that still perplexed us was the task of setting up artillery positions at Nhon Trach to bring Tan Son Nhat airfield under control. The Bien Hoa airfield had been shut down by our artillery positions at Hieu Liem, and the enemy had to shift their planes to Tan Son Nhat and Binh Thuy (at Can Tho). We would shorten the enemy airplanes' range—shifting it 150 kilometers to the south—if they took off from Binh Thuy. But Tan Son Nhat airfield still allowed the enemy to continue committing their crimes, and from there all kinds of transport aircraft were carrying American and quisling leaders abroad at a rapid pace, with no letup.

The order of battle sent to all the eastern wings was

clear: on April 27, or at the latest on the 28th, we must capture Nhon Trach to set up positions for our 130mm artillery to fire on Tan Son Nhat. But Nhon Trach was far to the southeast of Saigon, twenty kilometers from Saigon as the crow flies. We would have to take care of Nuoc Trong base and Long Thanh district town before we would have a way to come down and capture Nhon Trach district town and bring the artillery down to set up there. If we could do this as we intended, not only could we paralyze the airfield, but we could shut down the Long Tau River and keep the enemy from fleeing down river to the sea. But if there were any "breakdown," and the positioning of the artillery were delayed, it would affect the coordinated plans for the campaign.

On the afternoon of April 25, after hearing the report from Senior Colonel Hoang Ngoc Dieu, deputy commander of air defense-air force troops, on the situation of captured enemy airfields from Thanh Son (Phan Rang) on the north—particularly that our pilots and mechanics at Da Nang air force base, under the command of Colonel Tran Manh, deputy chief of staff, had quickly learned how to fly and maintain the enemy A-37 aircraft—we decided we would use enemy airplanes piloted by our men to strike Tan Son Nhat airfield. This was a positive initiative to bring the airfield under control. It would be especially useful because it would stimulate further confusion in the enemy's already confused morale, prevent their leaders from fleeing easily, and signal them that our air force was making its appearance at the front and the skies of the whole South belonged to us. And this would also be a method of keeping the enemy from taking along airplanes still at Tan Son Nhat, while on the other hand creating the opportunity and conditions for our air force fighters to take part directly in this historic campaign. From that they would gain more experience for our air force's future training, building, and fighting.

Before that, we also met with Senior Colonel Dao Dinh Luyen, deputy commander of the air defense-air force troops and air force commander, and heard his careful report on the situation of our air force. We discussed the post-liberation use of the three large airfields remaining in Nam Bo with him, too. At the same time, we assigned his branch the mission of making immediate preparations to ensure that our air forces could be deployed quickly to take control of the airspace both of the South and of the whole country, including that above our territorial waters and the system of offshore islands.

The question of letting our pilots practice using captured enemy airplanes had been posed since the time we had seized a number of airplanes and airfields in the enemy's II Corps and I Corps. We had often exchanged opinions with the General Staff and the air defense-air force command. The General Staff had given instructions to the air defense-air force command on the matter, and they had been carried out. I turned to Hoang Ngoc Dieu, "The time for preparations is very short. We must hit Tan Son Nhat airfield in the next few days. Can you do it?"

He answered, "We are determined to carry it out. I ask permission to set out right away, tonight, for Phan Rang, and propose that you immediately cable the order to comrade Le Van Try, commander of the air defense-air force branch, who is now in Hanoi, to send pilots, mechanics, and airplanes from Da Nang to Thanh Son airfield."

The first rains of the season had begun in eastern Nam Bo, and the sky was dark with the blowing rain. Hoang Ngoc Dieu stood up and saluted me before leaving. Taking his hand, I cautioned him, "You must work urgently, really urgently. There are only three days left. If April 28 arrives and you cannot strike, you will have no other opportunity. Your combat air forces will have only one day, only this one time to score your victory."

We had to set the day specifically because according to the campaign plans, on April 28 our long-range artillery would be able to fire on Tan Son Nhat from the Nhon Trach position, and this would also be the day all the thrusts of our offensive struck toward the center of the city, so units would be entering Tan Son Nhat airfield. And they would surely not have time enough to prepare to strike earlier, before April 28.

At dawn on April 26, we got in cars to go to the advance campaign headquarters, located in an old base of one of our special action units from Saigon, northwest of Ben Cat. From this base our special action forces had over the years organized many attacks into Saigon, causing heavy casualties to the Americans and their valets. Our headquarters was a group of modest thatched huts, with the wind blowing in from all sides, and sitting inside the houses, looking out from under the roofs, we could see some patches of blue sky. Two days later, on April 28, Le Duc Tho and Pham Hung arrived together at the advance headquarters because the Ho Chi Minh campaign had begun the afternoon of April 26, the situation was very urgent, and sitting at the rear, three hours by car from us, they were anxious, and felt that we should concentrate at one end of things so we could take quick joint action whatever circumstances might arise.

Thus, after twenty-four days and nights of intense work since we had arrived at the B-2 command from the Tay Nguyen, at 17:00 hours on April 26, the first guns of the Ho Chi Minh campaign opened fire on the eastern approach. The plan specified that on the morning of April 27 there would be a barrage of attacks from all directions on the outskirts of Saigon, and the southwestern thrust would have to cut off Route 4 at many places from the Ben Luc bridge to the My Thuan ferry. On April 29 the barrage of attacks on the center of the city would begin.

In order to ensure attacks at the appointed time, all five thrusts had to overcome a great many difficulties. From the northwest, north, and southwest, forces, especially those with heavy technological weapons, had to cross the Be River and the eastern Vam Co River, and surround or force the surrender of the network of enemy outposts in Hau Nghia, Cu Chi, and Phu Loi. This would enable us to bring the combined deep-strike units rapidly into position at the gateways for their advance into the city center. From the east and southwest we had to capture Bien Hoa, Ba Ria, Vung Tau, and Long Thanh, and set up an artillery position at Nhon Trach to carry out the campaign encirclement and division before the April 29 barrage of attacks into the center of the city.

Back on April 24, when we were still at the base headquarters, we received a cabled report from Le Trong Tan, deputy campaign commander, who was commanding the two army corps of the eastern thrust, informing us that he and his troops agreed with the mission and the method of attack, and would strictly implement the order of battle of the campaign headquarters. But as for the timing, if the eastern wing struck with the other thrusts on April 27, it could not also strike along with the barrage of attacks on the city center beginning April 29, as its forces would still be fifteen to twenty kilometers from the outskirts of town. The enemy had also concentrated there in great numbers, and they would have to cross two large rivers, the Dong Nai and the Saigon. So Le Trong Tan proposed that the eastern thrust be allowed to open fire first, attacking at 17:00 hours on April 26. To present the matter more thoroughly, the eastern wing had selected Lieutenant-Colonel Le Phi Long to return to headquarters the night of April 25 to meet the campaign command and report.

Seeing that this proposal would have no effect on the overall plan, and in order to guarantee the strength of the barrage of attacks on the city center, we cabled our agreement with Le Trong Tan's proposal. At the same time, campaign headquarters also reminded all the other thrusts about the unified timing for the campaign as a whole and the timing of the eastern thrust so they would know and take appropriate action.

During the night of April 26 and the day of April 27, we concentrated on following and directing the activities of the eastern thrust, while at the same time we urged the northern and northwestern thrusts to concentrate their firepower to wipe out the enemy artillery positions and urgently organize their deep-strike forces. And for the southwestern thrust the critical problem was to organize the movement of their tanks and heavy 130mm artillery across the Vam Co river and to be thorough in cutting Route 4.

On the night of April 27, after a day and night of fighting, campaign headquarters summed up the situation. On the eastern thrust, the Second Army Corps opened fire exactly at 17:00 hours on April 26. Nearly a dozen artillery battalions poured a torrent of fire on the heads of the enemy. As soon as the cannon fire had stopped, our troops rushed out of the rubber forests following the sound of bugles echoing through the woods. Within less than two hours, the 304th division had captured the armor training school and part of Nuoc Trong base. Saigon armored officer students and officers from Thu Duc were there for exercises at the time and mounted an obstinate resistance and counterattacked throughout the day of April 27. We organized many successive attacks but had not yet been able to finish them off. Our troops had to fight back the enemy troops on the ground, and at the same time strike at the frenzied enemy planes which were dropping bombs all over the place. The sun was bright and harsh, the dry earth was hot as a griddle, and our fighters were so thirsty their throats were raw. All units had to send vehicles to carry drinking water to the soldiers who were fighting.

In coordination with the 304th division, the fighters of the 325th division captured Long Thanh subsector, crossed Route 15 to liberate Phuoc Thuong, and surrounded Long Tan. The 3rd division from Zone 5, which was now under the command of the Second Army Corps, with the direct support of tanks and heavy artillery, attacked like a hurricane. After three hours of fighting, they captured Duc Thanh subsector and then, at 15:00 hours on April 27, after completely liberating Ba Ria town, were moving on toward Vung Tau when the enemy destroyed the Co May bridge. The 3rd division had to stop to wait for the bridge to be repaired. In coordination with the main-force units, the regional forces and militia of Ba Ria had captured outposts, district towns, and subsector headquarters and liberated a vast section of Ba Ria province.

The Fourth Army Corps was operating along Route 1. Using the power of its combined units, it captured Trang Bom subsector and moved on toward Bien Hoa, but was blocked by the enemy, who had set up a defensive line there, and for the first time in the history of the Indochina war, had constructed a line of tank traps.

The sapper units had captured the Rach Chiec and Rach Cat bridges, the Ghenh bridge, and the Saigon River highway bridge, to welcome the main-force troops as they entered. But the enemy stubbornly mounted continuous counterattacks. There were places like the Rach Cu bridge and the Dong Nai River highway bridge where we and the enemy tussled back and forth desperately, striking and recapturing them several times, but in the end our sappers held all these extremely important bridges. This dazzling exploit by our sappers was a great aid to opening routes for our main forces to enter Saigon. It was also during these days that our long-range artillery at Hieu Liem paralyzed the Bien Hoa airfield. The enemy had to evacuate their airplanes to Tan Son Nhat, and the headquarters of Saigon's Third Army Corps had to flee to Go Vap the afternoon of April 28.

On the southwestern thrust, we cut Route 4 from the Ben Luc bridge to the Trung Luong crossroads north of the My Thuan ferry, and the section from Cai Lay to An Huu, blocking and drawing off forces from Saigon's 7th, 9th, and 22nd divisions, and creating favorable conditions for the actions of the other thrusts. The 232nd force had used one division to open the way to capture a bridgehead at An Ninh and Loc Giang on the Vam Co River, to send the essential assault forces—the 9th division and the technological weapons—across the river. The difficulty they faced was that of ensuring that the technological weapons, which were still running behind schedule, could get across the river. The 24th and 88th independent regiments were moving up, south of ward 8.

On the northern thrust, the First Army Corps wiped out a number of enemy artillery positions and took control of a segment of interprovincial road 16 to move its forces into position for the deep strike, and had come down to within seven kilometers of the north edge of Thu Dau Mot.

On the northwest thrust, the Third Army Corps, in a single day and night, destroyed eleven of eighteen enemy artillery positions, cut Route 22 and Route 1, blocked the regiments of Saigon's 25th division at Tay Ninh as they tried to regroup toward Dong Du, and forced one battalion of the 50th regiment to surrender. A sapper unit and the Gia Dinh regiment overran and took control of a section of the loop road around Saigon from the Binh Phuoc bridge to Quan Tre, and opened a gate around the barricades north of Tan Son Nhat airfield in preparation for the attack by our main-force troops.

Our general evaluation was that all the thrusts had basically carried out the plan, but the east and the southeast had encountered a number of difficulties that they had to overcome by April 28, especially in setting up the artillery positions at Nhon Trach. On the eastern and northwestern thrusts, the enemy fought back desperately, trying to keep us from capturing Nuoc Trong base and Ho Nai to open the road and position our forces for the strike deep into the city center, and they tried to keep us from cutting the 25th division's contacts between Tay Ninh and Saigon. But the time had come when there was no way their efforts could halt the wholesale unraveling of their defense system. One combat operations cadre made a delightful comparison: "The enemy's April 28 in Saigon is like their March 9 at Ban Me Thuot."

On the afternoon of April 28, Saigon's quisling administration played out the final act of the drama. After much controversy, posturing, and bargaining, and under pressure from his foreign guiding mandarins, Tran Van

Huong resigned, yielding the presidential chair to Duong Van Minh. The new president immediately called on the Saigon army: "Protect our territory," and "Do not lay down your weapons." At headquarters, meanwhile, as we were listening to a telephone report from Kim Tuan, deputy commander of the Third Army Corps, on the results of preparations and deployments for the attack on Dong Du, a combat operations cadre entered, his face radiant. He reported that at 15:40 a flight of five A-37s piloted by our comrades, with Nguyen Thanh Trung leading the way, had taken off from Thanh Son airfield to strike Tan Son Nhat.

It was magnificent coordination, the most perfect combined-forces strike ever by our troops, at an extremely important time which would have a great effect on the development of the campaign. I remembered what I had said to Hoang Ngoc Dieu the afternoon of April 25, and remembered his promise before we parted. And indeed there was "only one day, only one time." The air defense-air force command had been profoundly clearsighted and had actively implemented this resolution. Their commander, Le Van Try, had himself come to Thanh Son airfield and, along with our comrades there, had organized, supervised, and encouraged the men before they took off to carry out their mission. When our planes had reached the airspace of Tan Son Nhat, the enemy control tower stared and asked, "A-37s, what squadron are you from? What squadron? What squadron?" Our fighters answered "American-made planes here!" What followed was one bomb run, two bomb runs, many bomb runs against the rows of enemy aircraft. The explosions shook Saigon, and big pillars of smoke rose high into the air. Our daring bombing raid descending on Tan Son Nhat airport destroyed or damaged a number of enemy airplanes, including American planes on evacuation missions, throwing the enemy into a new fit of panic and confusion. The enemy no longer had any place which was secure, no place to go to escape our punishing blows.

Among the ranks of the enemy, some knew that we had used their airplanes to strike them, but there were others who, confused, thought that it was their own air force carrying out a coup. Even in our headquarters, a number of people who had not been told about this, when they heard that Tan Son Nhat had been bombed, said that this was "a second Nguyen Thanh Trung."

We also got a report that our troops' activities at sea had brought good results. After the mainland of Zone 5 was liberated, with timely direction from the Political Bureau and the Central Military Committee, the standing committee of the zone party committee and the Zone 5 command proposed a continuation of the offensive out to all the islands in our territorial waters as the number-one mission for their armed forces. The beautiful and sacred waters were the subjects of many literary works by our forefathers, and had witnessed many illustrious feats of arms by our fighters and people during the two wars of resistance. The seas were a frequent course for convoys of our ships and boats carrying arms and ammunition, food, and cadres from North to South and from Nam Bo up to Trung Bo, the graceful islands serving as rest bases for troops and transfer points for goods. Rich in bird nests, fish, and all kinds of ocean products, the seas were indeed a section of the Ho Chi Minh trail on the East Sea.

Carrying out the directive of the zone party committee and command, the Hoi An regional forces, along with guerillas, on March 30 coordinated with a popular uprising to liberate Cu Lao Cham Island. On the same day, the Cung Son (Cu Lao Re) Island party section led that island's people in an uprising to liberate the island, and welcomed the soldiers coming out to take over administration. On April 1, the people of Cu Lao Xanh Island also rose up to liberate their island. On April 10, a sapper unit from Khanh Hoa province and a battalion of the 968th division liberated Hon Tre Island.

With the overall situation developing favorably, on April 9 the General Command issued orders for the Zone 5 command, in coordination with the naval command, to use forces appropriate for a surprise assault to liberate the islands of the Truong Sa chain, which were being held by Saigon troops. So beginning on April 10, our forces consecutively liberated Song Tu Tay, Son Ca, Nam Yet, Sinh Ton, An Bang, and Truong Sa islands. On April 27, we used a sapper force and an infantry unit from the 968th division to liberate Cu Lao Thu Island, completing the liberation of most of the coastal and seaward islands of Trung Bo.

The liberation of the islands was a special exploit of the people's armed forces of Zone 5 and the naval forces. They used an extremely cunning, daring, and unexpected manner of attack, and with talented leadership and command, firmly grasped the opportunity and won big victories, quickly and determinedly.

Reviewing the situation on the night of April 28, campaign headquarters saw that the enemy were completely confused, their command in an uproar, and their III Corps command at Bien Hoa gradually disintegrating. In the first two days and nights of the campaign, all wings of our troops had completely implemented the plans, so we issued orders for a general offensive on the whole front for the morning of April 29, to advance into Saigon.

At 5:00 A.M. on April 29, when all wings of our troops had simultaneously opened fire for the attack, we received a long cable from the Political Bureau, containing a message and instructions.

1. OUR WARMEST PRAISE FOR ALL THE UNITS WHICH HAVE SCORED BIG EXPLOITS IN RECENT DAYS, SMASHING THE DEFENDING GANG ON THE EAST, NORTH, NORTHWEST, AND SOUTHWEST, CUTTING OFF ROUTE 4, ATTACKING THE ENEMY'S LARGE AIRFIELDS, AND OPERATING WELL ON THE OUTSKIRTS OF SAIGON AND INSIDE SAIGON.

WE CALL ON ALL CADRES AND FIGHTERS, PARTY MEMBERS, AND MEMBERS OF MASS ORGANIZATIONS, TO STRIKE WITH THE GREATEST DETERMINATION STRAIGHT INTO THE

ENEMY'S FINAL LAIR WITH THE HEROIC SPIRIT OF AN ARMY
WITH A HUNDRED VICTORIES IN A HUNDRED BATTLES,
SMASH THE ENEMY'S POWER TO RESIST, COORDINATE OF-
FENSIVES WITH UPRISINGS, AND COMPLETELY LIBERATE
THE CITY OF SAIGON-GIA DINH.

AT THE SAME TIME, YOU MUST MAINTAIN STRICT DIS-
CIPLINE, THOROUGHLY CARRYING OUT EVERY DIRECTIVE
AND ORDER; PROTECT THE LIFE AND PROPERTY OF THE
PEOPLE; UPHOLD THE REVOLUTIONARY NATURE AND VIC-
TORIOUS TRADITIONS OF OUR ARMY, COMPLETE YOUR EX-
TRAORDINARY MISSION, AND ACHIEVE COMPLETE VICTORY
FOR THE CAMPAIGN WHICH BEARS THE NAME OF OUR GREAT
UNCLE HO.

2. WHILE YOU ARE CONCENTRATING YOUR COMMAND AND
LEADERSHIP TO CARRY OUT YOUR MISSION OF LIBERATING
SAIGON-GIA DINH, YOU MUST DIVIDE UP RESPONSIBILITY
FOR CHECKING PLANS AND PREPARATIONS TO TAKE RAPID
ADVANTAGE OF OUR POSITION TO WIPE OUT AND DISPERSE
THE REMAINING ENEMY FORCES IN OTHER REGIONS ESPE-
CIALLY IN THE MEKONG DELTA AND ON CON SON AND PHU
QUOC ISLANDS, AND LIBERATE THE WHOLE OF THE SOUTH.
YOU MUST THOROUGHLY MOBILIZE YOUR REVOLUTIONARY
SPIRIT AND FIGHT CONTINUOUSLY UNTIL COMPLETE VIC-
TORY, OVERCOMING ALL THOUGHTS OF COMPLACENCY.

3. ON ENTERING THE CITY, CADRES AT ALL LEVELS MUST
GIVE IMMEDIATE ATTENTION TO THE LIVES OF THE WORKING
PEOPLE. BECAUSE OF THE EXPLOITATIVE POLICIES OF THE
OLD REGIME AND PLUNDERING BY THE COMPRADOR
BOURGEOISIE, IN ALL STRATA OF LABORERS AND WORKING
PEOPLE THERE ARE MANY FAMILIES WHO HAVE NO RICE
LEFT, OR WHO DO NOT HAVE ENOUGH MONEY TO BUY RICE.
YOU MUST IMMEDIATELY TAKE RICE FROM THE ENEMY'S
WAREHOUSES TO DISTRIBUTE TO FAMILIES WITHOUT
ENOUGH TO EAT, AND IF POSSIBLE, SOLDIERS SHOULD SHARE
THEIR RICE RATIONS WITH THE PEOPLE.

We knew that our troops were already carrying out the directives and call of the Political Bureau. We also knew that at this time the center was sending a large troop of cadres from all branches as reinforcements who could give timely service in the rapidly developing situation, and that Le Van Luong, head of the organization section of the party Central Committee, along with the other cadres responsible for this task, were working urgently to send them in quickly.

Cadres and fighters on the whole Saigon-Gia Dinh front knew this was the most decisive battle of this final phase of the general offensive and uprising that would conclude the war against the United States. Before their eyes were the last ramparts of the most obstinate and reactionary band of lackeys of the U.S. imperialist aggressors, the enemy we had to destroy. In the days just past, suffering, danger, and wounds had not made these comrades hesitate or slow the tempo of the offensive, and up to this time the campaign plans had been carried out in fine style.

The tasks of political mobilization and ideological education had been carried out continuously and creatively in our armed forces, so that our cadres and fighters had become all-around people, strong and wholesome in mind and body, with a strong will to struggle, and a consistently high tactical and technical level. As we entered the Ho Chi Minh campaign, political work held an extremely important position. At this time, Le Quang Hoa, deputy director of the General Political Office, was dispatched from the eastern wing of troops to return to help Pham Hung in his special concern for political work. He was fearless, going right along with all the units, and as soon as he returned to take up his assignment at headquarters, he and the cadres of the Political Office drafted a directive on political work in the campaign. After it had been approved by headquarters, he and the other representatives of the General Political Office took it to each wing of troops.

We had many forces, spread across a broad battlefield.

But those taking part in this campaign shared a single aspiration. Each unit had its own specific mission, as well as its particular record and traditions, yet because of good preparations from the first, supplemented by still more appropriate forms of political work, each and every person had, in the end, only one will, one unified objective: "Liberate Saigon. Liberate the South."

Besides the various forms of political work carried out by party committees, party members, youth league branches, and political officers from the time they received their assignments until just before the day the guns fired, campaign headquarters also sent a "mobilization order" to each person, drafted by the Political Office, ammended by each person in campaign headquarters, and finally approved by Pham Hung. The order was printed and distributed to all units in time. The call of the Political Bureau and the mobilization order from campaign headquarters stimulated every person, so all entered the battle with extremely high resolve.

It had been more than three days and nights, and hundreds of thousands of our fighters and cadres had overcome many hardships and dangers and were rushing forward, taking advantage of their victories. Since the opening of the Tay Nguyen campaign, many of our precious sons had sacrificed their lives for victory. And now, before the open gates of Saigon, yet other comrades fell, offering up their lives for the cause of the revolution. Still other comrades were wounded and had to let their guns slip from their hands. When we met local leaders, and when we assigned missions to the various units, we always reminded them that they must strictly implement the party's policies for fallen heroes and their families, and give perfect care to our wounded soldiers.

It must be said that in this work the doctors and other military medical personnel made a very important contribution. The military medics always stuck close to the soldiers during high-speed operations and battles, and alongside the scientific successes, there were outstanding examples of devoted service by our "good physicians and mothers."

Sitting in headquarters, we went over the "knotty" points for each wing. On the eastern thrust, the 325th division had taken control of Nhon Trach sector and Thanh Tuy Ha and moved on toward the Cat Lai ferry, preparing to send troops across the river into ward 9. The long-range artillery position set up at Nhon Trach fired a volley of more than 300 shells at Tan Son Nhat airfield. Those artillery explosions, which shook the very streets of Saigon, were the proclamation of the end of the quisling administration's regime. Their accurate fire coordinated with the rockets of the sapper troops. We had never used airplanes to direct our artillery fire, but with the help of the local people, we had sent our observers to slip in next to the enemy to direct our artillery, which was firing from quite a distance, so that it hit its mark.

The 304 explosions had just ended at Tan Son Nhat when the deep-strike force from the Second Army Corps arrived northwest of the Dong Nai River highway bridge and made contact with the 116th sapper force, which was still firmly holding the bridgehead after beating back many counterattacks by an enemy battalion. On the right-hand wing of the Second Army Corps, the 304th division organized a determined dawn attack on the enemy still remaining at the infantry school at Nuoc Trong base. Just before noon, our troops took control of the whole position and continued along Route 15, and by dusk arrived south of Long Binh base. Toward Vung Tau, we had taken control of most of the town on the afternoon of April 29.

At that time a deep-strike unit including one tank brigade and one infantry regiment assembled secretly in a rubber forest south of Dau Giay to await the order to advance into Saigon. Our fighters were sitting ready in trucks, wearing neat new uniforms, and all had red armbands so they could recognize each other easily when they entered the city. With leafy branches camouflaging people and vehicles, the whole unit roared off at 15:00 hours on orders from the Second Army Corps command, truck after truck stretching out in a long line, bravely advancing toward the center of Saigon. That imposing and historic sight as they moved out for the concluding attack of the war was truly unprecedented.

The Fourth Army Corps was engaged in fierce fighting. After capturing a number of objectives along Route 1, our troops moved on in three spearheads toward Ho Nai on the outskirts of Bien Hoa, and into Saigon's III Corps command and the Bien Hoa airfield, where they were blocked. This was the most vital point in the eastern part of the enemy's defense lines around Saigon, so they risked their lives to hold it. Many extremely fierce battles took place there. Advancing behind the Fourth Army Corps was the 52nd brigade from Zone 5, which had just moved down at top speed from Qui Nhon in motorized transport so they would be in time to take part in the campaign and serve as the reserve unit for the Fourth Army Corps and the whole eastern wing. This was a well-trained unit that had scored many battle exploits in the Tay Nguyen and in Zone 5, such as Ba To, Suoi Do, Tien Phuoc, Phuoc Lam, and Quang Yen. The troops of the brigade were sitting ready in nearly a hundred large touring cars clustered along Route 1 awaiting the order to advance on Saigon.

On the northern and northwestern thrusts, one unit of the First Army Corps had surrounded Phu Loi base, and one element had even captured Tan Uyen on the road to Lai Thieu, thereby setting up conditions for their deep-strike unit to advance toward Saigon's General Staff headquarters and the headquarters of their various armed services at Go Vap.

The Third Army Corps mounted determined attacks and defeated all enemy counterattacks, and by 14:00 hours on April 29 was in control of bases at Dong Du and Trang

Ho Chi Minh Campaign
April 26–April 30, 1975

KEY 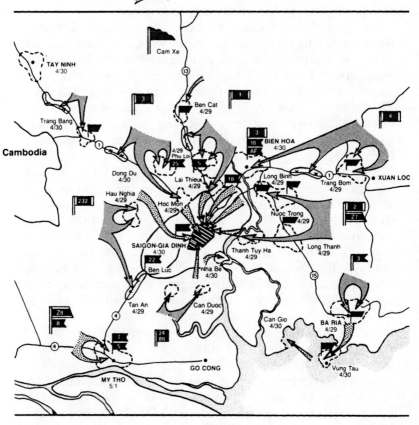 17:00 hours, April 26 -11:30, April 30, 1975

Cam Xe

TAY NINH
4/30

3

1

Ben Cat
4/29

Trang Bang
4/30

4

Cambodia

3
18
AF

BIEN HOA
4/30

4/29
Phu Loi

5

Dong Du
4/30

25

Lai Thieu
4/29

18

Long Binh
4/29

1

Trang Bom
4/29

XUAN LOC

232

Hau Nghia
4/29

Hoc Mon
4/29

Nuoc Trong
4/29

2
Z7

SAIGON-GIA DINH
4/30

Thanh Tuy Ha
4/29

Long Thanh
4/29

3

22

Ben Luc

Nha Be
4/30

Tan An
4/29

Can Duoc
4/29

Can Gio
4/30

15

BA RIA
4/29

Z8
B

7
5

24
88

GO CONG

Vung Tau
4/30

MY THO
5/1

Bang. Saigon's 25th division had fallen apart and been wiped out, and its commander, Candidate-General Ly Tong Ba, was captured. During the night of April 28, sapper troops had captured the Bong and Sang bridges on Route 1, and thanks to that, the deep-strike unit of the Third Army Corps rapidly vaulted past Hoc Mon, forcing the entire Quang Trung Training Center to surrender. The unit then advanced straight down to Ba Queo. Along the way our troops knocked out many enemy tanks, armored cars, and troops north of Cu Chi and at the Bong bridge and Hoc Mon. Because they heard our artillery still exploding at Tan Son Nhat and were following the joint plan, the unit did not attack right that night, but called a temporary halt and made urgent preparations for the attack on the airfield.

Along the southwest thrust, we finished capturing Hau Nghia province town, knocked out Duc Hoa district town, forced the enemy out of Duc Hue and Tra Cu, and opened a corridor along the eastern Vam Co River. As the enemy remnants from Hau Nghia fled toward Cu Chi, we blocked off and captured over 1,000 of them. The deep-strike unit of the 232nd force had crossed the eastern Vam Co River with all kinds of heavy equipment and assembled in the My Hanh area, with one regiment going to the Ba Hom region. Forces from the outskirts of town, special action units, and sapper units captured the river bridges and attacked the Phu Lam radar base, and at the same time fired rockets into Tan Son Nhat airfield, in preparation for the main-force troops' advance into Saigon.

The armed security forces on many of the thrusts joined with the people to neutralize traitors, chase down remnant enemy troops, and coordinate with the soldiers to prepare people and resources to lead our troops into the city center. Along Route 4, we kept the road cut and beat back many enemy counterattacks.

As we listened to the overall report on the situation as it had developed during the day of April 29, we all felt that after one day of carrying out the general offensive over the whole front, the situation had worked out quite well, just as laid out in the campaign plans. The units in all thrusts had moved ahead to capture enemy bases and positions in the outer perimeter; they isolated, encircled, blocked off, wiped out, and scattered the bulk of the 5th, 25th, 18th, 22nd, and 7th divisions deployed in the outer perimeter, and had prepared positions on the fringes of the central city and captured the important bridges around Saigon.

General Cao Van Vien, chief of Saigon's General Staff, had fled before the ink of his signature was dry on the order to "defend to the death, to the very end, the portion of land that remains." Major-General Vinh Loc took over. On April 29, Saigon's leading commanders met at night at their General Staff headquarters, and seeing how many generals and field officers had fled, decided to use the radio station to appeal to them to return and present themselves. The commander of Saigon's 18th division told us that his division had suffered heavy casualties and was in such disorder that it could not hold on past 8:00 the next morning. The commander of Saigon's 3rd cavalry brigade told us that the armored unit was out of ammunition and gas and could no longer mount any resistance. The commander of Saigon's Third Army Corps and the candidate-general who commanded their 22nd division had also abandoned their units and fled. Only their Fourth Army Corps, whose division had not yet suffered many casualties, still retained its command structure. Within Saigon city there were only two paratroop battalions left guarding the Bay Hien crossroads. The quisling president ordered his troops to hold the Phu Lam and Quan Tre radio-communications centers as best they could, but they did not have enough troops left to hold on.

Ho Chi Minh campaign headquarters was bustling with activity the night of April 29. Flashlights, hurricane lamps, and headlights burned bright in every hut and along every road. Gray heads bent over black heads as they pored over the maps, watching the vivid red arrowheads being drawn longer and longer, pointing straight toward the big objectives which we had chosen inside Saigon. Behind the combat operations room a battery of combat telephones worked incessantly.

All our radios were sending their signals out into the air, carrying supplementary directives from campaign headquarters down to all units before midnight—00:00 hours, April 30, 1975:

—Telling the 130mm artillery at Nhon Trach to stop firing into Tan Son Nhat airfield.

—Carefully checking the signals for coordinating fighting within the center of town.

—Assigning an additional mission to the Third Army Corps, to send one wing over to Saigon's General Staff headquarters after they had fought their way into Tan Son Nhat so they could coordinate with the First Army Corps.

—Telling the deep-strike units to advance quickly and go straight for their assigned targets, avoiding other targets along the way, not allowing themselves to be distracted, thus slowing down the speed of the advance.

By 24:00 hours on April 29, 1975, the body of forces for the attack on Saigon was poised like a divine hammer held aloft, and the enemy about to be dealt a punishing blow shook and trembled in fright watching that hammer descend.

17

Total Victory

As it unfolds our history occasionally repeats itself. As with our forefathers in those nights before final strategic general offensives against foreign invaders, our fighters on the Saigon front on the night of April 29 and early the next morning were restless, determined to win lightning victory. In these sacred hours, in this final day of the period determined by the Political Bureau for the liberation of Saigon, the fighters wrote on their helmets, on their sleeves, on their gun slings the immortal proclamation of President Ho Chi Minh:

Forward! Total victory is ours!

The sound of guns echoed over the whole front. Watching the flashes of light from our advancing wings of troops, or the light of flames rising from enemy bases around Saigon as they burst into fire, everyone could see that the dawn of our day of total victory was approaching. Le Ngoc Hien was on duty at headquarters listening to the cabled reports from all units. The spearhead from the Third Army Corps that had advanced farthest during the night had reached Ba Queo; that from the First Army Corps had closed in on Lai Thieu; that from the Second Army Corps had moved up close to the Dong Nai River highway bridge; that from the Fourth Army Corps was on the outskirts of Bien Hoa; and that from the 232nd force was in the Ba Hom area. Thus, the spearheads of our assault were only ten to twenty kilometers from the center of Saigon, the final few kilometers before we could rejoin our land in a single span, to carry the Ho Chi Minh trail through to the center of the city bearing his name. The routes of advance had worked out exactly according to the campaign plan, and were giving form to our shrewd style of attack, which even in the final days held many surprises for the enemy.

Saigon still hoped to rely on their remaining divisions to block our troops, whiïe they tried to "negotiate" with us to preserve the structure of their administration and armed forces. A number of retired Saigon generals and colonels also jumped in now with their schemes and plans to rescue the situation. At 2:00 A.M. our military delegation at Camp Davis cabled campaign headquarters to report,

THERE ARE THREE PEOPLE HERE THAT THE SAIGON AD-MINISTRATION HAS SENT TO DISCUSS A CEASEFIRE.* COM-RADE VO DONG GIANG MET THEM AND TOLD THEM OUR STAND AND PRINCIPLES AS STATED IN THE GOVERNMENT DECLARA-TION OF APRIL 26.** AFTER THAT, THEY ASKED TO LEAVE AND RETURN HOME. WE SAID THAT OUR TROOPS' ARTILLERY WAS FALLING HEAVILY ON THE AIRFIELD, THAT IT WAS VERY

* Father Chan Tin, one of the members of this delegation, published his account of the visit in the April 1976 issue of *Dung Day*, the monthly magazine of which he is publisher, in Ho Chi Minh City. In that account he says: "The military delegation of the Front [the National Liberation Front] warned that they would not meet with us if we were people sent by Mr. Duong Van Minh—because negotiations on a ceasefire had ended at 4 P.M. But because we correctly and determinedly insisted that we *were not a delegation sent by Mr. Duong Van Minh,* we were received happily, in a different, deeper bunker."

** On April 26, the Provisional Revolutionary Government issued a declaration elaborating on an earlier statement which had called for complete U.S. withdrawal and "a new administration standing for peace, independence, democracy, and national concord, and seriously implementing the Paris Agreement." The new declaration called specifically for the dismantling of Saigon's army and police apparatus.

DANGEROUS, AND THAT THEY OUGHT NOT TO GO. IN THE
END ALL THREE OF THEM AGREED TO STAY. THEY ARE
NOW IN THE BUNKER WITH US.

At this time, the heads of the quisling administration
were sitting anxiously waiting for their three messengers,
and seeing they still had not returned, called to each other,
bewildered and puzzled. A few hours before they sent
these three to Tan Son Nhat to meet us, they had chosen
four other "messengers" to call on our delegation, also
about a ceasefire. Our cadres had invited them to eat some
bananas which our men had grown themselves, then
explained our government's April 26 declaration to them.

In those final days of April, our military delegation witnessed the end-of-the-line haste and bewilderment of the
Americans and their protégés. In the past, our delegation's headquarters had often been blockaded and pro-
voked, and had suffered many difficulties, like having
electricity and water cut off, or not being allowed contact
with the outside. But during these days, this was the place
the enemy came most often seeking favors. Ambassador
Martin asked to meet a representative of our delegation.
We declined. And the quisling administration asked our
delegation for permission to appoint a person to fly to
Hanoi to negotiate a ceasefire. We turned that down, too.

Nguyen Duy Trinh sent a telegram to inform us that the
Americans' and puppets' cunning diplomatic plans coming one on top of the other, coupled with threatening hints
to us, were aimed at blocking our troops' general offensive
on Saigon, and showed all the more that we must fight
more urgently, attack more quickly, and make the best
use of each hour, each minute for total victory.

When it was almost light, the American news services
reported that Martin had cleared out of Saigon in a
helicopter. This viceregal mandarin, the final American
plenipotentiary in South Vietnam, beat a most hasty and
pitiful retreat. As it happened, up until the day he left
Saigon, Martin still felt certain that the quisling adminis-

tration could be preserved, and that a ceasefire could be arranged, so he was halfhearted about the evacuation, waiting and watching. He went all the way out to Tan Son Nhat airfield to observe the situation. Our barrage of bombs and our fierce shelling had nearly paralyzed this vital airfield, and the fixed-wing aircraft they had intended to use for their evacuation could no longer operate. The encirclement of Saigon was growing tighter by the day. The Duong Van Minh card* which they had played far too late proved useless. When Martin reported this to Washington, President Ford issued orders to begin a helicopter evacuation. Coming in waves for eighteen hours straight, they carried more than 1,000 Americans and over 5,000 of their Vietnamese retainers, along with their families, out of the South. Ford also ordered Martin to evacuate immediately "without a minute's delay."

The American evacuation was carried out from the tops of thirteen tall buildings chosen as landing pads for their helicopters. The number of these landing pads shrank gradually as tongues of fire from our advancing troops came closer. At the American embassy, the boarding point for the evacuation copters was a scene of monumental confusion, with the Americans' flunkies fighting their way in, smashing doors, climbing walls, climbing each other's backs, tussling, brawling, and trampling each other as they sought to flee. It reached the point where Martin, who wanted to return to his own house for his suitcase before he fled, had to take a back street, using the rear gate of the embassy. When "Code 2," Martin's code name, and "Lady 09," the name of the helicopter carrying him, left the embassy for the East Sea, it signaled the shameful defeat of U.S. imperialism after thirty years of intervention and military adventures in Vietnam. At the height of their invasion of Vietnam, the U.S. had used 60 percent of their total infantry, 58 percent of their marines, 32 percent of their tactical air force, 50 percent of their strategic air

---

* This refers to the final move of putting Minh in power.

force, fifteen of their eighteen aircraft carriers, 800,000 American troops (counting those stationed in satellite countries who were taking part in the Vietnam war), and more than 1 million Saigon troops. They mobilized as many as 6 million American soldiers in rotation, dropped over 10 million tons of bombs, and spent over $300 billion, but in the end the U.S. ambassador had to crawl up to the helicopter pad looking for a way to flee. Today, looking back on the gigantic force the enemy had mobilized, recalling the malicious designs they admitted, and thinking about the extreme difficulties and complexities which our revolutionary sampan had had to pass through, we were all the more aware how immeasurably great this campaign to liberate Saigon and liberate the South was.

Dawn broke clear and cool, and extraordinarily beautiful. The earliest news broadcast from the Voice of Vietnam read the April 30 editorial from *Nhan Dan:* "The army and people of Saigon-Gia Dinh are shouldering a historic mission which is extremely heavy but exceptionally glorious, stepping up attacks and uprisings, smashing the nerve centers and the final dens of the U.S. quisling administration, and completing the task of liberating the land. People throughout our land are turned toward Saigon-Gia Dinh, awaiting news of victory in this magnificent battle, confident that the army and people of this heroic city will surely complete their glorious mission for the Fatherland."

The campaign headquarters' meeting at the change of watch that day was crowded and lively, with no one having to call for anyone. Everyone arrived at the meeting room early, and every person who had a radio brought it along. We looked at the lines marking the routes of our advancing troops on the map: five wings of troops like the five points of a big star coming together in the city bearing Uncle Ho's name. The five army corps were not just simple numbers added up. They had taken on a very new, very powerful substance. We knew that the members of the Political Bureau and the Central Military Committee, who

had given their close and talented leadership and direction to the fighting for the past fifty days and more, must
also be gathered to follow developments on a map of
Saigon. We also knew that throughout the whole country
at that hour, people of every region would be milling
around maps of the Fatherland, waiting for news of victory so they could solemnly color in the revolutionary flag
above Ho Chi Minh City.

We heard some of the information the enemy had just
reported to each other. Saigon's Special Capital Zone
headquarters reported to the enemy at Long An: "Thu Duc
has been overrun by communist troops. Communist troops
are advancing on Saigon from Hoc Mon, and they even
have T-54 tanks. Why haven't we seen any orders from our
superiors at all?" They didn't know that their chief of staff
had fled early that morning. The Saigon fleet announced
to all stations attached to it that the naval command had
already fled, and that they should no longer contact them,
but if anything came up they should make direct contact
with the fleet out at sea.

The more the situation developed, the clearer it was that
our field positions were extremely threatening, but the
enemy were completely wiped out. They knew that the
principal direction of our attack would be from the north
and northwest of Saigon, so they had placed their 5th and
25th divisions there. The enemy were vacillating between two ideas: defending Saigon at a distance, from the
outside, or pulling their forces back into Saigon. If they
held the outside, then the inside would be neglected, because they didn't have enough troops. And if they abandoned the outside and pulled back in to hold the inside,
then the lesson of the Tay Nguyen showed that there
would be a panic and they would all the more quickly find
themselves in a position where they would be wiped out.
Either way they were dead. But the field positions on the
morning of April 30 were such that even if Saigon's 5th
and 25th divisions had wanted to pull back to Saigon, they
could not have done so, because we had them tightly

boxed in on the outer perimeter, and had simultaneously launched powerful assault spearheads striking straight for the center of town. Their 25th division was stationed at the Cu Chi base, also called Dong Du. This base had been set up in 1966 by the U.S. 25th "Tropic Lightning" division sent from Hawaii to block our route of advance on Saigon and destroy the foundations of our footholds in the area. The 25th division's commanders had now used barbed wire to block off all entrances and exits to keep their soldiers from fleeing, and had raised the slogan "defend to the death." On the morning of April 29, our Third Army Corps used tanks to strike directly into the position, rushing straight toward the division commander's bunker. The enemy staff fled in confusion. The main gate had opened, and enemy officers and soldiers vaulted past barricades—even barbed wire and mine fields—to flee. Our troops fired into the air to force them to halt and surrender. The division commander escaped, but later he was captured, too.

When they lost Dong Du, the enemy were very confused and wavering. Enemy forces blocked off toward the northwest had no way to pull back to Saigon. Seizing that opportunity, the 316th division of our Third Army Corps deployed roadblocks to cut the road, surrounded enemy units on each section and, moving onto the offensive in time, captured the artillery position at Lap Tao, then continued on to hit Phuoc Hiep, Suoi Sau, Tra Vo, Ben Muong, Bau Nau, and Cam Giang, wiping out and scattering Saigon's whole 46th regiment and capturing 600 of them.

The 10th division, the deep-strike division of the Third Army Corps, captured Hoc Mon, the Quang Trung camp, and Ba Queo on April 29, then, taking advantage of its victories, struck straight at the Bay Hien crossroads on the morning of April 30. After that, they captured Gate 5 of Tan Son Nhat airfield and the enemy paratroop command. The same morning they began to attack Tan Son Nhat airfield, and one element of their forces coordinated with the First Army Corps to strike toward Saigon's General Staff headquarters. From 8:00 to 8:30 our artillery sent rapid, concentrated fire into the airfield. Flames and smoke rose into the skies. As soon as the sound of artillery stopped, the 24th infantry regiment, sitting in tanks and armored cars, rushed in to take the Bay Hien crossroads, and taking advantage of their victory moved on to Gate 5 of the airfield. There the enemy mounted a desperate resistance, even using airplanes to bomb our battle formations. Our troops reinforced for continuous assaults until 9:30, when they captured the airfield gate. Meanwhile, another wing of troops captured the enemy paratroop command and made contact with our military delegation Camp Davis. A third wing of troops struck straight into the communications area, the command of the 5th air force division, and the enemy air force command. Coordinating with the 24th regiment, at 9:30 the 28th regiment also began to strike directly at the main gate of Saigon's General Staff headquarters.

Saigon's 5th division, which still held the Lai Khe base on Route 13, fifty kilometers north of Saigon, also came under fierce attack from our First Army Corps. This was another U.S. base, set up by the 1st "Big Red 1" division in 1965. When the division commander, Candidate-General Le Nguyen Vy, lost contact with Saigon's Third Army Corps headquarters and saw the general situation in Saigon was very dangerous, he issued orders to gather all vehicles to move the whole division back to Saigon. But we held the road to Saigon, and he and his unit were blocked inside their base. Then one element of our First Army Corps struck straight at the Lai Khe base. Le Nguyen Vy killed himself, his deputy fled, and the entire 5th division staff was captured.

Another wing of the First Army Corps, the 312th division, wiped out and forced the surrender of all enemy troops at Phu Loi base between 5:00 and 10:00 A.M. that day. These included the forces of Binh Duong sector and an element of Saigon's 5th division.

Correctly anticipating the enemy's retreat route, our units deployed blocking forces in the vicinity of An Loi on Route 14, so they captured all thirty-six vehicles, and 1,200 enemy surrendered. In the Bung region on Route 13, our troops captured 7,000 of the enemy's 5th division who were fleeing toward Lai Thieu.

Meanwhile, the 320th division, in coordination with the specialized branches of the First Army Corps, captured Lai Thieu and advanced toward the Binh Phuoc bridge, which sapper troops had captured and held since dawn. Along the route of advance, at 8:30 this unit had damaged, destroyed, or captured 180 vehicles of all kinds belonging to Saigon's 3rd cavalry brigade, and after that moved on toward the command compound for the various branches of the enemy armed forces in Go Vap. Another wing, also between the deep-strike division, attacked the enemy from the intersection at the Binh Phuoc bridge and the Binh Trieu bridge, wiping out and scattering all the remaining forces of the 3rd cavalry brigade, and capturing enemy tanks to lead the way for our advance on Saigon's General Staff headquarters.

On the combat operations map at Saigon's General Staff headquarters, someone had written one question: "And where is the 308th division?" This was one of our heroic elite main-force divisions, which the enemy had not yet seen appear on the front. Among their fears, one derived from bourgeois military doctrine: "The thing to fear most is the silence of the opposing forces." Saigon's 18th division troops were terrified when they saw our troops standing blocking their way as they fled toward Thu Doc. The commander and his crew of staff officers disguised themselves to blend in with their panicked remnants and fled secretly toward Saigon.

The Fourth Army Corps concentrated its forces from 7:00 to 9:00 A.M. to capture the headquarters of Saigon's Third Army Corps at Hoc Ba Thuc, next to the Bien Hoa airfield, scattered resisting enemy troops at Ho Nai and Tam Hiep, and prepared to strike into Saigon.

The Second Army Corps wing, after a night of readjusting its formations for improved coordination, sent its deep-strike unit across the Dong Nai River highway bridge on the morning of April 30, with fire support from three positions. They moved ahead, aiming straight for the heart of Saigon. Along the way the army corps used its fire power to wipe out nests of enemy resistance at Thu Duc and north of the Rach Chiec bridge. At 9:30 the advance element reached the Rach Chiec bridge, which had been captured ahead of time by our special action forces, and held until main-force troops arrived.

Leading elements of the 232nd force on both the southwestern and southern thrusts were approaching the Special Capital Zone headquarters and Saigon's Directorate-General of Police. We advanced actively on Route 4, wiping out and scattering the whole of Saigon's newly re-formed 22nd division and the 6th ranger group. We liberated Tan An town, and captured Thu Thua subsector.

Trying to rescue something from the situation, the Saigon quisling administration convoked a meeting of all their ministers at "Independence Palace" for a presentation ceremony for the new cabinet at 10:00 A.M. on the morning of April 30. But it was far too late. Right at 9:25 they got the news that they had lost four divisions—the 5th, 18th, 22nd, and 25th—and all their marine squadrons. Our troops had fought into Tan Son Nhat and the General Staff headquarters, our tanks had crossed all the bridges on the Saigon River, and the city had been totally cut off from the enemy Fourth Army Corps in the Mekong Delta. Faced with that situation, they saw that there was virtually nothing left, and they were forced to issue an announcement asking for a ceasefire. That announcement was written and recorded at "Independence Palace," and sent to the radio station.

While this whole final "imperial court" of the regime set up by the United States was sitting in "Independence Palace," the door of the room opened. They all stood up, thinking it was the Liberation Army arriving. The person who stepped in was the French General Vanuxem, who had come alone, of his own accord. He dashed up to the room where the "cabinet" was sitting to intercept the tape the quisling president had recorded for broadcast, and presented a plan to block our general offensive into Saigon.

Vanuxem's diabolical plots were truly laughable, actions that were indeed brutal and cynical. It is not yet convenient to say much about them, but even they could not have helped the quisling administration reverse the situation. The tape was taken on for broadcast, proposing "a ceasefire . . . to discuss the transfer of power." Even now the enemy were using schemes to halt our troops' advance to total victory!

Faced with that situation, the Political Bureau immediately directed the front: "Continue the attack on Saigon according to plan, advancing in the most powerful spirit, liberate and take over the whole city, disarm enemy troops, dissolve the enemy administration at all levels, and thoroughly smash all enemy resistance." And the Ho Chi Minh campaign headquarters, after a collective discussion, issued battle orders to all zones, army corps, and units to 1) continue advancing the offensive rapidly into all the predetermined objectives in the city and other regions; 2) call on enemy troops to surrender and turn in their weapons; arrest and gather together all enemy officers from the rank of major on up; 3) attack any enemy resistance at once and wipe it out immediately.

Even before they had received the orders, right after they heard the news that the enemy had requested a ceasefire, every unit on the front continued its rapid advance along the streets of Saigon. Our soldiers said to each other, "There won't be any ceasefire. Keep up the attack. This is a once-in-a-thousand-years chance." We were very glad to see that our cadres and fighters were so mature and politically sharp. They had a strong will to win, a spirit of discipline and responsibility for the fate of the nation, and they fully grasped the strategic resolution of the Political Bureau.

The most extraordinary thing about this historic campaign was what had sprouted in the souls of our cadres and fighters. Why were our soldiers so heroic and determined during this campaign? What had given all of them this clear understanding of the great resolution of the party and of the nation, this clear understanding of our immeasurably precious opportunity, and this clear understanding of our unprecedented manner of fighting? What had made them so extraordinarily courageous and intense, so outstanding in their political acumen in this final phase of the war?

The will and competence of our soldiers were not achieved in a day, but were the result of a continuous process of carrying out the party's ideological and organizational work in the armed forces. And throughout our thirty years of struggle, there had been no campaign in which Uncle Ho had not gone into the operation with our soldiers. Going out to battle this time, our whole army had been given singular, unprecedented strength because this strategically decisive battle bore his name: Ho Chi Minh, for every one of our cadres and fighters, was faith, strength, and life. Among the myriad troops in all the advancing wings, every one of our fighters carried toward Ho Chi Minh City the hopes of the nation and a love for our land. Today each fighter could see with his own eyes the resiliency which the Fatherland had built up during these many years, and given his own resiliency there was nothing, no enemy scheme that could stop him.

Our troops advanced rapidly to the five primary objectives, and then spread out from there. Wherever they went, a forest of revolutionary flags appeared, and people poured out to cheer them, turning the streets of Saigon into a giant festival. From the Binh Phoc bridge to Quan Tre, people carrying flags, beating drums and hollow wooden fish, and calling through megaphones, chased down the enemy, disarmed enemy soldiers, neutralized traitors and spies, and guided our soldiers. In Hoc Mon on Route 1, the people all came out into the road to greet the soldiers, guide them, and point out the hiding places of enemy thugs. Everywhere people used megaphones to call on Saigon soldiers to take off their uniforms and lay down their guns. The people of the city, especially the workers, protected factories and warehouses and turned them over to our soldiers. In all the districts bordering the city—Binh Hoa, Thanh My Tay, Phu Nhuan, Go Vap, and Thu Duc—members of the revolutionary infrastructure and other people distributed leaflets, raised flags, called on enemy soldiers to drop their guns, and supplied and guided our soldiers. Before this great army entered the city, the great cause of our nation and the policies of our revolution had entered the hearts of the people.

We were very pleased to hear that the people of the city rose up when the military attacks, going one step ahead, had given them the leverage. The masses had entered this decisive battle at just the right time, not too early, but not too late. The patriotic actions of the people created a revolutionary atmosphere of vast strength on all the city's streets. This was the most precious aspect of the mass movement in Saigon-Gia Dinh, the result of many years of propaganda, education, organizing, and training by the municipal party branch. When the opportune moment arrived, those political troops had risen up with a vanguard spirit, and advanced in giant strides along with our powerful main-force divisions, resolutely, intelligently, and courageously. The people of the city not only carried flags and food and drink for the troops, but helped disperse large numbers of enemy soldiers, forced many to surrender, chased and captured many of those who were hiding out, and preserved order and security in the streets. And we will never forget the widespread and moving images of thousands, of tens of thousands of people enthusiastically giving directions to our soldiers and guiding them as they entered the city, and helping all the wings of troops strike quickly and unexpectedly at enemy positions. Those nameless heroes of Saigon-Gia Dinh brought into the general offensive the fresh and beautiful features of people's war.

As we looked at the combat operations map, the five wings of our troops seemed like five lotuses blossoming out from our five major objectives. The First Army Corps had captured Saigon's General Staff headquarters and the command compounds of all the enemy armed services. When the Third Army Corps captured Tan Son Nhat they met one wing of troops already encamped there—our military delegation at Camp Davis; it was an amazing and moving meeting. The Fourth Army Corps captured Saigon's Ministry of Defense, the Bach Dang port, and the radio station. The 232nd force took the Special Capital Zone headquarters and the Directorate-General of Police. The Second Army Corps seized "Independence Palace," the place where the quisling leaders, those hirelings of the United States, had sold our independence, traded in human blood, and carried on their smuggling. Our soldiers immediately rushed upstairs to the place where the quisling cabinet was meeting, and arrested the whole central leadership of the Saigon administration, including their president, right on the spot. Our soldiers' vigorous actions and firm declarations revealed the spirit of a victorious army. By 11:30 A.M. on April 30 the revolutionary flag flew from "Independence Palace"; this became the meeting point for all the wings of liberating troops.

At the front headquarters, we turned on our radios to listen. The voice of the quisling president called on his troops to put down their weapons and surrender unconditionally to our troops. Saigon was completely liberated! Total victory! We were completely victorious! All of us at headquarters jumped up and shouted, embraced and carried each other around on our shoulders. The sound of applause, laughter, and happy, noisy, chattering speech was as festive as if spring had just burst upon us. It was an indescribably joyous scene. Le Duc Tho and Pham Hung embraced me and all the cadres and fighters present. We were all so happy we were choked with emotion. I lit a cigarette and smoked. Dinh Duc Thien, his eyes somewhat red, said, "Now if these eyes close, my heart will be at rest." This historic and sacred, intoxicating and completely satisfying moment was one that comes once in a generation, once in many generations. Our generation had known many victorious mornings, but there had been no morning so fresh and beautiful, so radiant, so clear and cool, so sweet-scented as this morning of total victory, a morning which made babes older than their years and made old men young again

The Political Bureau cabled us:

RECEIVED NEWS WE RAISED FLAG ABOVE "INDEPENDENCE PALACE." SEND YOU ALL CONGRATULATIONS ON THE GREAT VICTORY. POLITICAL BUREAU IS MOST HAPPY.

And there was even a voice from the heart of the Fatherland on the telephone for us: "Congratulations on the great victory. Can you hear the sound of the fireworks going off down there? Fireworks are echoing all through Hanoi."

All of Hanoi poured out into the streets lighting firecrackers, throwing flowers, waving flags. Hanoi, the capital of the whole country, heroic Hanoi, home of Uncle Ho and our party, had accomplished this victory, along with the entire country. Forests of people, seas of people, flooded the streets singing. The whole land turned out in the streets to breathe deep the air of this perfectly happy day. The entire land danced to celebrate the day of true peace after thirty years of war, the day our division had been wiped out and the suffering of separation ended.

All the people, except for the clique of traitors, were overflowing with pride and excitement, and raised high the songs of victory. Their faces had never been so beautiful as today. Our heroic people were worthy of this great exploit, and this historic victory had itself depended heavily on their immense labors and great sacrifices. From now on, our land was unified in one span, our net-

work of mountains and rivers again one, peace truly un-
ambiguous, independence truly complete. Families would
be brought together, and the nation, too, would be reunited.

Vo Xuan Sang, the cadre who is my guard, is a
photographer—not a professional, but he did record the
exuberant scene at headquarters in that first moment of
total victory. We were so happy we forgot about eating and
sleeping. And we wept. Yes, those tears were reserved for
this day of total victory which so many generations had
fought for with all their devotion and with all their pas-
sion, committing their lives to it.

Our thought, our first thought, in that first moment of
victory was of our beloved Uncle Ho, whose fame had
been linked with this historic campaign, linked with every
victory of our people. Our people and army could happily
report to Uncle Ho that his admonition had been carried
out in fine style. Today the bell still echoed in Uncle's
house on stilts, reporting the news of victory at the front.
The bugle call of total victory still wafted through the
windows and doors and slipped in among the pages of
poetry on Uncle's desk. Uncle's arm was still beckoning
affectionately, calling us to his embrace. Uncle's form
was still there on this glorious day of total victory, beating
time for us as we sang.*

Le Duc Tho, Pham Hung, and I leaned on our chairs
looking at the map of Ho Chi Minh City spread out on the
table. We thought of the welter of jobs ahead. Were the
electricity and water in Saigon still working? Saigon's
army of nearly 1 million had disbanded on the spot. How
should we deal with them? What could we do to help the
hungry and find ways for the millions of unemployed to
make a living? Should we ask the center to send in
supplies right away to keep the factories in Saigon alive?
How could we quickly build up a revolutionary adminis-

---

* Ho Chi Minh was especially fond of leading groups in singing "*Ket
Doan*"—"Unity."

tration at the grassroots level? What policy should we take toward the bourgeoisie? And how could we carry the South on to socialism along with the whole country? The conclusion of this struggle was the opening of another, no less complex and filled with hardship. The difficulties would be many, but the advantages were not few. Saigon and the South, which had gone out first and returned last, deserved a life of peace, plenty, and happiness.

The liberation of Saigon-Gia Dinh established decisive conditions to force the enemy Fourth Army Corps to surrender, and to finish the liberation of the Mekong Delta. In early April 1975, COSVN and the regional headquarters had issued a directive to the Mekong Delta front to prepare quickly for a general offensive and uprising, coordinated with the Saigon-Gia Dinh front. The directive specified a barrage of offensives and uprisings beginning April 29 with the motto, "Provinces liberate provinces, districts liberate districts, villages liberate villages, and zones liberate zones with their own forces." At the same time, in accordance with the directions of the Political Bureau and the Central Military Committee, our Ho Chi Minh campaign headquarters still intended to use a portion of our main-force troops and technological weapons to advance into the Mekong Delta to finish off the enemy Fourth Army Corps if they were still stubbornly resisting after the liberation of Saigon.

All of the delta provinces carried out their offensives and uprisings according to plan. Since the beginning of the dry season, the armed forces and the people of the Mekong Delta, had focused on smashing the enemy's pacification efforts throughout the region. They mounted a continuous series of attacks and uprisings so that before the Ho Chi Minh campaign they had established new positions and a new balance of forces, and had inflicted casualties on Saigon's Fourth Army Corps and weakened them. The liberated zone was expanded, the zone under enemy control was narrowed, and the enemy's reserve forces were knocked flat. By contrast, our armed forces increased by leaps and bounds, and were positioned right next to the important targets. Political forces developed, and the masses were mobilized and organized into units ready to rise up when they got the opportunity and the signal.

When the Ho Chi Minh campaign went into the phase of the general offensive into the central city, especially after the night of April 29, the main-force troops of Zone 8 and Zone 9, in coordination with the regional forces and guerilla militia, surrounded My Tho and Can Tho and cut Route 4 in many places. After Saigon was liberated, while the enemy were in complete confusion and uncertainty and were falling apart, the armed forces of Zone 8 and Zone 9, following plans already prepared, mounted a series of attacks under the direct leadership of the local party branches. Coordinating these attacks with uprisings by tens of thousands of the masses, they liberated all cities and towns, captured all big military bases, all district towns and subsectors, and all enemy outposts. They knocked out all units in the enemy's IV Corps and forced them to turn in their weapons and surrender, and completely toppled the quisling administration from the province level down to the villages, liberated the Nam Bo delta, and liberated the islands at great speed. Their offensives and uprisings took many rich and creative forms.

The final hours of the enemy troops in IV Corps were truly pitiful. Enemy forces included three main-force divisions, the 7th, 9th, and 21st, along with armored units, artillery, riverine groups, and security and civil guard units. The enemy 21st division had primary responsibility for protecting the Fourth Army Corps headquarters in Can Tho, and on the morning of April 30, they put up a desperate resistance on the outer perimeter of the town. Even when the Saigon president proclaimed surrender, Brigadier-General Nguyen Khoa Nam, commander of their Fourth Army Corps and concurrently commander of IV Corps, still obstinately issued the order: "Hold your positions, cease firing, but if you are attacked, resist." At 16:00 hours that same day, Nguyen Khoa Nam summoned Candidate-General Mach Van Truong, commander of the enemy's 21st division, to a meeting to discuss schemes to deal with us. But because of our increasing pressure, their 31st, 32nd, and 33rd regiments, along with most of the staff sections at divisional headquarters, had, on their own initiative, discarded their weapons, thrown away their uniforms, and returned home. There were only a few highranking puppet officers left to surrender to us at 20:00 hours that same day.

The enemy's 7th division had the primary mission of breaking through the blockade of Route 4. The division commander, Candidate-General Tran Van Hai, assembled his commanders for a meeting at Dong Tam (My Tho) base as soon as he heard the news that Saigon had been liberated. While that was going on, his soldiers deserted their units and flocked back to their homes. At night the enemy officers of all ranks fled, too. Depressed and discouraged, Tran Van Hai killed himself at 3:00 A.M. on May 1. Thus, the 7th division, the strongest division of Saigon's Fourth Army Corps, fell apart completely.

Finally, the enemy 9th division, commanded by Candidate-General Huynh Van Lac, had responsibility for breaking the blockade of Route 4 in the vicinity of Long An. When they got the news that their president had surrendered, and when they saw our victorious army and people attacking and rising up everywhere like a torrential waterfall, the officers and soldiers of the enemy 9th division were thrown into absolute confusion, entirely lost their spirit, and spontaneously fled. By 4:00 A.M. on May 1, they had completely scattered. Confronted with the strength of the offensives and uprisings of the army and people in the Mekong Delta, with the collapse and rapid disintegration of the whole of the Fourth Army Corps, and with this terribly bitter and shameful defeat, the quisling generals who commanded the Fourth Army Corps and its divisions entered their deadend street in many different ways: some surrendered, some fled, and one killed himself.

We began to load tanks and artillery on ships to prepare for a combined assault with the navy and the air force on Con Son Island, our first joint air-naval battle. But as the ships were about to leave the docks we got news that the patriotic fighters on Con Son had risen up and liberated the island themselves. The Zone 9 command had plans to reinforce and liberate Phu Quoc, and our naval vessels were ordered to go to the islands to greet our patriotic fighters who had just escaped from enemy prisons.

On May 1, the Ho Chi Minh campaign headquarters celebrated the complete liberation of the South and commemorated International Labor Day. Candies, cakes, and soft drinks were set out on the table. And when he saw that there was a bottle of liquor, Pham Hung asked in surprise where it had come from. Dinh Duc Thien "let out the secret": "Today, which conveniently happens to be comrade Van Tien Dung's birthday as well, this liquor has been sent to him from the 'rear.' " I had also drunk this liquor on May 1, 1972 in Quang Tri.

In these forests on the front lines, where the silence of the guns was a signal that our Fatherland had entered the age of spring, Pham Hung happily invited everyone to lift their glasses in a toast to the day of total victory. This glory belongs to President Ho Chi Minh! This glory belongs to our heroic party, to the Central Committee, and to the Political Bureau! This glory belongs to the perfectly heroic people's armed forces of our whole land! This glory belongs to the great and heroic people of our land! This glory belongs to all the heroes and martyrs who have fallen for the cause of independence, reunification, and socialism for the Fatherland!

We took a car to Saigon, past areas and positions so vital for the liberation of the city, like Trang Bang and Cu Chi, and past areas which had been revolutionary bases for many years, since the founding of the party, like Hoc Mon and Ba Diem. Along the highway, in the villages, and in the city streets there was no sea of blood, only a sea of people in high spirits, waving their hands and waving flags to welcome peace and the revolution. That sea of people, mingling endlessly with the long lines of our soldiers' trucks, tanks, and cars, in itself proclaimed our total victory. The sides of the road were still clogged with uniforms, rank insignia, guns and ammunition, boots, helmets, vehicles, and artillery the puppet army had abandoned in defeat. Spread out around us were not only the relics of a military force that had been smashed, but the relics of a reactionary political doctrine that had unraveled, the doctrine of a crew of imperialists so arrogant about their wealth and so worshipful of possessions that it blinded them. It was ironic that at every enemy base and barracks a sign had been erected, painted in large letters with the words, "Honor–Responsibility–Fatherland." What the enemy did not have, they had to shout about loudest. The main road into Saigon was very good, built by the enemy in the past to serve their operations. All of the enemy bases and storage depots were vast. The banks, the American billets, the hotels, many stories tall, were imposing advertisements for neocolonialism, implying that it would stand firm here, that it would stand for time without end. In 1968 Westmoreland boasted, "We will always be in Vietnam. Our bombs and bullets will prove it." But in fact the proof was exactly the opposite. We went into the headquarters of Saigon's General Staff. Here, as at the enemy Directorate-General of Police, the files of the enemy commanders' top secret documents remained. Their modern computer with its famous memory containing bio-data on each officer and soldier in their million-plus army was still running. American computers had not won in this war. The intelligence and will of our nation had won completely.

From Saigon's General Staff headquarters we went to Camp Davis at Tan Son Nhat airfield. In our delegation's former press conference room, Ho Xuan Anh "supervised" the first meeting since total victory of the campaign headquarters, with the commanders and political officers of all four army corps, the 232nd force, and the 559th force, to give them specific assignments for each unit to carry out during the period of military administration of the city, and to divide up the work of assuming administration of the enemy's military structure.

Only seventeen days before, when we assigned each army corps its mission for the attack on Saigon and divided up the work of continuing the administration of the city, we discussed it over maps. Today, sitting in the midst of liberated Saigon, we had seen it with our own eyes, had come right to the place to discuss and assign missions "on the spot." One comrade burst out, "So fast! It's more beautiful than a dream."

A few days later, Le Duan and Vo Nguyen Giap flew from Hanoi to Saigon and landed at Tan Son Nhat airfield. Under the brilliant May sun of Ho Chi Minh City, our beloved first secretary stepped down from the plane, his hand holding a handkerchief to wipe away the tears. From the hardship of his many years of activities on the battlefields of the South, he had a deep understanding of the value of today's great victory. When he met Le Duc Tho, Pham Hung, Tran Quoc Hoan, our comrades from COSVN, and myself, as well as the many other people who had come out to meet him, Le Duan embraced us warmly, referred to the job that had been done, and reminded us of the many important new tasks that needed to be done.

On the day President Ton Duc Thang led the delegation from the North to Ho Chi Minh City for the victory celebration, Le Duc Tho and Pham Hung, comrades from COSVN, Chairman Nguyen Huu Tho of the Central Committee of the National Front for the Liberation of South Vietnam, President Huynh Tan Phat of the Provisional Revolutionary Government of the Republic of South Vietnam, personages from the Vietnam Alliance of National, Democratic, and Peace Forces, and many other people of note, along with thousands of Saigonese of all ages came out with flags and flowers to meet Uncle Ton at Tan Son Nhat airfield. Le Duc Tho, Hoang Quoc Viet, and I were also members of the delegation from the North. As soon as the plane's wheels had stopped, amid the welcoming cheers of the people, we boarded the plane to greet Uncle Ton at his seat. I stood at attention:

"Comrade President, I can report that the Vietnamese people's armed forces have fulfilled their mission of liberating Saigon and liberating the South."

I choked up and could say nothing more. Seeing Uncle Ton, I remembered Uncle Ho. Our glorious country, our beloved South was completely liberated, but Uncle Ho was not here. The South had always been in his heart. I suddenly remembered one day in 1969, before I left for a fraternal socialist country, when Uncle Ho had admonished me to remember to visit two young guerilla girls from the South—one of whom, Kien, had been captured by the enemy and had one leg cut off—who were being treated in that friendly country. After I returned to our country, during an evening meal with Uncle Ho and Uncle Ton on August 7, 1969, I reported to Uncle Ho on the health of the two girls, gave him pictures taken with them, and letters the two had sent him. He seemed reassured. He seldom ate well or slept peacefully while our compatriots in the South continued to suffer. Now the night had passed, the sky again was light, yet the compatriots of the South could not welcome him. But his will and his thought would live on for a thousand autumns with the nation, with the land, and with each and every Vietnamese.

After the victory celebration in front of "Independence Palace," which had become the headquarters of the city's military administrative committee, and the commemoration of President Ho Chi Minh's birth anniversary, all of our comrades from the Ho Chi Minh campaign headquarters, and the highranking cadres of all the unit commands, offices, and branches which took part in the campaign, went to Da Lat for a conference to sum up the campaign. The weather in Da Lat in May reminded me of Hanoi in the fall. It had been just five months since the

Political Bureau had assigned us the mission of opening a general offensive and uprising.

The conference met at the Palace Hotel, the biggest building in Da Lat, overlooking the Xuan Huong Lake and the whole central area of town. It was here that, twenty-nine years before, during the talks with France, the French colonialists had stubbornly demanded the detachment of Nam Bo from Vietnam and the reimposition of their old rule under a new form. Today, here, we had representatives from all the units of the People's Army of Vietnam which had gained total victory in the Ho Chi Minh campaign and had restored complete peace, independence, and unity to the nation. These comrades who had combined to fight closely, side by side, on every thrust of the campaign, on every battlefront of the totally victorious general offensive and uprising—some going ahead, others following behind—were now all meeting together for the first time, shaking hands, their faces happy. Looking at all these faces we were so fond of, we remembered their voices and the lines they had written, which we had received over the radio or by telegram in the solemn or tense, high-spirited or anxious moments of the long months of this campaign fought with no rest.

Pham Hung, political officer, on behalf of the Ho Chi Minh campaign command, convened the conference: "The completely victorious Ho Chi Minh campaign was the high point of the earthshaking general offensive and uprising by our army and people which, between the beginning of March and April 30, rapidly smashed the final den of the enemy, liberated Ho Chi Minh City in a very short time, wiped out, scattered, and captured the whole of the enemy's forces in III Corps and IV Corps, including their general reserve forces, all branches and specialized services, and all main-force and regional units. We have confiscated all their weapons, captured all their ports, airfields, and supply depots. toppled the whole lackey administrative system from central to local level, concluded the general offensive and uprising throughout the South in total victory, and carried out the historic mission of the people's national democratic revolution in the whole country. If in the past we defeated French colonialism with the Dien Bien Phu campaign, today, with the total victory of the Ho Chi Minh campaign, we have ended United States neocolonialism in our land, Vietnam, and completely fulfilled the sacred testament of our beloved Uncle Ho. Since the beginning of the party, through nearly a half century of continuous struggle, the people's national democratic revolution has now been carried out throughout the whole country. This victory fully establishes basic, favorable conditions for our people to build a peaceful, unified, independent, democratic, and prosperous Vietnam, and to contribute to the preservation of peace in Southeast Asia and in the world."

Le Duc Tho, on behalf of the Political Bureau, reviewed the great exploits of our army and people, profoundly and thoroughly analyzed the significance of and the reasons for the victory of the general offensive and uprising in general, and especially of the totally victorious historic Ho Chi Minh campaign. He said, essentially, that we won for many reasons. The main thing, the most essential and decisive element in every victory, is the correct and talented leadership of the party. Our victory also springs from many causes having to do with the patriotic traditions and the spirit of unity of our people, the spirit of heroic struggle of our people's armed forces, and the help of the fraternal socialist countries and our friends around the world.

In speaking of the leadership of the party, he said that we must see that the leadership of the Political Bureau and the Central Military Committee in the process of this general offensive and uprising was precise and incisive. Today's victory is the result of the long process of thirty years' resistance. Our entire country resisted for thirty years, and those years trained us as people, trained our soldiers, and gave us much precious experience. The victory of the August Revolution established conditions for our victorious resistance against the French. The victorious resistance against France created conditions for us to build the North into a firm revolutionary base for the whole country to defeat the United States. When we chased the American troops out, it finally created conditions for us to topple the puppets. And in this general offensive and uprising we carried the struggle on to achieve total victory. Our liberation of Ban Me Thuot blasted a strategic opening, and the liberation of the Tay Nguyen established a position from which to strike the enemy in Hue, Da Nang, and the whole of Zone 5, and smash the enemy's plans to regroup. All these victories, along with the chain reaction of offensives and uprisings in the jungled mountain areas and the Nam Bo countryside, created an extremely favorable opening for the final decisive battle—the Ho Chi Minh campaign—to achieve total victory.

In the process of many years of resistance against the U.S. imperialists, we surprised them many times. After signing the Paris Agreement, Kissinger told us that America had been surprised twice. The first time was when they attacked Highway 9 in southern Laos in 1971; they did not expect that we could dispatch troops there so quickly or that our antiaircraft defenses there would be so strong. The second time was in 1972, when they did not expect that we would send tanks so far south as An Loc. Yet it was not just at An Loc. In 1972 we had attacked on a number of other fronts of the southern battlefield with tanks, too. And those two were not the Americans' only surprises. The Tet Mau Than offensive was also a surprise to the Americans, causing them great casualties and forcing them to change their strategy. The North's victory over the B-52 strategic bombers was another surprise: the United States intended to destroy us, but instead we dealt them a heavy defeat. That was a victory that greatly strengthened our delegation at the conference table in Paris. And in our 1975 general offensive and uprising, the enemy received many big surprises. But the biggest surprise for the Americans was the U.S. imperialists' leap into Vietnam itself. That was their fundamental surprise and their strategic error.

The U.S. imperialists were always obstinate, and they would have to bear the consequences of their errors. Right after the signing of the Paris Agreement on Vietnam, and again in June 1973, in Paris, we told Kissinger frankly that it was America that had seriously violated the Paris Agreement on Vietnam, continuing its neocolonial war of aggression. It was completely unreasonable for the United States to violate the agreement intentionally and cynically and yet demand that we respect the agreement. We made it clear we would never sit with folded arms and watch them violate the agreement. We would not let them do whatever they pleased, or retreat into a passive defense. We reserved for ourselves the right to freedom of action in the face of U.S. violation of the agreement.

This was something we had warned the Americans about long ago. But the United States and their crew of lackeys singlemindedly continued their systematic efforts to destroy the agreement, and continually stepped up the war and increased their operations of terror and repression against the people of the South. In order to protect the fruits of the revolution and smash their encroaching operations, our only recourse was revolutionary violence, relying on our military forces and political forces, resolutely counterattacking and attacking the enemy, in order to proceed to the total liberation of the South.

Lenin once taught that the thing to be most avoided is, once victorious, becoming intoxicated by that victory. Once intoxicated it is easy to become self-satisfied and lose vigilance. The U.S. imperialists have been defeated in Vietnam, but their dark schemes have not ended. Along with the forces of reaction, they have constantly sought means to destroy the fruits of our revolution. They have constantly interfered most viciously, and engaged in the most savage destruction. So we must raise our vigilance and build a mighty national defense, a powerful army ready for battle and always with a high will to win, in order to protect our Fatherland.

Moreover, we must absolutely avoid all thoughts of our personal importance or position. As Le Duan has said, this victory belongs to our party, to our great President Ho Chi Minh, to our people and all our heroic fighters, and to the martyrs who sacrificed their lives for the Fatherland. This victory is one of the whole country; it does not belong to any one person or unit or locality. The strength of this total victory is the strength of the whole country, of every person and every family, the strength of the spirit of patriotism and of socialist idealism.

Le Duc Tho also gave a very profound analysis of Vietnam's unique military arts, especially the art of the campaign in this final battle. I then presented a report summing up the Ho Chi Minh campaign. Clearly the whole party, army, and people had given us a great many unique experiences which, after we put them all together, would enrich Vietnamese military science many times over and help us develop our martial arts. They would help us build a revolutionary, modern standing army which could protect the independence, long-lasting peace, and socialist construction of the Fatherland, and which would be prepared to fulfill the internationalist responsibilities of a revolutionary army, of a true Marxist-Leninist party, our ever-victorious Vietnam Workers Party.

The total all-around victory of the General Offensive and Uprising of Spring 1975 was the greatest and most illustrious victory in our nation's 4,000-year history of building and preserving the country, opening a new age full of promise for our Fatherland. This victory, in the spirit of our history and of the times, was extremely fast. Was it because the U.S. imperialists had mistakenly or accidentally abandoned an ambitious war that they had to accept consequences which would in the long run be harmful to them in many ways? Was it because the heads of the Saigon army and administration had accidentally committed errors that their imposing war machine with its army of over a million built up over twenty years suffered destruction, dissolution, and great defeat in less than two months? No, it was not that. The defeat of the enemy had been inescapable, and it was we ourselves who had caused their defeat. Our strategy and tactics, the field positions and methods of attack we used, forced the enemy into a dilemma where either way they had to lose, and there was no way they could turn the circumstances around.

The strategic resolve of the Political Bureau was from the first to liberate the South, the sooner the better. They concluded that if the Americans came in again, we would still attack with determination, strike even harder, and win greater victory. We had prepared sufficient forces and had plans and measures ready to mete out still heavier blows to the Americans. The United States had mobilized gigantic forces for many years to carry on their invasion of our land, but in the end they were pitifully defeated and had to pull out. If they had returned, what hope would they have had of reversing the positions? And one thing certain was that they would have brought upon themselves greater and more shameful defeats. The United States did not give more aid in weapons and dollars to the puppets not because they had no more forces, not because they made a mistake, but primarily because in the face of the strength of our attack, in the situation they faced at home and abroad, they were well aware that no matter how much aid they gave to their protégés, they could not save that crew of flunkies. No matter how much more the United States had supplied to the quislings in weapons and munitions in 1975, they would certainly still have collapsed, and our troops would have confiscated all the more war booty.

Our methods of fighting also forced the Saigon army into a complete deadend, where any way they turned they were finished. It was not accidental that they pulled out of the Tay Nguyen. And if they had not pulled out, would they have avoided defeat? After we liberated Ban Me Thuot and wiped out the counterattacking enemy troops, we prepared to attack Pleiku and Kontum, because the Political Bureau's strategic plan beginning the first of 1975 was a resolution to liberate the Tay Nguyen. Facing the strength of the troops we had in the Tay Nguyen in March, the enemy knew that if they remained in Pleiku and Kontum they would certainly be wiped out in a big way, so they calculated many aspects before deciding on a withdrawal to preserve their forces. When they withdrew, we blocked them and wiped out most of that force. But even if they had not withdrawn, we would still have attacked Pleiku and Kontum in a few days, and they would surely have suffered the same fate as they did fleeing. Whether the enemy had pulled out or not, whether they had held Pleiku and Kontum or not, they would still have been wiped out and the Tay Nguyen would certainly have been liberated. That was because our troops were strong and held the initiative. Enemy mistakes were absolutely not the sole cause of their defeat. They were the only ones surprised by their defeat and collapse. We had calculated it in advance, and knew in advance the basic principles of warfare. The victory of the general offensive and uprising was rooted in the clearsighted leadership of the Central Committee which was trained and led by President Ho Chi Minh; in the mature, incisive, creative, and resolute leadership of the Political Bureau and the Central Military Committee; and in the extraordinary efforts of the army and people of our whole country.

On the basis of the results achieved through a long and arduous process of struggle by our army and people under the leadership of the party, we created an important opportune moment. The Political Bureau and the Central Military Committee made flexible use of the laws of revolutionary warfare, firmly grasped the rules of the enemy's war of aggression in the final phase of the war, stimulated the situation so it would develop by leaps and bounds, shifted to a strategy of lightning-speed general offensives and uprisings, maintained the strategic initiative, and controlled the enemy troops from beginning to end, surprised them and caused them to make mistakes, dealt them defeats one on top of the other, and carried them to total collapse. The hearty strength of the whole country and the talent for organization that led to this historic total victory will surely lead to accomplishments in the task of building socialism in our whole country.

On behalf of the campaign headquarters, I commended the outstanding successes of all the zones, the army corps, the specialized arms and branches, the divisions, all the units and offices that had taken a direct part in the campaign and also all the units that had guarded the stability of the North. I thanked all the branches, all the civilian offices, all the forces and regions for the support and cooperation they had extended to the army.

We had the coordinated strength of the army and the people of the whole country, of the rear and the front lines, of the material and the spiritual, of people and weaponry, of courageous hearts and intelligent minds. Our mastery of ourselves and our mastery of technology led to mastery of the battlefield and mastery of our nation's fate.

With that coordinated strength, in the spring of 1975 the army and people of our whole land plucked the colorful, fragrant bouquet of total victory which bloomed in the glorious light of the truth: "Nothing is more precious than independence and freedom."

May I respectfully offer it now to President Ho Chi Minh, the great leader of the Vietnamese nation, the person who led our army and people from victory to victory.

May I respectfully offer it to our beloved party, a firm Marxist-Leninist party, which has passed through many challenges, victorious in every battle, a resolute unit in the ranks of the international communist movement.

May I respectfully offer it to all our beloved comrades, fellow soldiers, and compatriots who sacrificed their lives for the revolutionary cause, who went before us to open the way to today's victory.

And let me pass this bouquet of total victory on to all our

compatriots throughout the country, to all patriotic citizens, the nameless heroes of the resistance, to old and young, to our people who for many years have tightened their belts, divided their bowls of rice in two, with each person working for two to contribute their labor and their goods to the resistance against the United States to bring it to total victory today.

Let me pass it on to the mothers and sisters of Vietnam, courageous, gentle, loyal, resourceful, who sent their husbands and sons and nephews off to fight the enemy, sacrificing all, with boundless endurance.

Let me pass it on to the manual and mental workers who produced, created, and invented under the thunder of bombs and shells to add material and moral strength to our whole people and our whole army as they fought the enemy.

Let me pass it on to all the cadres and fighters of the people's armed forces down South and up North, the young men and women who so deserve our love, who came from fields and factories, schools and families, picked up their guns to fight the enemy, passed through so much suffering and danger, endured so many hardships and privations. So many groups of people constantly coming forward, fathers and sons, brothers old and young, wives and husbands, who have gone through these thirty years from Tan Trao and Cao Lang through Dien Bien Phu down to Ho Chi Minh City and on to Ca Mau.

Let me pass it on to all our brothers, sisters, and friends on all the five continents, people who regarded the Vietnamese people's resistance against the United States as their own, who stood in the trenches with the people of Vietnam, who gave their support, moral and material, to Vietnam to defeat the United States.

And let me pass on to all of you, my readers, this spring of great victory which I cannot possibly relate to the full.

From the base of the heavens, there shone forth a sun bright red like the revolutionary truth and the spring of great victory which our nation had lived.

Afterword

The first time I met a Vietnamese was in London on May 12, 1965. I had addressed a public meeting earlier in the day, expressing alarm over the escalation of America's war against Vietnam. I had never been to Vietnam, never met a Vietnamese, but I could not believe that whatever was happening there constituted a threat to our national security and warranted such a military response. Many mothers shared my fears, and as Women's Strike for Peace we sought support from women around the world to join an effort to end the war.

A London friend led me up the narrow stairs at Netherhall Gardens to a small apartment where a strikingly beautiful Vietnamese woman, about my age, sat with her youngest child on her knee. She was married to a journalist, and they were among Hanoi's first "unofficial" representatives in the West.

"We are prepared to fight until our grandchildren's generation for independence and peace," she said, looking at her seven-year-old son. It was the first time I understood the determination of her people to be free.

Eleven years later, when my husband and I were visitors in reunified Vietnam and arrived in Ho Chi Minh City, that same woman greeted us in the Majestic Hotel. Her son is in the university now, and she works with the

Front Committee of Saigon, escorting foreign visitors
through her hometown. She embraced me with strength
and love, and we cried out of a sense of relief and joy. We
too had been reunited.

Now, having made four trips to Vietnam—including one
by jeep from the China border through the northern provinces and a recent one by bus from Hanoi to Ho Chi Minh
City—I more deeply understand how the Vietnamese won
their freedom. I witnessed the determination of the
Vietnamese people not to be defeated by B-52s or pacification programs.

A half hour out of Da Nang, on Route 1, before you get to
the dismantled Chu Lai airbase, is the district of Dien
Ban. The ricefields look like salvage dumps, houses are
repaired with U.S. army surplus, flowers are watered from
pails made in Hoboken. We stopped in a small village to
allow our bus to return to Da Nang for some things that
were left behind. The early afternoon sun was sharp and
intense, and we quickly sought shelter in a house chosen
at random. We were welcomed into a room, where many
beds indicated a large family. We sat at the usual central
table, before an altar on which incense was burning in
honor of family ancestors, and a large photograph of Ho
Chi Minh. Our arrival attracted the village children and
soon the owner was summoned to receive his unexpected
guests.

Mr. Le Tu Cong is sixty-five years old and sports the
familiar wispy beard, white pants, and white jacket. On
May 1, 1975, he was liberated from Con Son Island, where
the discovery of the tiger cages in 1970 became a turning
point in the history of the U.S. antiwar movement. Mr.
Cong was held chained to other prisoners for two years in
a former ox stable. Rice was shoveled through ceiling
bars, to be eaten from the floor, and lime was thrown at
the prisoners when they protested. They had organized an
underground communication system to keep in touch
with other prisoners and to relay messages to their
families at home. They had heard about the spring upris-

ing and prepared a celebration for the moment of liberation. They made a flag from their clothes. Mr. Cong's
nephew, also a prisoner, tore up his shirt and drew his
own blood to write a slogan. "We freed ourselves before
the liberation army could reach us," Cong proudly told us.
The chairman of his village today was also in Con Son
prison. Why, we asked, were so many farmers arrested
from this quiet hamlet? "Many of our men were in prison.
I worked against the Saigon government since the
French. My brother was killed in the liberation army.
Thieu arrested so many of us. I am an old man now—
retired. But happy to be alive. If the village committee
needs help, they call on me. The government helps us
now. Prices are high, but the government is building an
irrigation project for us. There is water now. The government repaired our church. I have spent eleven years in
prisons. Our whole village supported the liberation struggle."

Resistance to the U.S.-supported Thieu regime was evi-
dent all over Vietnam's ricefields, in its factories. In village after village we asked people how they had spent the
last ten years; so many said they had been arrested. For
every person arrested, Thieu lost the support of an entire
household.

It has been twenty years since Dien Bien Phu, when the
United States replaced France as the imperialist power in
Indochina. It has been thirty years since the August Revolution, when Ho Chi Minh read Vietnam's Declaration of
Independence in Hanoi's Ba Dinh Square, and Vietnam
was unified for twenty-five days. It has been forty-seven
years since Ho Chi Minh formed the Indochinese Communist Party. And finally, in only fifty-five days and fifty-
five nights, the Vietnamese people's last struggle reached
its Great Spring Victory.

In the fall of 1973 Don Luce and I visited the liberated
areas of the South. American troops were gone, but the
barrier dividing North from South at the 17th parallel
remained. We crossed a temporary pontoon over the Ben

Hai River in a DRV jeep, and were met at the "border" by
PRG friends we had known from the Paris peace talks.
The changing of the escorts ceremony took a short time,
but the two flags—DRV on the north side of the river, PRG
on the south—the customs house, and the only sign we
ever saw in English, "Welcome to the Republic of South
Vietnam," made the demarcation clear.

In 1976 a new bridge spanned the Ben Hai, with no
signs, no flags, and no customs house. People walk or
cycle back and forth with a naturalness which belies the
division of the past. Many are finding relatives and friends
they had not heard from for twenty or thirty years. Reunification is a daily excitement enjoyed by all those long
separated by war, invasion, and political struggle—
virtually all the people of Vietnam.

The border and its trappings of separation never served
the purpose the Franco-American policymakers had
intended—to prevent the spread of a people's movement
for liberation. Throughout the war, materials, people, and
munitions successfully moved south. A gas pipeline was
built in the midst of the heaviest bombing of any war.
Cadres from the south often walked for weeks from their
liberated zone to the "border," then on to Hanoi and to
board airplanes to take them to international conferences,
to visit Canada, Sweden, France, Italy, England, and
socialist countries. The people of Vietnam insisted on
keeping contact with support groups around the world to
maintain the solidarity movement.

Equally remarkable was the effort by the American
people to maintain links with the Vietnamese people. For
four years during the heaviest bombing of the North,
Americans traveled to Vietnam in every single month except one, and that was because of severe flooding. These
trips not only yielded insights and information that gave
new momentum to the antiwar movement, but often provided news that our government was unable to obtain,
such as the names of American prisoners of war. On one

such trip, in October 1973, Don Luce and I met Le Duc Tho and General Chu Van Tan.

General Dung has described Le Duc Tho's arrival in Nam Bo to provide the political leadership for the military offensive. Tho, who directed the peace talks for North Vietnam from October 1968 to their conclusion in January 1973, made frequent flights to Paris to meet secretly with Henry Kissinger. He is not a young man. Impeccably groomed, he met us at 8:00 A.M. for a three-hour informal talk. During the entire conversation, which ranged from nostalgic stories about Paris and his adversary to a current political analysis, Tho remained sedately at ease, in contrast to his restless American guests. He focused his remarks on the U.S. obligation to "heal the wounds of war," specified in the Paris Peace Accords. He told us how Vietnam had helped formulate that phrase, avoiding the use of words like "reparations" so as not to attach a sense of guilt to postwar aid.

He also reminisced about his ability to emerge unruffled from a sixteen-hour session with Kissinger, who appeared fatigued and a bit disheveled by contrast. Thus we were not a bit surprised to read of Tho's arrival by motorcycle in the woods of Nam Bo, or to learn that he remained with the offensive, despite the rugged conditions, until its victory in Saigon on April 30, 1975.

Our trip to Vietnam in November 1973 followed the Peace Accords, but still preceded the war's end. It offered us a unique opportunity to meet with those directing the battle. We were driven over a circuitous route in the Viet Bac region, home to many of the northern ethnic minority groups. Generals Chu Van Tan, then second highest ranking military official in the North, and Nguyen Bang Giang met us at a large "Pentagon" building hidden in a mountainous hardwood forest. Over beer (for us) and lemonade (for the generals) we found them as articulate on the subjects of crop rotation and reconstruction needs as on military tactics. Chu Van Tan gave his appraisal of

American military strategy so essential to campaign planning. "The United States is big, it is richer and has a professional army, advanced industry, science, and technology. We had to study all those aspects. We also had to know the weak points of the enemy. It may be strong in technology, but it is weak in other areas.

"During its two hundred years of history the United States did not lose any war with any country before it came to Vietnam, and it lost the war in Vietnam, although it tries to deny that. But the fact is that it had to get its troops out of Vietnam without fanfare.

"The weak point is that justice was not on its side. Despite its material strength, the United States waged an unjust war. The more prolonged the war, the more isolated it became. Second, the United States lacked political support for the war. Third, it tried to use maximum strength to crush us, hoping to make a quick war to occupy our country. For this it sent half a million troops and resorted to electronic and chemical warfare. Fourteen million tons of bombs exploded here, equal to two hundred Hiroshimas."

In 1944 General Nguyen Bang Giang had rescued an American pilot, shot down by the Japanese occupying Vietnam while he was flying the "hump" to attack Japan. Giang, who spoke no English, walked the pilot for twenty-seven days and nights to Pac Bo, the cave near the China border where Ho Chi Minh was organizing the independence of Vietnam. English-speaking Ho, who had visited New York in 1914, had discussions with the pilot which resulted in a relationship between the Office of Strategic Services (OSS) and the Vietminh. Between June and August 1944 American intelligence officers worked with Vietminh guerrillas tracking Japanese planes over Vietnam.

So Vietnam was not always Washington's enemy. We once had a consulate in Hanoi, the only building with a red-brick New England fireplace, which housed the special representative of the Provisional Revolutionary Government during the war years. As Hanoi is now the capital of reunified Vietnam, the Vietnamese might offer to return it to its original occupants once negotiations toward recognition succeed.

Le Duc Tho spoke often of Vietnam's interest in "resuming" normal relations with the United States. It is two years since the war's end, four years since American troops and prisoners of war came home. Tens of thousands of Americans have contributed millions of dollars for postwar reconstruction aid—a symbolic gesture pending more significant amounts from the U.S. government. Yet the most powerful nation on earth has isolated itself from the rest of the world by rejecting Vietnam's admission to the United Nations for two years in a row.

Vietnam's Paris negotiator, Xuan Thuy, told us in Hanoi this summer, "We are ready to forget the past. We have fought for so many years we want a long and lasting peace. If the United States shows good will we are ready to set up relations." The Vietnamese have great respect for American achievements in science, agriculture, and technology. They admire the millions of people who helped bring an end to America's longest and ugliest war. They want to be friends with those who wish friendship, to trade with those who seek markets, to share scientific research, engage in cultural exchanges, and participate in the deliberations of the world.

We have a great deal to learn from the Vietnamese people, from the way they waged their war, from their determination to be independent and free, from their readiness to forget the past and build for a future of peace. That readiness, and an openness not seen with any other nation, is apparent in General Dung's account of the last campaign to end the war. Never has so much been revealed so soon after battle. It is time to make peace with Vietnam, and with ourselves.

—*Cora Weiss*
April 1977

• • • •

"I've always acted alone," Henry Kissinger once told Italian journalist Oriana Fallaci in an unguarded moment. "Americans admire the cowboy leading the caravan alone astride on his horse . . . a Wild West tale, if you like."

Our Great Spring Victory tells a very different story about decision making, describing the care taken to be sure that every person felt a part of the process. There were no cowboys leading the caravan alone. I was in Hanoi in October of 1972 as a special correspondent for ABC news and saw an example of this.

I walked into a dining room of the Thong Nhat Hotel for breakfast at 8:00 A.M., to find all of the waiters and waitresses huddled around one table. They were discussing a mimeographed sheet outlining the nine-point proposal that had been agreed upon by the United States and the Vietnamese in Paris. One of the waitresses told me that the United States was backing down on the agreement. At noon, ambassadors from other countries were given that document, and at 3:00 that afternoon I was invited, along with other foreign correspondents, to a press briefing on the release. The decisions were discussed with the people first, with ambassadors and foreign journalists afterward.

The next day I was in a village forty miles from Hanoi. The village radio was being played loudly and everyone was interested. Kissinger's famous "Peace is at hand" speech was being translated. I noticed that several villagers were digging their bunkers deeper as they listened and I asked why.

"Whenever we hear speeches like that, we get bombed," an old man carrying dirt told me.

The villagers were right in their caution. Less than two months later, the U.S. air force began the massive Christmas bombing of Hanoi and Haiphong. Later, I filmed the destruction of Hanoi's largest hospital, Bach Mai. I proceeded carefully, without emotion. I had seen it all before. Most of the hospitals, schools, roads, and other infrastructure in North Vietnam had been destroyed.

I turned to Paul Washburn, the Methodist Bishop of Chicago, who was with me at the time, to ask him a question. He was crying. The impact of the war was great for those of us who were there during those years of bombing. If each American could have spent five minutes beneath the bombs, we would have stopped the war years earlier. We would have found a way!

When we passed three workers pounding rocks into little stones for cement for the hospital foundation, Bishop Washburn took one of the hammers and started to help. Afterward he explained his feelings: "I just decided to help. The workers didn't seem to mind. In fact, I think they liked it. They smiled. I couldn't tell what they thought because I can't speak Vietnamese. But I had a good feeling for those few moments that we pounded rocks together. When I got up to leave, I looked back at the pile of rocks. It seemed exactly the same size as when I started. If we are really going to help Vietnam, we must be more than symbolic."

The destruction of Vietnam was massive. There are 83,000 amputees, 8,000 parapalegics, 30,000 blind, 10,000 deaf. A total of 13,457,822 Vietnamese were killed, wounded, or made refugees. Thousands of mines are scattered throughout the countryside—farmers look for them by prodding the soil with pointed bamboo sticks.

Much of the damage can be repaired. Many of those paralyzed from torture and shackling in the Saigon regime's prisons will be able to walk again if they are given the right treatment. The unexploded bombs and mines can be found with metal detectors and defused. The back-to-the-farm movement has already begun.

Our participation in this rebuilding is important not only to Vietnam but to us. Dick Hughes, who spent many years working with Saigon's shoeshine boys and remained in

Vietnam for a year after the war was over, spoke to this point in a *New York Times* article:

> When my scheduled flight left Tan Son Nhut airport on August 7, 1976, I not only felt a debt to the Vietnamese people, I knew the kids I loved were finally finding people who cared.
>
> The postwar problems we often only give lip service to are, in fact, enormous. I saw them. . . . And I'm at a loss how to tell my own people that Vietnam's needs are our remedy—to say that what the Vietnamese people have to offer us—as they did me—is so great that for our own sake we must help them.

Our Great Spring Victory was written for the Vietnamese. It tells the story of the skill and sacrifice of a whole people in defeating the U.S. military might. It does not say much about Americans who protested the war. But we should not only remember the vast destruction that our massive military machine caused. We can also be proud of helping to stop the destruction. We have more heroes from the war in Vietnam than any other war in our history: Dr. Howard Levy, who refused to train the Green Berets, Don Lawson, who refused to fly more B-52 bombing raids over Cambodia, and Mike Heck, who refused to continue the Christmas bombing of Hanoi. There were thousands of men who refused to cooperate with the Selective Service system—and millions of women, men, and children who marched the streets of Washington, New York, Peoria, Boston, and San Francisco, shouting "Stop this war."

The United States continued the war year after year because our government never understood Vietnamese nationalism or the feelings of the average Vietnamese farmer and worker. We never had an ambassador in Vietnam who could even say "hello" in Vietnamese. The only one who even tried was McNamara. He learned to say "long live Vietnam!" but when he made his speech in the huge Saigon Square, he mixed up the tones. He raised his arms in the victory symbol before 30,000 university and high school students who had been ordered to come and cheer. Then he shouted, not "Long live Vietnam," but

"The southern duck wants to lie down!" Our officials never could get the intonation right.

One of the people who suffered most from the war was a high school student, Thieu Thi Tao, who spent years in the tiger cages of Con Son Island. I met her there in 1970, along with two congresspeople and a congressional aid, Tom Harkin. She was paralyzed from shackling and suffering from pinkeye. Nearly five years later, still remembering our fleeting visit, she wrote me a letter and inquired about Tom: "I still remember the gentleman who spoke with me in the tiger cages. I don't know his name, but he seemed very nice. If you happen to meet him, please remember me kindly to him."

—*Don Luce*
April 1977

Cora Weiss and Don Luce meeting with Generals Chu Van Tan and Nguyen Bang Giang in Thai Nguyen, North Vietnam, November 1973.

LaVergne, TN USA
08 September 2010
196259LV00002B/35/A